**possible ?**

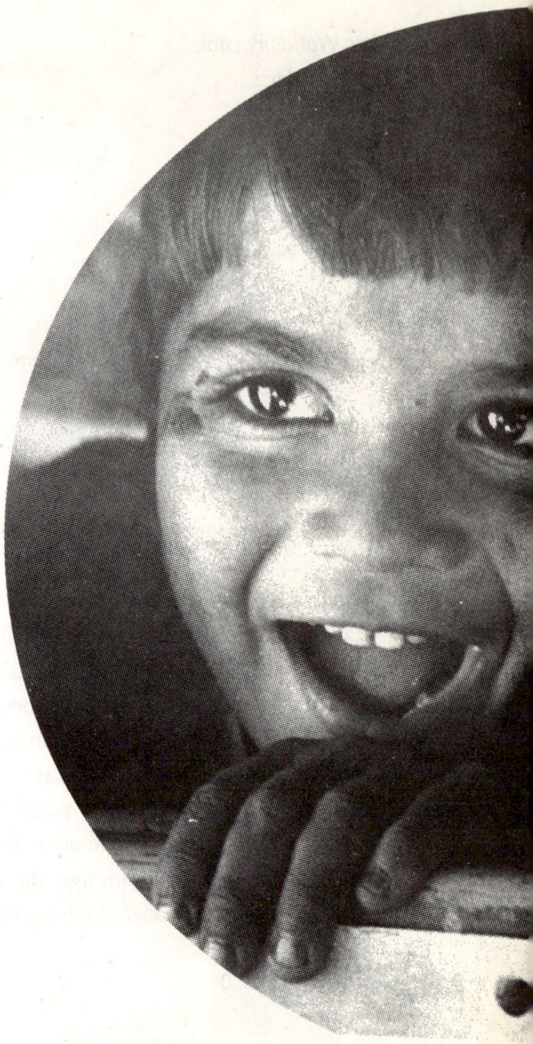

*Are Other Worlds Possible?*
*Talking New Politics*

Published (2005) by

Zubaan
K-92, First Floor,
Hauz Khas Enclave,
New Delhi – 110016
Email: zubaanwbooks@vsnl.net
Website: www.zubaanbooks.com



Zubaan is an independent feminist publishing house based in New Delhi, India, with a strong academic and general list. It was set up in March 2003, as an associate of the well known feminist house Kali for Women, and carries forward Kali's tradition of publishing world quality books to high editorial and production standards. "Zubaan" means tongue, voice, language, speech in Hindustani. Zubaan is a non-profit publisher, working in the areas of the humanities, social sciences, as well as in fiction, general non-fiction, and books for young adults. Zubaan is committed to publishing works on and by women, which will challenge, entertain, delight and inform our readers all over the world. Its aim is to ensure that the voices of women, particularly from the South, are heard, and to reversing the flow of information, which is traditionally from the North to the South, the West to the East.

ISBN 81 89013 27 0

DESIGN: Shuka Jain, Design Works
COVER PHOTOGRAPHS: Jai Sen
MAP: Mappa Atlantica di Luis Texeira, 1600 circa

Printed at Frontline Imaging Pvt. Ltd.,
D-14/7, Okhla Industrial Area, Phase I, New Delhi - 110020

TALKING
NEW
POLITICS

# CONTENTS

# CONTENTS

# INTRODUCTION

## Interrogating the World Social Forum and its Culture of Politics

**Jai Sen**

Are other worlds possible? More open, just, peaceful and joyful worlds than what we know today; less violent, divided, and exploitative worlds?

These questions formed the central concerns of a series of seminars that took place at the University of Delhi, India between August-December 2003. Conceived as a set of discussions, the 'Open Space Series' as it was called, addressed itself to the overall theme: 'Are Other Worlds Possible? Cultures of Politics and the World Social Forum', and acted as a run-up to the World Social Forum, held in Mumbai in January 2004. [1] The idea behind the discussions was to provide information about the Forum, to develop a critical engagement with it and the ideas it professes, and to encourage and build a culture of critical engagement with our own lives. In the way they were structured, the seminars also attempted to be what the Forum says it wants to be, 'an open space' for the free expression and exchange of ideas. [2]

As organisers, we were pleasantly surprised by the response to the seminars. Each session had large numbers of students attending and actively participating; the speakers brought both depth and quality to the debate; people said good things about the discussions; and we hoped that in some measure we had succeeded in extending the boundaries of the Forum in India. These were boundaries that had been threatening to close in (for instance, through the unfortunate fact of the growth of manipulative power politics, a lack of transparency with the organising committee, and the progressive introduction of restrictive rules of participation, as I also elucidate below). [3] We heard, too, of similar initiatives being taken up in universities elsewhere in India and abroad. It was these responses that convinced us that it was important to take the idea further, and to give it more permanent shape, which the reader will find in these books, collectively titled Are Other Worlds Possible?

This Introduction attempts to place the seminar series - and this series of books - in some perspective. [4]

The World Social Forum was initiated in Brazil in January 2001 as a challenge to the World Economic Forum in order to put forward another view of the world and its possibilities. It is now widely seen as being a highly significant world initiative. The motto the World Social Forum has coined for itself is 'Another World Is Possible!' But: are other worlds really possible? What would be involved – what kinds of changes would we have to bring about – to make these other worlds a reality? Is this merely a utopian idea, or is there something that the World Social Forum can bring to the task of building other worlds? If so, what can be learnt from it?

These questions, that lay at the heart of the process that created the WSF, were precisely the ones that we wanted to explore in our seminars. In particular, we hoped to be able to critically examine and interrogate the culture of politics that the Forum has formulated and posited, and that it is professedly practising. In other words, not merely the what of politics, but the how. And through this, we also proposed to interrogate and critically reflect on the cultures of politics that all of us practise every day, in our daily lives, in the institutions and organisations and movements we ourselves work in.

In the Charter of Principles that is said to be its guiding philosophy, the Forum has declared itself to be an 'open space' for the free exchange of ideas amongst those who are opposed to neo-liberal globalisation and its impacts. (This is the letter of the Charter; in reality, this has been interpreted to also include those who are not necessarily opposed to it but critical of and/or concerned with it, and about the social, economic, and political order more generally.) In this relatively undirected 'open space' people from a wide range of streams of thought and action can meet and interact, without feeling that they have to agree with the views of the organisers or that they have to subscribe to particular ideas or prescriptions. Beyond this, and consistent with the idea of an open space, any formulations and statements that emerge from the Forum come out of this interaction. They appear in the names of the participants and not of the World Social Forum, which itself takes no positions or 'leadership' on any issues beyond what is given in its Charter of Principles. [5]

Both these propositions are, in many senses and at many levels, very different from conventional organisational culture, and contain and constitute deep challenges to all those who take part in the process. But what is the actual experience of the Forum in this area? And how do these propositions address questions of actually existing social structure and power in society, in different contexts across the world at this point in history and in transnational, 'global' space?

In many ways, the answers to these questions are contained in the evolving history and shape of the Forum. From being a single and then a regular, major event each year, (in Porto Alegre in Brazil, and timed to challenge the annual World Economic Forum at Davos, Switzerland), the Forum has become an efflorescence of protest, reflective analysis, and the celebration of alternatives, across the world.

In November 2002, the first European Social Forum was held in Florence, Italy, and some 500,000 - one million people marched in a peace rally to protest the threat of the US-led war on Iraq. In early 2003, before the third World Social Forum in Porto Alegre in late January, four regional fora were held in various parts of the world – the Asian Social Forum in Hyderabad, India, the Palestine Social Forum, an African Social Forum in Addis Ababa, Ethiopia, and a Pan-Amazonian Social Forum in Belém, Brazil. This is aside from several thematic, national, and also city and college fora in many countries of the world. This extraordinary

efflorescence has continued through 2003 and 2004 and affirms both the need and the importance of creating such a space, locally, regionally and internationally. (For details of recent, current, and upcoming programmes, see http://www.forumsocialmundial.org.br/main.asp?id_menu=11_1&cd_la.)

There are also several 'side' or 'peripheral' events that take place during the Forum, some planned, many unplanned. These peripheral spaces play very important roles in defining the overall culture of the Forum, and in preserving (and elaborating) its openness. These include, for example, the Youth Forum and parallel events by civil and political entities that wish to relate to the Forum but prefer to maintain a little distance, as well as more formal 'parallel' events such as the World Parliamentary Forum, the World Forum of Mayors and Local Authorities, and the World Education Forum.

The steady growth in numbers attending the world event – from 25-30,000 people at the first one, to 50-60,000 at the second, to 100,000 at the third and perhaps 130,000 at the fourth — attest to the relevance of the Forum to people all over the world. But while there is cause for optimism here, there is reason for concern too, for it is not numbers alone that count. This growth has also brought its own share of organisational and management problems, both at the events themselves and also in the evolution of policy and strategy for the Forum as an idea, sometimes tending to overwhelm it.

The third world meeting, in January 2003, is widely considered to be the point at which organisers, participants and observers began to seriously talk about how to practise alternatives to economic globalisation and to reflect on the extent to which the Forum is practising the principles it preaches. Also — coincidentally — the January 2003 meeting marks the moment when serious organisational problems began to show up. [6] And the fourth edition, held in Mumbai, saw — for the first time — the public staging of major events in opposition to the Forum, challenging its legitimacy both in terms of opposition to economic globalisation and as an open space. (These included the Mumbai Resistance; see www.mumbairesistance.org.)

The Forum is therefore becoming aware of its own globalisation, as regional and problem-specific Forums mushroom worldwide. But are the Forum's ruling bodies, structures, and processes appropriate and adequate to a phenomenon growing exponentially and spreading globally?

The Mumbai Forum was also marked by two new developments: by mass participation — of Dalits (earlier referred to as 'untouchables') and of Adivasis ('tribals') — and also by a far greater participation of women than has been the case for the earlier editions of the world meeting, in Brazil. For this reason, the Mumbai Forum is regarded — within Forum circles — as being something of a landmark.

All this — the new developments as much as the opposition — suggests that there is reason to think that the WSF has struck at the level of meaning. It seems to have been able to announce at a world level, in a manner that had perhaps

so far not been achieved, that there is an alternative to economic, capitalist globalisation – indeed, and quite crucially in conceptual terms, that there are many alternatives; and – importantly – to demonstrate and make manifest and public the reality that people all over the world are today mobilising to define and to live those alternatives. In this way, the WSF – along with all the other forms of global civil action that are also taking place — is arguably playing a major role in freeing people all over the world of the shackles of the colonisation of the mind.

But this also raises questions that the Forum must ask itself: most centrally, how can it most effectively realise the potential of the world transformative power that it is speaking to — and crucially, that it is gathering?

## BEYOND BRAZIL

This is ground that is difficult enough, but there is more. During 2002-3, as we discuss below, the International Council of the World Social Forum also made the historic decision, after prolonged debate, that the fourth world meeting of the organisation and process called 'the World Social Forum' would, for the first time, be held outside Brazil, in India.

The Brazilians chose India because it is, like Brazil, a large country with a more or less functioning electoral democracy and with strong and vibrant traditions of civil and political movement. It is also strategically located in Asia, the most populous continent in the world – and which had till then been very poorly represented at the World Social Forum.

To this, Samir Amin, of the Third World Forum and member of the WSF International Council added another dimension. He argued, at the meeting of the International Council in Porto Alegre in January 2003, that it was evident that Asia was the arena of the next strike of the US imperium, and so it was not just important but essential for the Forum to now be held there – and that if so, India was really the only choice, especially given the role it has historically played in South-South solidarity, and especially in terms of Afro-Asian politics. [7]

Informal preliminary discussions took place at meetings in Europe during the second half of 2001, The then-still forming International Council decided at its second meeting in November 2001 to send a delegation of members of the Brazil Organising Committee and the International Council to India, to explore possibilities. A first meeting with a handful of Indians from different civil formations took place in Bangalore in mid-December 2001.

However there was sharp disagreement at this meeting, regarding the possibility of holding the Forum in India, and especially regarding who should organise any such meeting and how this should be decided, and the participants agreed that another larger meeting should be called to consider these questions. This meeting, which was in effect the first national consultation on the WSF in India, was held in New Delhi on January 9-10, 2002. With the discussions given some structure and direction by an independently prepared

paper that analysed these and other related questions, the consultation debated the questions at length and came to the conclusion that the meeting could, and should, be organised in India but only in January 2004, and not in 2003 as had been proposed by the IC; and it established a Preparatory Committee to initiate the work.

There were two reasons behind this decision to accept the responsibility of organising the world meeting, but only in 2004. One, the meeting recognised that the deeper, underlying reality of civil and political movement in India was that they, despite vibrancy, also deeply divided, and people needed time to come together. Two, because general elections were scheduled for the country in 2004, it was felt that strategically this offered the possibility both for using the Forum as a vehicle for building a broader secular civil platform, and for building the Forum itself. This perspective was generated within the understanding that the rampant religious nationalism we were then faced with in India was as dangerous as capitalist globalisation, and that the two in fact intertwine. The Delhi meeting also urged the International Council to look at the World Social Forum more as a process that took place throughout the year than as only an annual event; and towards this, it offered to help organise a regional Social Forum somewhere in South Asia in late 2002 or early 2003. [8] The IC accepted these proposals, though only after considerable debate, first at its meeting in January 2003 and then again in January 2004. As one keen observer (and member of the WSF's International Council) commented, "The decision made in Porto Alegre to hold the next main World Social Forum meeting in India, in January 2004, [has] been the most difficult decision ever made by the IC." [9]

Holding the Forum in Asia and in India was, therefore, a major and ambitious initiative towards the globalisation of the World Social Forum as an idea and as a culture, and constituted a major landmark in its history. Although the fifth world meeting is again to be held in Porto Alegre, Brazil, holding the meeting in India has set a precedent that will almost certainly be followed in later years. So, quite aside from the challenges of the roles that the World Social Forum can potentially play in world politics, it was, and remains a crucial testing time for the Forum, in both organisational as well as political-strategic terms.

Finally, there is the global context within which all this is taking place. Over the last three to four years, which are precisely the years in which the World Social Forum has taken shape, some very important developments have also taken place internationally. One of the more audacious acts of militancy took place on September 11, 2001 — which, let us recall, was during the very first year of the Forum. In reaction, wars have been unilaterally launched by some nations against others in declared pre-emptive defence of their self-interests, in defiance of world public opinion and the opposition from a majority of nation-states, brazenly bypassing the multilateral world order that has been built up over the past century. The-then US President even seized the opportunity to declare those who criticised so-called 'globalisation' and 'free trade' as being

enemies of his country, and consequently, targets for this war. And in the name of the 'war on terrorism' that has been launched by nation-states across the globe, 'security' and surveillance measures have been relentlessly tightened, as much against civil and political protestors as against 'terrorists'.

Stepping further back, we can see that in the past decade, the US has moved decisively to the right; Europe has often seemed to be moving that way; and Hindu, Islamic, Christian, and Jewish fundamentalisms are rampant in different parts of the world, including of course in India and other parts of South Asia. Even as the economy unravels within its heartland, capitalist globalisation is riding triumphant across the world, and the shadows of imperialism and authoritarianism are increasingly evident.

It is in this larger context too, that we wanted to locate and look at the World Social Forum and what it could potentially mean. Specifically, what was it that the Forum and the upcoming world meeting could do towards addressing these issues and objectives?

## INTERROGATING THE FORUM

As we saw it, organising the Forum in India was not only a historic step, but also a historic opportunity, and a historic juncture, for civil politics and social movements at the world level and in India. But we felt we had to ask the question: Had the World Social Forum, and the manner in which it was organising the world meeting in Mumbai, grasped the significance of the moment?

Specifically, we felt it was important to critically examine the vocabulary and culture of the politics of the Forum, and what it, in fact — and not only in theory — constitutes and represents. When it was formed, and as still stated in its Charter of Principles, the singular position of the World Social Forum was opposition to neo-liberal globalisation, and implicitly also to a politics of violence. Over time, and especially in the world context that emerged in the period immediately following its formation, this also came to include opposition to war and militarism. But this vocabulary was then dramatically expanded once it was decided that the world meeting was being held in India, to also include opposition to caste, communalism, and patriarchy.

As already mentioned, the first formal consultation held in India (Bhopal in April 2002, following the first one in Delhi in January 2002) came to the conclusion that these three contradictions, and empires, also constituted fundamental elements of the framework in relation to which the WSF must conduct itself, at least in India and South Asia. While the relevance of patriarchy was never contested, the proposal to include caste and communalism (or religious fundamentalism) was seen by some in the WSF International Council to be only Indian and South Asian concerns, and therefore not appropriate for inclusion as themes for the world meeting of the Forum.

After much debate at its meeting in Miami, in June 2003 however, the International Council approved this widened vocabulary for the World Social

Forum in Mumbai. In principle therefore, and even if all these new formulations have not yet been formally incorporated into the WSF Charter of Principles even now, the International Council in one sense took the first step of accepting this much-widened vocabulary as the Forum's vocabulary: for the world meeting in Mumbai after all, would be — and was — seen as 'The World Social Forum' speaking, not just WSF India.

On the one hand, this expansion very substantially changed the Forum, its constituency, and its politics. But what is significant is that during this same period, the WSF also became 'stricter' and more demanding in terms of its politics, in a way mirroring what was happening in the wider world. During 2003, both WSF India and the WSF International Council formally decided that organisations wanting to be members of its bodies have to give their written declaration of adherence to the WSF Charter of Principles. This stern organisational discipline was perhaps not a new idea (it is common in the more organised political parties, both of the left and the right, as well as in fundamentalist groups), and had been earlier reflected in positions articulated here and there by some of its more prominent leadership; [10] but this now became accepted policy even in a professedly open, democratic and new-generation initiative such as the Forum.

In our eyes, these developments were crucial for the culture of the Forum. Several questions emerged: given these developments, how was the Forum any different from all the other modes of political organisation that we are more familiar with? What purpose was this widening vocabulary and growing conditionality serving? Most fundamentally, were these changes going to actually help in building a new world — 'another' world? Were they helping to persuade more people in the world of the value of opposing these empires, or were they in fact restricting — closing down — the 'open space' that the Forum was said to be? Is mere opposition to x, y, and z enough for building other worlds — or does one not also need to stand for something?

All this taken into account, what implications did these conditions have for the initiative as an initiative? And beyond the taking of these positions by its leadership, just how were these conditionalities contributing to helping the Forum more effectively confront and contest these empires — and to contribute to building other worlds?

Given the highly volatile world context within which the Forum was taking shape, the important initiatives and positions that it itself was taking, as well as the major challenges it was facing at that point in time, we believed that there was reason to think that the WSF was at a critical juncture. It seemed to us that the Forum, as well as the thousands of organisations from across the world that are participating in and supporting it, would perhaps do well to take a step back and get a view of the larger picture of which they are only one part, one frame, one moment.

## THE OPEN SPACE SERIES

The Open Space Seminar Series was seen as a small contribution to developing such a perspective. At the time we embarked upon it, the Forum was hardly known in India, either as an organisation or an initiative, or indeed as the 'movement' that it was by then widely seen to be elsewhere in the world. Nor was its interesting culture of politics — the culture of 'open space' — familiar to many in India. Despite the fact that the Asian Social Forum had been held in Hyderabad in 2003, and that it was seen, by and large, as having been a success, there had, till then, been very little critical examination in India of the Forum, either as an idea or as a significant world institution. [11]

Beyond this, the experience of the Forum over the past year and a half also strongly suggested that both within India and internationally, the Forum was already tending to become a tightly controlled domain, and not the open space that it claimed to – and indeed wanted to – be; and where the organisers seemed to have lost sight of one of the great insights and contributions of the Forum of creating an open space in the deeply troubling world in which we live today. As organisers, we saw the seminar series as playing a small role in this, just by being an open space.

The twelve seminars that took place (in reality, eleven out of the twelve originally planned, and one after the Mumbai Forum) were organised in two interweaving streams. (See the Programme at the end of the book.) One stream dealt with the structural issues that the World Social Forum had till then been concerned with and in many senses is organised around — economic globalisation, and militarisation and war — and also with the new issues that were then added to this vocabulary by it being held in India: Religious fundamentalism and communalism, caste, race, and patriarchy. In short, all the empires that confront us and attempt to bind us, from outside and inside; all the empires that the Forum has formally declared that it proposes to confront, both implicitly and explicitly. This we called 'Stream B'.

The other stream — alternating and intertwining with the 'first' — dealt with the relationship of the Forum to such issues and to such empires, but was organised not in terms of the issues but of themes that we suggested were crucial to understanding the evolving culture of politics that the Forum offers: the question of what is now widely referred to as 'new' politics in relation to 'old' politics, including the relationship of political parties and movements affiliated to them and independent social movements (and where the Forum's Charter of Principles specifically excludes parties from taking part); the increasingly contested question whether the Forum should be a space or a movement; the crucial question of the Forum's relationship to and understanding of violence (and where the Charter again excludes those who believe in armed action as a means of addressing issues — but has thereby also excluded movements such as the Zapatistas, which has inspired social and political movements around the world and, many say, the global solidarity and justice movement itself, of which

the Forum is a part); and the challenge that 'the Forum', though commonly understood only as a world meeting that takes place each year, is – like much transnational civil movement - in many senses a construct in virtual space. This was Stream A.

The series closed with two very stimulating sessions that broke out of the structure that we had otherwise adopted for the series: one, examining the question of whether socialism is really the only possible other world, and the other looking critically at the University as an open space, which is of course what it is meant to be all about, in classic liberal doctrine; and beyond this, and anticipating certain answers, exploring the possibility of whether The University as an institution could adopt this radical culture of politics and organisation, of 'open space'.

The actual experience of the series was extraordinary. Most seminars had a hundred or more people in the audience; almost all had rich discussions after the presentations, and therefore often took up to three hours each (and in one case, went on for seven hours, including the screening of a film and the discussion around that); and from the feedback we got, we believe that the speakers enjoyed the sessions as much as the audience did.

The speakers at the seminars came from many different fields and persuasions, some well known, others less so, but all with important and fresh contributions. Beyond this, one of the main objectives of this initiative was to involve and engage students in the idea and process of the World Social Forum. By involving them in many aspects of the organisation of the series, the initiative was not restricted to a series of seminars alone.

These efforts paid off, in more ways than we had expected. They led to the formation of two discussion groups among students in Delhi — Apunba (a Manipuri word meaning 'we', in the sense of 'us, a community') and the Radicals' Collective. They led not only to significant numbers of Delhi University students attending the World Social Forum in Mumbai but to their taking part, from all reports, in a critical, engaged manner — thereby contributing strongly to that larger world. And they seemed also to challenge the organisers of the WSF in India — the WSF India Organising Committee — to come down from their mountain and try harder, in various ways, to reach out to these and other constituencies.

As the series progressed, we also received several enquiries from teachers and students in colleges from other parts of the country about the possibility of our organising similar seminars there (which sadly, we have been unable to manage till now); but in the one case where the locals simply took up the initiative, the series also led to the formation of what has become a major project in itself: the 'Other Worlds Educational Project' organised by young educationalists at the University of Nottingham in the UK. In a sentence, this initiative has launched a web-based course on critical engagement with cultures of politics that was, in its own words, inspired by the Delhi series – but there is much, much more to it. For details, see http://www.nottingham.ac.uk/home/taxvoa/OtherWorld/template2/-index.html.

The Open Space Seminar Series was co-organised by Mukul Mangalik, Reader in History at Ramjas College, University of Delhi, the writer, and Madhuresh Kumar, a former student of Mukul's and by then working with me; and with the help of Janaki Abraham, Lecturer at the Delhi School of Economics, several other teachers at other colleges, and several students. The series as a whole was organised under the auspices of The History Society, Ramjas College, and drew heavily on the social capital and popularity Mukul — member of the Society — enjoys in the university community.

Aside from the seminars themselves, we also published a Reader for the series (Are Other Worlds Possible? The Open Space Reader on the World Social Forum and its Engagement with Empire), and organised an 'Open Spaces Concert' towards the end of the series.

## THE OPEN SPACE BOOKS

When planning the books that might come out of the Open Space Series, we elected to distribute the fairly large amount of text that came out of the twelve seminars into three easy-to-purchase, easy-to-carry, and easy-to-read books. While there are obvious attractions to making all the material accessible in one book, we felt that there were many more advantages to presenting the material as a series, but where each book also stands by itself.

We accordingly decided to use a structure similar to that of the series, as mentioned above, and also to break past it. Book One — this volume — focuses on what, in a way, the series was all about and is called, Talking New Politics. It is made up of some of the material from what had labelled as the 'Stream A' seminars and also the additional session we organised after the Mumbai Forum, in February 2004, looking back at the Forum and how it is – or is not – helping to build other worlds.

Starting with a discussion of the idea of the WSF, and more generally of 'envisioning the world' as a concept, it goes on to look deeply at two key underlying concerns of the Forum: the relation between new (social) movements and old (political) movements, and the question of violence and non-violence and the boundaries and interfaces of violence, looked at from several points of view. With all the contributors being from India — albeit from many backgrounds — the book then moves to presenting three very different analyses of the roles that the Forum is today playing in the world, presented by contributors from three very different parts of the world: Argentina, Australia, and France.

This volume, like the others in this series, also contains a detailed Glossary of all the particular and somewhat specialised terms used in the Forum and in social and political movements, in the hope this can help all readers to equally engage with the ideas explored here. This is perhaps one of the first such glossaries in this field, and we would welcome feedback as to its usefulness.

Book Two, Interrogating Empires, is based entirely on the presentations and discussions in the 'Stream B' seminars in the series, and focuses on the structural

issues that the World Social Forum had till then been concerned with and in many senses is organised around: economic globalisation, militarisation and war, and also the new issues that have then been added on to this vocabulary as a result of the world meeting being held in India, as discussed above: patriarchy, communalism, and caste.

And Book Three, Imagining Alternatives, looks at how different people perceive and imagine what might, or could, be the 'other worlds' that they struggle for, and that some argue are already here, if we only care to look: The world of cyberspace, the world of socialism, and the world of the university, as an open space

This series as a whole therefore attempts to encompass the issues and concerns of the World Social Forum, and to look at why and how the issues being confronted by it are world issues; and also at how and why the 'internal' issues it faces are in fact generic issues, pertinent to all civil and political institutions — academic, activist, professional, and government. It also looks at how these issues are intertwined, and what their implications are, separately and combined; it attempts a critical examination of existing cultures of politics, and of what the alternative culture of politics proposed by the Forum — the idea of open space, of plurality and openness — can offer us, given the state of the world and of politics today; and it tries to open a discussion of the importance of openness in our own actions in daily life, and of attempting to practise a culture of critical engagement and open space.

The seminars did not come to clear conclusions on any of the issues discussed, and nor was this their objective; nor do these books attempt any prescriptions. In their own way, they also attempt — within the limits of what books can be — to be open spaces that challenge us to engage with ourselves and the worlds around us.

Through the collective efforts of the Are Other Worlds Possible team, we have tried to design the books so that they reflect some of this character. We have taken a somewhat unconventional approach to the format and have also included a tear-out sheet for your feedback and comments. Please feel free to contact us, at any of the e-addresses in the form for any further information or with any further suggestions!

We look forward to hearing from you - and to working together with you, towards other worlds.

**New Delhi, November 15, 2004**

## NOTES

1 See the Background Note to the seminar series, Mukul Mangalik and Jai Sen, with Madhuresh Kumar, (2003) – 'Are Other Worlds Possible? Cultures of Politics and the World Social Forum'. A Background Note for the "Open Space" Seminar Series at the University of Delhi, August – December 2003', then published in: Jai Sen with Madhuresh Kumar, compilers, (2003) - *Are Other Worlds Possible? The Open Space Reader on the World Social Forum and its Engagement with Empire*, pp 9-13. And see the Open Space Seminar Series Programme in this book, for an overview of the series as it took place.

2 For a discussion of this concept of 'open space', see: Francisco Whitaker, (2001) – 'World Social Forum: Origins and Targets'. Typescript in English. Available on the World Social Forum website, http://www.forumsocialmundial.org.br. Originally appeared as an article in Portuguese, in *Correio da Cidadania*, January 22, 2001. Translated by Jesus Bengoetxea and Sandra Guimarães; Chico Whitaker, March 2003 – 'Notes about the World Social Forum'. Revised version, dt March 17, 2003; and, for a critique: Jai Sen, 2004, as above.

3 For details, see Jai Sen, (2004) - 'The Long March to Another World: Reflections of a member of the WSF India Committee in 2002 on the first year of the World Social Forum process in India', in Jai Sen, Anita Anand, Arturo Escobar, and Peter Waterman, (eds. 2004) *World Social Forum: Challenging Empires*, New Delhi, The Viveka Foundation pp 293-311. Available at http://-www.choike.org/nuevo_eng/informes/157.html.

4 This Introduction is based on an article on the Open Space Seminar Series, 'Are Other Worlds Possible?' that appeared in *Seminar* (New Delhi) 530 in October 2003. The article was in turn based on the Background Note to the series authored by Mukul Mangalik and Jai Sen, as above. The stance in this Introduction is therefore not entirely personal but rather represents a loosely shared viewpoint. I acknowledge my debt to Mukul and Madhuresh. For my own analysis and views on the Forum, see: Jai Sen, (2002) 'On Building Another World [Or: 'Are other globalisations possible?]: The World Social Forum as an instrument of Global Democratisation'. A Paper for the NIGD (Network Institute for Global Democratisation) Seminar at the World Social Forum, on 'Global Democracy? A North-South Dialogue' held on February 4, 2002, at Amarzem, Porto Alegre, Brazil. Available at: http://www.nu.ac.za/ccs. http://www.forumsocialmundial.org.br/eng/tbib.asp, and http://www.choike.org/cgibin/-choike/links/page.cgi?p=ver_informe&id=977; and: Jai Sen, (2004) – 'How Open? The Forum as Logo, the Forum as Religion - Scepticism of the Intellect, Optimism of the Will', in Sen, Anand, Escobar, and Waterman, op.cit.

5 For a detailed discussion of the concept of the Forum, see Boaventura de Sousa Santos, (2003) – 'The World Social Forum: Toward A Counter-Hegemonic Globalization'. First draft, March 2003. Presented at the XXIV International Congress of the Latin American Studies Association, Dallas, USA March 27-27 2003. Published in edited form in Sen, Anand, Escobar, and Waterman, op.cit.

6 While the WSF has itself followed a practice of encouraging reflection and assessment and of placing such documents on this website, the January 2003 world meeting perhaps marked the point when several more major papers were prepared either before or immediately after. These include: Michael Albert, (2003) 'The WSF's Future', on ZNet, February 2 (http://www.zmag.org/content/showarticle.cfm?SectionID=41&ItemID=2956); Nikhil Anand, (May 2003) - 'Bound to Mobility?', as above; Jacklyn Cock, (2003) 'A Better or Worse World? The Third World Social Forum, Porto Alegre

2003'. Centre for Civil Society, Durban, South Africa, Research Report 5; Boaventura de Sousa Santos, (March 2003), as above; Arturo Escobar, (2003) - 'Other Worlds Are (Already) Possible: Cyber-Internationalism and Post-Capitalist Cultures. Draft Notes for the Cyberspace Panel', Life after Capitalism Programme, World Social Forum, Porto Alegre, January 23-8'. (www.zmag.org/lac.htm); and Peter Waterman, (forthcoming) - 'Second Thoughts on The Third World Social Forum, Porto Alegre, January 23-28, 2003: Place, Space and the Reinvention of Social Emancipation'. First and second drafts in circulation. All of these papers have now appeared in edited forms in Sen, Anand, Escobar, and Waterman, op.cit.

7 For an elaboration of Samir Amin's arguments, see: Samir Amin (Third World Forum), interviewed by V. Sridhar, January 2003 – 'For struggles, global and national', in *Frontline*, volume 20 issue 2, (http://www.flonnet.com/fl2002-/stories/20030131008201200.htm); republished in Sen, Anand, Escobar, and Waterman, op.cit.

8 For a more detailed discussion of this history, see Jai Sen, March-April 2002 - 'On Building Another World', as above, and also 'The Long March to Another World: Reflections on the World Social Forum process in India and internationally' (January 2003); op.cit.

9 See Teivo Teivainen, Network Institute for Global Democratization, July 2003 – 'Toward India, Toward (At Least Some) Rules'. Report of the WSF International Council Meeting, Miami June 2003. First Draft, 5.7.2003, Lima, Peru.

10 For instance, by Samir Amin, of the Third World Forum, in: Samir Amin, January 2003, as above. (Amin is highly regarded; to quote from the introduction to this article, he is "an intellectual who is regarded as one of the foremost thinkers on the changing dynamics of capitalism, [and] was among those assembled at the "Anti-Davos in Davos" [in January 2000]. Since then he has been actively associated with not only the WSF but also the regional forums that have evolved as a challenge to imperialist globalisation. He is director, Third World Forum (TWF), located in Dakar (Senegal) and Cairo and in Belgium, a network of social scientists and intellectuals from developing countries. Amin has also played a key role in the formation of the World Forum for Alternatives, which was launched in 1997.')

11 The few articles that appeared in the more important national press included: Devaki Jain, (January 2003) 'The Empire Strikes Back: A Report on the Asian Social Forum', in *Economic and Political Weekly*; Sukumar Muralidharan, 'Globalising Resistance', in *Frontline*, Volume 20, Issue 2. (http://www.flonnet.com/fl2002/stories/20030131009100400.htm); and: Jai Sen, (January 2003) 'The Long March to Another World', in *The Hindu*, January 29 and January 30, 2003. p 13. Also available on T*ransnational Alternativ@s* (http://-www.tni.org/tat/index.htm). All of these were subsequently reprinted in edited form in Sen, Anand, Escobar, and Waterman, op.cit.

In September 2003, a major monograph appeared on the political economy of the World Social Forum, but despite this being the first (and still most comprehensive) analysis of the Forum in these terms it seems to have received only limited circulation, at least in India. See: RUPE (Research Unit for Political Economy), (2003) *The Economics and Politics of the World Social Forum: Lessons for the Struggle against 'Globalisation'*. 'Aspects of India's Economy' series, no 35. Available at: www.rupe-india.org.

# A SALUTE

## MUKUL MANGALIK

There were times during the 1960s – coming to a head in the late 60s and early 70s, and carrying on well into the 80s – when it became possible for huge numbers of people across the globe – men and women, students, youth, ordinary working people and people without power – to dream impossible dreams.

It became possible for them to feel that it was they – their daily chores, their routine, their invisible, everyday labour – not money, that made the world go round; that far from being powerless, they could in fact dare to live out their desires and change the world, their own, as well the bigger wider world; beyond, much beyond the bounds of languages, origins, cultures, nations, and nationalism.

And they shouted

London, Paris, Rome, Berlin

We shall fight, we shall win!

Ho Ho Ho Chi Minh!

These were slogans that could have been spawned only by those feelings, during those times. The world was the stage. At least one of the major goals was a better life for all. Che Guevara, though not universally loved even among rebels, was, not surprisingly, an icon.

By the end of the 1980s, doors began to close – the doors to newer, better worlds. Into the 90s, massacres ruled the world. Dreams turned into nightmares of blood and gore, the cries for revenge, exclusion, death to democracy.

Hidden, veiled as it were, in the din and all this sound and fury, the empire of capital, the US in the lead, dug in its claws across the globe, profit its prime concern, the defence of human rights the ruse, Islam and terror held up as demons to be exorcised. If the attack on civil liberties, the massive spilling of the blood of innocents and the increasing risks of nuclear annihilation are the costs the world must bear, so be it.

It is into this frightening world that the World Social Forum has come like a breath of fresh air, a whiff of hope on a global scale after the crash of the dreams of the 60s and the 70s. This is the reason we met in a series of 12 seminars and discussions, aimed at exploring and interrogating as much as possible about the WSF.

The idea of the seminars was to talk about the Forum and deal with issues that the Forum is taking up; to feed new issues into these discussions; to weave songs, poems, plays, and films into the entire process.

The hope was that once the series got rolling – starting off in Ramjas and then moving from college to college, that these concerns, this spirit, would at some level become a part of everyday life on our campus.

That was a hope, an idea. It worked.

So, these books, to help the hope, our dreams, along.

# A SALUTE

## MUKUL MANGALIK

There were times during the 1960s — coming to a head in the late 60s and early 70s and carrying on well into the 80s — when it became possible for huge numbers of people across the globe — [illegible] women, students, [illegible] ordinary working people and people without power — to [illegible] impossible dreams.

It became possible for them to feel that it was they — their daily chores, their routine, their invisible everyday labour — not money, that made the world go round; that far from being powerless, they could in fact dare to live out their desires and change the world, their own, and a [illegible] wider world, beyond, much beyond the bounds of languages, origins, cultures, nations, and [illegible]onalism.

And they [illegible]...

[illegible] fighting [illegible]

We shall fight, we shall win

Ho Ho Ho Chi Minh!

[illegible] were [illegible] only have been [illegible] only by [illegible] during those times. The world was the stage. At least one of the major goals was a better life for all. Che Guevara, [illegible] everywhere [illegible] was, not surprisingly, an icon.

By the end of the 1980s, [illegible] began to close — the doors to newer, better worlds. Into the 90s, [illegible] the world. Dreams turned into nightmares of blood and gore, the [illegible] [illegible] death of democracy.

Though, victorious it were, in the din of all this sound and fury, the empire of capital, the US in the lead, [illegible] its claws across the globe, profit its prime concern, the defence of human rights the ruse, Islam and terror held up as demons to be exorcised. If the attack on [illegible] liberties, the [illegible] of the [illegible] and the increasing [illegible] of [illegible] are [illegible] to be [illegible].

[illegible] the World Social Forum, has come like a breath of fresh air, a [illegible] on a global scale after the [illegible] the dreams of the 60s and the 70s. This is the reason [illegible] seminars and discussions aimed at [illegible] and [illegible] as much as possible about the [illegible].

The idea of the seminars was to [illegible] about the Forum and deal with issues that the Forum is taking up, to [illegible] issues into these discussions, to weave songs, poems, plays and films into the entire process.

The hope was that once the series got going — starting off in [illegible] and then moving from college to college, that these concerns, this spirit, would at some level become a part of everyday life on our campus.

That was a hope, an idea [illegible].

So, these books, to [illegible] the hope, our dreams, along.

# ENVISIONING THE WORLD

BREAKING BOUNDARIES

ALTERNATIVE FRAMES

REDEFINING THE WORLD

OPEN FORUM

> We need to see the Forum not just as an event or a meeting that takes place once a year, or three times a year. It is a process of a formation of a culture, which is important; it provides an open space for free exchange, of mobilising on a sustained basis.

# breaking boundaries

**Jai Sen**

*Jai Sen has worked as an architect and urban designer, a civil campaignist, a researcher and writer, on dwelling, labour, planning and rights related issues. More recently, he has involved himself in research on the history and dynamics of popular movement in India, and a great deal of his recent work has also focused on the internationalisation and globalisation of civil movements, on cultures of politics, and on the Forum's concept of 'open space'. Among his publications are an edited volume (co-edited with Anita Anand, Arturo Escobar and Peter Waterman)* World Social Forum: Challenging Empires *(New Delhi, 2004). For the moment, he sees himself as an installation architect.*

*jai.sen@vsnl.com*

At some risk of overstatement, it is possible to argue that the World Social Forum (WSF) is one of the great ideas of our times and of the past century. Many have compared it to grand world ideas. Noam Chomsky has been attributed as saying it could be seen in terms of being a fifth International. I don't know if you are aware of the history of the Left and of the four Internationals that we have seen in the last century and a half, but the formation of 'Internationals' is a major idea in terms of the Left's conception of the future. Others, like Michael Hardt, have compared it to the Non Aligned Movement, yet others to the New International Economic Order. The WSF has provided grand visions, alternative ways of looking at history and of struggling with the empires that we confront and that confront us.

The WSF is not something that's happened by itself. I will give you some detail on how it has risen, as part of a great movement, against the exigencies

of economic globalisation and war, and the vital space it is now providing for 'the world' to meet, to exchange and strategise. It has already had a significant impact, and it holds great potential. But that potential will unfold only if we engage with it. I think these discussions, in this series of 'open space' seminars, are a first step towards doing so; I hope they will provide a meeting of minds, and not just be a series of events.

We need to see the Forum in the context of the time at which it has arisen. Many of you will be aware, through your studies and reflection on the growing empire in the world today, that we face imperialism on a world scale that perhaps hasn't been known for a century or more. The sweeping manner in which this has taken hold of the world is almost shocking.

It is also a time of growing fundamentalism. The Empire — the US Empire and the so-called 'coalition of the willing' — is only one manifestation of fundamentalism. There is also religious fundamentalism, which we know well in this country, and there is widespread fundamentalism throughout the world — Hindu, Islamic, Christian fundamentalism, intertwining with the rise of fundamentalist politics. The United States itself is an example of how this is taking shape, but it is also on the rise in many other countries. It is a time of growing conflict, of inter-sectoral conflict, as people retreat under these assaults and assert themselves, reaching for their own identities. So, an identity conflict is rising. At the same time, more people than ever known in history are refugees and migrants, fleeing to other worlds in search of some security — but where they are also made insecure, precisely because they are seeking refuge — and where their insecurities are taken advantage of, by fundamentalists. These communities are growing and developing identities on a world scale, partly through the Internet and partly through sheer struggle, and are also learning to cope with what is happening in the world around them in ways they know and that they judge best, for the situations they are in. These are increasingly led and dominated by narrow, fundamentalist concerns.

> "We are living in exciting times and I believe the Forum is a manifestation of that excitement. We are the Forum. Not they. Not the people who are in the committees."

In other words, we live in an age where we are witnessing the emergence of worldwide networks of fundamentalisms: where we are beginning to see the crystallisation of 'networks of networks' in this area — of 'meshworks' — such as the interweaving of religion and arms and so on. Researchers speak of this happening in terms of the rise of global civil movements; but it is not only so-called 'civil society' that is experiencing this. So is what I term 'uncivil society' – the societies of those who are dominated and marginalised by those of us who like to call ourselves 'civil society', earlier within 'national' boundaries but now at a world scale. [1]

The historical mission of 'civil societies' all over the world, in the North as well as the South, has been to 'civilise' the uncivil. It is now a time in history however, when the uncivil all over the world are realising and asserting their identities, and fighting back – which makes this a very important moment, and movement, in world history. But while this much is good, there is much reason for all those who celebrate this to also be concerned: Precisely because these movements are struggling to articulate and assert their identities at a stage in history when they are also struggling against the serial impacts of capitalist globalisation, they are highly vulnerable – and their struggles are all too often being co-opted by fundamentalists and others, with radically different visions of the future.

We are living through a time of tremendous tumult. It is a phase of history where what are called 'social movements' are widely seen to have made a range of successful impacts on politics and history, such as in the field of human rights. We have seen major advances since the 1960s, in areas of women's rights, and on environmental, indigenous people's and Dalit questions, as well as on more specific questions and issues such as land mines or child labour rights. There are so many areas — housing and many others — where major ground has been broken. But when you look at all this within the larger history of the period, at what else has also been happening and taking shape, such as fundamentalism, it all seems to pale. The issue then becomes: how do we deal with what is happening? This is one of the issues we'll be looking at in these discussions: old versus new politics — parties, social movements and civil groups, how different ways of interacting, of addressing issues are going to take place.

## AN ALTERNATIVE WORLD

So, just what is the idea of the Forum? As I see it, in essence, it's very simple. The idea was conceived in 2000, and the first World Social Forum took place in January 2001, as a challenge to the World Economic Forum that takes place in Davos, in Switzerland, each January, the annual meeting of global corporations with heads of State.

The World Social Forum was conceived of as a place to think about and formulate an alternative world, a world different from the one we are living in today. That is why it has coined for itself the motto, 'Another world is possible'. More accurately it should have said, 'Other worlds are possible', but the slogan formally is: 'Another world is possible', in the singular.

The WSF saw itself as a challenge to Davos, and to the argument that neo-liberal globalisation is the need of the world and that this is the manner in which the world must move — that everything must be subordinate to the economy. So the idea, very simply, was a focus on the 'social', not on the economic. Therefore, the World Social Forum. This is a concern of all kinds of people in the world: students, youth, and professionals, ordinary people who are living at home and are struggling to deal with the world — not just those who are actively involved in movements.

This was where it all started. But to do this, the Forum also coined an interesting concept: it created the idea of an 'open space', for free and relatively undirected exchange between people of many different persuasions, backgrounds, contexts. It has therefore come to allow a cross-fertilisation that perhaps has never been dreamt of in history before, and it has manifested itself spectacularly.

Let me repeat something to underline it: This idea was conceptualised in the year 2000, which is the year immediately after the big first demonstration that took place in Seattle, around the World Trade Organisation, in November-December 1999. This was therefore a time when many discussions were taking place, about how to follow Seattle. In that same year there were also several other big demonstrations — in Washington DC, against the World Bank, in April 2000, then in Prague, against the G8, and in many other parts of the world.

What took place that year was therefore a kind of crescendo of the statement — of the assertion — of alternatives. Those who conceived of the World Social Forum, basically Brazilians and also some Europeans, argued that there needed to be a place where all these movements could meet, could talk

together, and could see how this emerging movement for another world could be sustained.

### A COLLECTIVE VOICE

But they made an important distinction: they said that no one "ism" should guide this initiative. It should be a free and open space. Consequently, the Forum should never speak as a forum. It should be completely open for those who meet to get together in groups — affinities — and to speak in collective terms, as they like. So, it may be the Greens, the feminists, those concerned with religion and faith, the communists or socialists who speak. It may be a special interest group that comes together — children's rights; indigenous people — and the Forum should help them speak within a country, at a regional level, and at a world level. This is what has actually now taken place, through the World Social Forum.

There was something called the 'Brazil Organising Committee' that was first set up by eight civil organisations of different backgrounds, CUT a landless workers' movement, MST, Movimento dos Trabalhadores Rurais Sem Terra, a big federation of trade unions in the country. There were religious organisations, associated with the church (which had a history of being very active since the 60s in the Brazilian struggle against the rule of the generals, and before that with local communities in urban areas and with the 'Indians' in Brazil), a women's organisation, a human rights organisation, and others, including a research organisation, IBASE. There is also a coalition called ABONG, which is the Brazil Association of NGOs.

After the tremendous success of the first World Social Forum in January 2001, this Organising Committee convened and set up an 'International Council' in June 2001. This is now made up of movements, trade unions, NGOs, and other like-minded people from all over the world. It continues to be constructed and expanded even today, some years later.

The first Forum was held in Porto Alegre, a city in the south of Brazil. This city had become quite well known in previous years for a process of participatory planning and budgeting, where families, households, and individuals took part in the planning of the city. This process transformed planning and the environs of the city. In part, this happened because of the fact that the Workers' Party, which is made up not only of socialists but is a very broad coalition, and which is in power now in Brazil, had come into power in Porto Alegre and in Rio Grande do Sul. And it was this party that led the process of participatory planning. So, when people from Brazil and Europe were thinking about where to hold the first Forum, they felt that it should be in Brazil and in this city.

Porto Alegre is a very rich city, and in general, the southeast of Brazil where

it is located, is a very prosperous part of the country, unlike the northeast, which is stricken by poverty and landlessness. So, it was a powerful experiment with alternatives. Then the city government, and the state government, who were hosts to the first Forum, became very important factors in its success. They provided infrastructure to the Forum organisers, and helped to make an important beginning for this new experiment.

We also need to briefly look at the history of the Forum. The Workers' Party has emerged in the last 25-30 years in Brazil. Since the seventies, it has been part of the resurgence of civil politics and of a new politics, if you like, that took root during the military regime in Brazil from 1964 to 84 when there was, during certain periods, ruthless suppression of all kinds of movements. It began as a resistance to this suppression. But once the military stepped down in 1984, because of the collapse of the country's economy and under pressure of the countrywide mobilisation that had by then taken place, this movement gradually took over leadership of civil and political society in Brazil. It now represents the cultural, social and political resurgence in the country as a whole. Many of the organisations of the Brazil Organising Committee, are members of this party, or associated with it.

But I also need to make clear that the World Social Forum is not a party-organised forum. It is quite separate from the party — it is a civil forum. At the same time, it is clear that the party (the Workers' Party) has been very closely associated with the Forum, and at times there have been many accusations that the party has used the Forum to grandstand itself, such as at the first inauguration. There were party banners everywhere. So much so, it was difficult to know whether it was a party forum or not!

This is an important issue for the Forum because in its Charter of Principles, which it adopted in 2001, the Forum has said clearly that it is a world forum for social movements and organisations, and that it does not want any organisations that are political parties. It also does not allow members of governments to come in, as members of government (they can come in as individuals), and it does not allow any members of groups that are involved in armed struggle or are sympathetic to armed struggle.

These are the three proscriptions of the World Social Forum. So, in that sense, the Workers' Party being there is in one sense a violation of the idea of the Forum as a free civil space.

## INTERNATIONALISING THE FORUM

The idea to internationalise the Forum came up in 2001. The Brazilians argued very strongly that the World Social Forum could not remain a Brazilian process. In their analysis, India was the place where it should next be held. They took the initiative to do this in 2001, the very first year of the Forum,

and began speaking at different meetings to Indians whom they knew, about the possibility of organising the Forum in India. Intense discussions took place, for instance, at a World Assembly of Citizens in France in mid-2001.

The first, more formal, preparatory discussions on India as a possible venue were held in Bangalore, in December 2001. The idea behind this thinking — of holding the meeting in India — was that in the world as it exists, there was a need to move away from Latin America — to involve Asia as it was the most populous continent in the world. Within Asia, it was important to locate the Forum in a country with strong traditions of movement and civil activism, which could sustain such a movement and could also give it an Asian and a regional perspective, and where the Forum would be tolerated by the government. In other words, they were looking for a relatively democratic country. Well, India is the only country in Asia that fits this bill well. So, negotiations on the Brazilians' proposal that the 2003 World Social Forum be held in India were started.

**THE INDIAN COMMITTEE**

The Indian committee, which was formed in early 2002, decided that it could not hold the Forum in India in 2003, as proposed by the Brazilians. For a variety of reasons, the Committee proposed that if the Brazilians wanted the world meeting to be held in India, it could only be done in January 2004. So, the first meeting of the WSF outside Brazil was planned for Mumbai, January 16–21, 2004.

In India, there is something called an India General Council, an India Working Committee, and an India Organising Committee. As you know, we are brilliant at creating these huge bureaucracies and infrastructures, and it's sort of pyramidical. It starts from a few hundred organisations in the general council, and goes up to the few people who are actually organising it. The Forum secretariat has so far been located in Mumbai, but there are a number of people from Delhi who are also very actively involved.

The World Social Forum has a Charter of Principles, which lays out its basic

> People are also talking about: who controls the Forum? Is it the socialists? Is it the anarchists? Is it the Trotskyites? Is it the Communists? Or none of them?

policy positions on what it is and how it sees the world. This document declares that the Forum is 'for all those opposed to neo-liberal globalisation'. This has now come to be seen as a kind of statement of adherence. In fact, the International Council of the Forum in June 2003 took a decision that all those who want to be members of the International Council have to declare their written opposition to neo-liberal globalisation.

With its coming to India, the whole agenda of the Forum has widened. Communalism, fundamentalism, caste and race, and patriarchy have now been brought in. These are not part of the world Charter, but of the Indian version, the 'India Policy Statement'. So we are seeing a shift in the world forum — not just opposition to neo-liberal globalisation, but also to these other empires.

There is also the question of war and militarisation, which the Europeans have brought out very strongly, and added to the Forum's agenda. The European Social Forum, held for the first time in Florence in Italy in November 2002, and then in Paris in November 2003, have added this to their agenda, and therefore to the WSF's agenda. So we now have five empires that the WSF is confronting.

## KEY CHANGES IN POLICY

The Forum has thus taken three or four key policy decisions since 2002, both in India and internationally. The first of these is to hold the world event outside Brazil, in Mumbai, the second, to oppose other empires.

Thirdly, the major organisational structure that is emerging is now very different from the previous one: there were only eight organisations to coordinate the Forum in Brazil; in the world process we now have 250 organisations represented, from all kinds of fields of activism. A shift is taking place from a non-representative committee to a representative one. This is happening even though the Forum's Charter makes clear that the Forum is not trying to 'represent' others, or to be a leader of world social movements. It has said clearly that it is not trying to be a world social movement, but is trying only to coordinate this meeting that takes place. And we are now getting to a situation where in India we have created a representative structure where workers, Dalits, women, tribals — all these 'sections' are now 'represented'. There is therefore a radical change that has taken place in the Forum. This is a conceptual change, as much as it is structural.

The fourth major change took place in India in 2002-03: the organisers had created a new space, in terms of the way the WSF was structured, where small organisations and individuals had a place in the committee. This wasn't there in the international committee and in the other processes. In other words, it was a much more free space, recognising that there were roles that small organisations and individuals play in society and history. But later in 2003, that space has been cancelled. It was taken away by the organisers of the World Social Forum in India; contradicting the most fundamental principle of the WSF that it is an open space, open to all.

The formal excuse that has been given by the Indian working committee is that the Brazilians don't provide for it, so why should we? But the reality is that the Committee which is dominated by large organisations, many affiliated to political parties, have found that individuals and small organisations raise awkward questions. This became very difficult to sustain, so they decided to enforce regularity and conformity; they chopped off that space. That big organisations – also corporate bodies – will do this, is perhaps only to be expected; but I think we need to look at how and why the smaller organisations did not protest in any way, and at how this is changing the culture of politics in the Forum, as well as in terms of world movements.

## THE IDEA OF THE FORUM

I would like to reflect briefly on the idea of the Forum. I think we need to see it at two levels. First, it is a world initiative. It can be compared to the United Nations and to the Non Aligned Movement, though the difference is that

both of these are, or were, inter-State initiatives. This is the first world-scale 'inter-civil' initiative. Nothing like this has ever taken place before. The civil campaigns that have taken place around different issues over the past decades — environment, women's rights, and so on — have been very important and they have strongly contributed to the growth of this culture of transnational civil politics, but none of them matches the ambition and realm that the World Social Forum has brought out. At the second level is what the Forum means, and what it can mean: it is building bridges, internally, in Brazil and in India. It allows us to speak across boundaries.

In India, we still enjoy a relatively open political space, even though those spaces are closing down today (personally, I argue that this is happening decisively in our times, in the world as a whole). In this context, the Forum allows many movements that normally don't get the chance to communicate with each other, to talk, to listen and to hear. For example, how does the women's movement conceptualise patriarchy? How can those of us who are not feminists understand the issue of feminism? The Forum now allows us to get a deeper understanding of this, because it encourages a discussion across boundaries. This is true for all kinds of movements.

The Forum also allows the building of bridges internationally — across regions, across the world. In the 50s and 60s there was a great efflorescence of internationalism, something that grew out of the experience of the Second

> We see the Forum as an event and it is an amazing event. It is truly an extraordinary celebration of life that goes on well past the six-day annual event that we know as the Forum. Despite its confusion, and even if all the systems may break down, it is still fantastic, in the sense that through all the meetings and possibilities, one has a chance of seeing the world in a microcosm.

World War in the 1940s, and of the horrors of nationalism (the Nazis, the Italian fascists), but that then died out to some degree – and was largely also restricted to inter-State internationalism; though the concept of universal human rights also grew out of that.

Today the Forum is a process where international action has become available to many, many more people. To a degree 'international action and thought' is already available to us, through the Internet. Many of us are doing this. But the Forum allows the world to come home, and we see the world in a richness that is otherwise difficult to perceive. Lastly, the Forum stands for the concept of 'open space', which is what I want to turn to now.

## AN OPEN SPACE

We need to see the Forum not just as an event. It is not just a meeting that takes place once a year, or three times a year. Much more than this, it is a process of the formation of a culture, which is important; it provides an open space for free exchange, and for mobilising on a sustained basis. These are its vital roles.

As I have already said, the Forum does not take place by itself. It has a history and a context; it has grown out of many major movements since the 60s. These — from human rights to the rights of tribal and indigenous peoples, to women's rights, and issues of war — have helped us understand the world as one. All this has been extremely important. The Forum is a part of this articulation of universalism.

Though the idea of universal rights is much older — for instance, during the French Revolution in the 18th century — it has really only been since the 1950s that the idea of certain concepts being universally valid and therefore universally applicable has emerged. One of the most important areas where this has taken place is in the field of human rights. Similarly, this idea of the Forum as a 'universal idea' has also emerged.

But there are also serious problems with this idea. Because, after all, even what is portrayed as universality grows out of and manifests a certain culture. We therefore have to look carefully at this concept: in a dictatorship, for instance, how much can a World Social Forum talk about openness? In other words, is the culture of politics – the culture of open space — proposed by the Forum really valid universally, to all peoples in all places?

Notwithstanding this, it is still important to recognise the Forum as one of the world's first truly global initiatives from the South. It is particularly important to recognise this in the post 9/11 context and its aftermath of war; of the rise of US imperialism.

In this context, the Forum offers a major space for free debate. This space is under assault today, all over the world. It is being grotesquely reduced

through the curtailing of civil liberties. Most specifically in the United States, where there has been a drastic curtailing of civil liberties, but also all over the world — from Australia, to Britain to Malaysia to Indonesia to Egypt to South America — new legislation is being brought in to control terrorists and militants, but is being widely used against all kinds of civil and political activists instead. We of course have our own version, POTA (the Prevention of Terrorism Act), and we know how it is being used and misused.

## PROMOTING CIVIL SPACE

We therefore need to perceive that the Forum is a part of a world process to promote open, civil space and to defend open, civil space. The point is whether the Forum is aware of this. I personally question this, as to whether it is sufficiently aware of its role in history.

Equally, are we sufficiently aware that Asia is the arena where the Empire has now struck so decisively — through the war on Iraq, where the Americans have now created a base for themselves in West Asia, and through this are seeking to control all of West, North and Central Asia.

This is therefore a very important development; but what perspective does it give us, with which we should view the Forum?

Remember that Latin America was where the Empire last struck. During the 1950s, 60s, 70s and 80s, Latin America was the backyard of the United States. That was where the Empire that we today know first entrenched itself, and still continues to do so. But today Asia is the target. Africa is to come. So how does Asia see itself, in terms of solidarity with past imperialism? And with the victims of the Empire?

We need to build that solidarity. It — Latin America, Africa, wherever — cannot be seen as 'another part of the world'. Our history is different, but it's a part of world history. So the Forum is a very interesting and important place to confront this larger reality.

Lastly, I want to briefly touch on the concept of virtual and real worlds. I have really only talked so far about the real world, not the virtual world. There is a great deal of exchange that takes place, around the Forum, on its web-site. We see the Forum as an event and it is an amazing event. It is truly an extraordinary celebration of life that goes on well past the six-day annual event that we know as the Forum. Despite its confusion, and even if all the systems may break down, it is still fantastic, in the sense that through all the meetings and possibilities, one has a chance of seeing the world in a microcosm.

## CRITICAL REFLECTIONS

I will wrap up with some critical reflections on some of the issues I have tried to raise.

One, 'open space' has been argued by its authors, primarily Brazilians and some Europeans, as being a neutral space. Many people have written about this, including myself. I have gone on record as saying that it's a wonderful, totally neutral space, allowing undirected discussions. After a year, however, I have realised that it's not that at all. It's a highly structured space. In one sense, no space is neutral. When any institution — whether it's a feudal landlord, or an industry or the State or a popular movement — creates a space, it sets some rules for this space. In the case of the World Social Forum, it is the Brazilian Organising Committee, and now the International Council, that sets the rules; and the Charter of Principles, of course are the rules.

There are also clear rules about who is excluded — who the Forum is not open to. People who have any doubts at all about opposing neo-liberal globalisation are not welcome; not only those who promote it. If you have questions about whether structural adjustment can help a country, you are not welcome. The Forum has drawn very tight boundaries around itself, and in my way of thinking, its unwillingness to engage with those who have questions in their minds is a big conceptual problem for it, in terms of its self-definition as an open space.

If you take the Forum's opposition to the five empires as an example, you could say that you actually want the 'perfect person' — the perfect, complete activist! Because the perfect Forum participant should, in fact, be consciously and knowingly opposed to all the empires, at once: to neo-liberal globalisation, to war, to patriarchy, to communalism, and to caste. And if you don't oppose all five, you don't get into that space. But clearly, none of us is

completely knowledgeable in all these areas, and so this is an important indication that the Forum is not truly an 'open space'.

Secondly, it's also not an open space in the sense that it is actually meant only for organisations. It is technically not for individuals. Even though individuals usually make up two-thirds of the participants at any given Forum, they (we!) have no role in any of the decision-making that takes place. Individuals are also registered differently, at the Forum as an event, and have different (meaning less) rights.

But the world is changing. Today, all the organisational forms that we know and use — trade unions, societies, trusts, and cooperatives — date from the 19th century. This includes political parties. They came out of a conception of social and economic relations of the 18th and 19th centuries, and from the potentialities of communication that pertained at that time. In case we have not noticed, the world has radically changed since then! These organisational forms, and the rules they represent and practise, do not arise from today's realities, from today's modes of production or communication.

Today, people associate in entirely new ways, in new networks, with new forms of associations. The Forum is a child of the 20th-21st century, and yet it's base is in old politics. It's a curious mix. And it doesn't know how to handle this mix. This is something that is resurging very strongly in the International Council, where by and large, it is old organisations that are ruling and who are setting rules to protect their places. These are very important conceptual issues that we need to look at.

Thirdly, the issue of power is coming up in the Forum. Today, the World Social Forum is seen as a power—nebulous, but a power all the same. Many people associated with the World Social Forum see it as having authored the big demonstrations that took place across the world against the Iraq war February 2003. I think that this is going a bit far. In February, after the demonstrations, the *New York Times* carried an article that said: "There is now a second world power — public opinion". The writer was clearly signalling the Forum and the big actions that had been taking place. This is a sign of public opinion about the Forum. It may be an overstatement, but it has gone to that degree.

People are also talking about: who *controls* the Forum? Is it the socialists? Is it the anarchists? Is it the Trotskyites? Is it the Communists? Or none of them? Is there some dark horse? Who controls the horse?

In other words, the World Social Forum is today seen as an arena of power struggle, but those who are in the leadership, in the co-ordination, are themselves jostling for power. They are trying to influence, and control, how things take place. So, although power and the contestation for power are not meant to be there in the Forum — it is meant to be neutral and open for everybody – they are very present. These are the contradictions that are

taking shape in the Forum. But the Forum has not yet engaged with the issue of power. And it doesn't even seem to have a concept of it. Nor does it deal with power in society; the realms of power — whether communal, fundamentalist, or economic.

So how does it want to actually bring about change? Like the world movement as a whole, it has abandoned the old two-stage theory of social transformation, of "take over the world and then transform it". But then, what does it want to do? What is its theory?

Lastly, there is the issue of — as I term it — 'the Forum as religion'. The Forum is starting to believe in itself. Increasingly, the Forum is asking only known, safe speakers to speak. I will give you a case in point. In December 2002, the Brazilians sent to the Indian Organising Committee a list of speakers they wanted from India for the Forum in Brazil, in January 2003. But a few members of the Indian committee vetted that list, struck off names and sent back their own list, because they were worried about the affiliations of some of the names on that list!

So, now we have this problem: only safe people — those who can be relied upon to say the right things — should be asked to speak at meetings. We then have a situation where only those who are already committed to a position come to meetings. So what do we have? A situation where the priests are talking to the converted and committed. But then, where is the debate that the Forum is meant to be about? Where is the open space?

The Forum is beginning to believe in itself, to close in on itself. We are seeing the process, not only of religion growing but also of corporatism growing. The Forum is being franchised across the world. The WSF's motto 'Another world is possible!' has become a logo. By believing in itself, the Forum is today constructing a corporate empire.

I think we urgently need to interrogate these developments. They represent a deeply problematic challenge to what was a brilliant idea. I think the WSF remains a brilliant idea, but I think we need to interrogate this idea in history; we need to struggle with those who are leading it.

We are living in exciting times and I believe the Forum is a manifestation of that excitement. We are the Forum. Not they. Not the people who are in the committees. We are the Forum. We can make it. Like we can make politics, we can remake the world. We have to believe in ourselves and the Forum as a possible vehicle, which can take this forward. But it's a problematic formulation that now needs critical review and reflection. ■

NOTES: 1. For Further explication of my concept of 'Uncivil' see my paper – 'Civilising Globalisation? Or Globalising Civilisation? Some reflections towards civil governance and a conscious, critical globalisation'. A Paper for a Presentation to the Opening Session of 'Helsinki Conference 2002: Searching for Global Partnerships' Helsinki, Finland, December 2-4 2002. Organised by the Crisis Management Initiative (Office of President Ahtisaari), on behalf of the Government of Finland. Available at: www.helsinkiconference.fi )

# alternative frames

**NIVEDITA MENON**

*Nivedita Menon has taught Political Science in Delhi University for over 15 years. She writes mainly on gender and politics, and her latest book is* Recovering Subversion: Feminist Politics Beyond the Law, *(Delhi 2004). She has been active in non-party, non-funded citizens' initiatives in Delhi around issues of secularism, peace, opposition to the nuclear bomb and for workers' rights for over a decade.*

*niveditamenon2001@yahoo.co.uk*

> "The purity that we demand of our allies is our greatest weakness."

I would like to use this opportunity to describe what the WSF represents for me at a very emotional level. Many of us, who were young in the 1980s, have had to come to terms very painfully with the idea that what we imagined would be progress has not gone the way we thought it would. We believed when we read, for example, *A Train to Pakistan*, a novel on the Partition by Khushwant Singh — I read it when I was about 15 or 16 — and I remember thinking, 'This is the past of the country, and we are now moving forward.' I read it and I was sad. But that was the sad *past* of the country.

I think many of you have been born into an age — and have come of age, in the 1990s — when such certainties were not available to you in the first place. You came into a world in which those old certainties — and the ways in which we thought the world would change — were already in question. Poverty was growing, imperialism was more powerful. There were wars. Now there are also ethnic fratricides, entire communities killing one another all over the world.

**A DISTILLATION OF VOICES**

So it seems to me that what the World Social Forum has done, is in some ways it has distilled — and for me it represents what it can represent at its best — certain kinds of voices of dissent, and voices that have challenged hegemonic commonsensical notions. The World Social Forum can, at its best, represent

that range of voices that have always questioned what common sense is.

I am reminded of Emma Goldman, the famous American anarchist whose voice of dissent was so dangerous for American democracy that she had to be imprisoned for many years. She was finally sent into exile. The greatest democracy in the world couldn't tolerate her voice of dissent. All she did was speak at forums, challenging mainstream notions of patriarchy, family and the State, and she was exiled. She said, "If there is no dancing in the revolution, I want no part of it." And I think this sense of dance, and power and poetry, which has actually marked voices of dissent and voices of revolt, is what I'd like to bring before you.

I'm trying to say that the World Social Forum could be a distillation not only of voices but also of different kinds of ways in which notions of development and progress have been challenged, at least from the mid-twentieth century onwards. Of course, from much earlier than that too. For example, if you think of the notion of an affluent society, you have the anthropologist Marshall Sahlins talking about affluent societies in a different sense. He says, "If an affluent society is a society in which everybody's needs are met, then in fact the simplest hunting-gathering societies are the most affluent because they have the simplest needs."

The whole question of need and development is challenged by this idea that affluence is not something you have to pursue. If you say that the so-called primitive hunting-gathering societies are affluent, you are denying it is the pre-ordained fate of human beings to consistently chase after unmeetable needs with scarce resources. Sahlins says, "It is to deny that the human condition is a pre-ordained tragedy in which the human being is a prisoner sentenced to the hard labour of living with perpetual disparity between his unlimited wants and his insufficient means." This kind of notion challenges the idea of development itself, makes you realise that chasing after perpetual prosperity is very problematic. We are not really talking about alternative forms of development here, but about alternatives to development that question the very idea of 'progress'.

There was this joke I remember reading, which some of you may have come across, and we laugh because it seems the response is so irrational, of a man in a rural, undeveloped poor locality, sitting and staring at the river, watching the sunlight play on the water. He is fishing, or perhaps just contemplating the river, when a man drives up in a car and says, "What are you doing?"

"I'm just relaxing", he says.

The other man says, "Well, why don't you go to work in my factory?"

He asks, "For what?"

"You'll make some money," he says.

"For what?"

The second man says, "You can make more money, you can save the money."

"And then do what?"

"You can relax," the man says.

"I'm relaxing now," the first man answers.

I remember thinking it was silly. We laughed, because obviously the man by the river doesn't get it. This is not relaxation. Real relaxation is when you've worked your guts out in somebody's factory and then saved up enough money to buy a refrigerator into which you have to earn enough to put this, that and the other ... and so on. This joke was funny because the response of the man by the river was utterly irrational. It was completely unreasonable, refusing to accept notions of what is the right thing to do and what is the right way to go. I think these are the kind of alternative frames in which the World Social Forum could enable us to look at the world.

I would like us to think about all the different kinds of ways in which that could happen.

## QUESTIONING THE CODES

There is another story which actually is a bit of a favourite of mine and like all people who have been teaching for a while, there is always a danger that everybody has heard this story before, probably from me. I promise never to repeat it again in any institution of Delhi University, but I must say it for one last time. It's a story supposedly about Picasso. I presume all of you are familiar

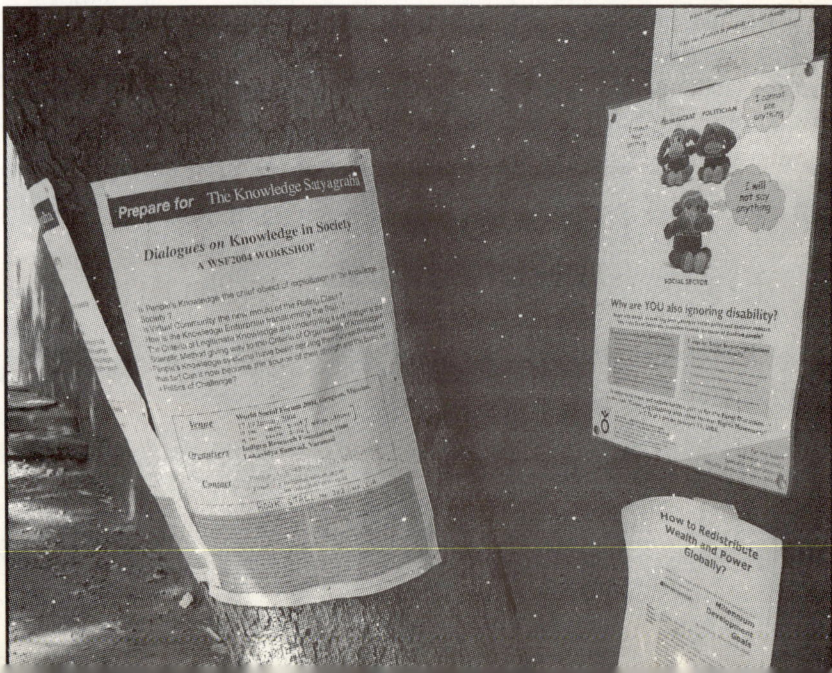

with Picasso's Cubist phase? But in case you have not seen prints of his work, let's just say his work is called 'modern art' in a pejorative sense. Basically, his painting in this phase is not realistic, not a straightforward representation of what we see as 'reality', although he has also done exquisitely realistic work and beautiful portraits in an earlier phase. So, this man goes to Picasso to get a portrait of his wife painted, and the wife does a couple of sittings. Then Picasso says, "All right, come back after two weeks." The man comes back after two weeks, excitedly, to get the portrait of his wife. Picasso unveils the painting, which is basically something like three triangles and a fish.

The husband says, "This is a portrait of my wife?"

And Picasso says, "Yeah, this is it."

The man says, "But this is not what my wife looks like."

Picasso says, "No? What does she look like?"

He is a very devoted husband, he has a little photograph of his wife in his wallet. He holds up the photograph and says, "This is what my wife looks like."

And Picasso says, "She looks exactly like that?"

He replies, "Yes, she looks exactly like that."

Picasso says, "Rather small, isn't she?"

Now, what is happening in this story is that Picasso's question is enabling us to understand that what we assume to be natural, real, rational and unchangeable appears to be so only by the functioning of certain codes. The moment those codes are questioned, you begin to understand that there has been a whole process by which the world has been naturalised in that way.

It is the whole development of the language of photography that enables us to say that three triangles and a fish doesn't represent this woman, but a small two-dimensional, black and white picture, which would actually be only as large as the woman's palm, is an exact representation of her. It's the power that the language of photography exercises in presenting itself as something that represents reality.

> "I would like to think of the World Social Forum as a space with enormous diversity and alternative visions."

What I'm trying to say with this story is that we need to really draw on resources which have continuously presented us with alternative frames for understanding the world and once you place this alternative frame upon the world, notions of rationality and irrationality, notions of what is reasonable and unreasonable, all these kind of ideas acquire a completely different meaning.

I mean, take for example the notion of progress, to which I think many of us still subscribe. To be progressive is to be good. We value progress. But what is the notion of progress? The notion of progress is that everybody is moving continually forwards and upwards, in a very clear way. This is a legacy of thought from the Enlightenment, coming down to us from Europe of the 18th century. Many of these ideas that we use unthinkingly, have come up in that particular historical context; for example, that progress of a certain kind is inevitable; that all societies move from poverty, illiteracy, ignorance, darkness and barbarism to rationality, riches, civilisation and so on.

But more importantly, the idea of progress has involved the important notion that you have to move from diverse and heterogeneous practices to one unified, rational, simple world. There is the whole notion that diversity and heterogeneity are wasteful and dangerous, that we need to continuously iron out diversity in order to produce a unified, simple, rational whole to avoid confusion. This is an idea that is inherent in the idea of globalisation.

What is the idea behind the Uniform Civil Code in India, for instance? That heterogeneous practices of communities are destructive for the nation State.

So there is a whole way in which the idea of progress involves the elimination of diversity. You can see how that notion is behind the idea that the WSF should move towards one platform of action, one voice. That you have to clean up the inside of the Forum and make that into a unitary space and not permit diversity there; diversity is dangerous.

But why is diversity dangerous?

It's the uncontrollability of diversity and the fact that diversity will generate energies that are not always going to fit into what you think is good, whether what you stand for is corporate globalisation or the World Social Forum. The fact that diversity will generate uncontrollable, unpredictable energies is something that is frightening for any order that seeks to impose one model on the universe. What has therefore happened, is that the ideas of 'progress' and 'development' have given States their raison d'etre, have permitted governance of populations, and therefore the idea of progress. And the unitary notion of progress has actually acted as a weapon to disenfranchise the powerless and marginalised.

If you take something very simple, in our context, to understand, like the Narmada Bachao Andolan — what is it challenging? It's challenging the idea

that there is one kind of progress and it's saying we don't want that progress. It's a challenge to the idea that there can only be one way in which human civilisation should move. Now, what this means effectively is that what we have called 'progress' and 'development', has in fact been the ideology to exclude large masses of people rather than bring in large masses of people.

## SUSTAINABLE DEVELOPMENT

Interestingly, each time there are voices that challenge development, they get incorporated into some kind of institutionalised framework. So, when you hear, for example, the term 'sustainable development', that sounds like a good thing, right? Sustainable development is okay because we can somehow manage through this to sustain the globe. But where does the notion come from?

It comes out of the realisation that in order to keep up development at the rate it is going, you need to have an unending supply of natural resources. So, sustainable development is not challenging the idea of development of this sort. It is simply saying: how can we manage growth and development in such a way that somehow we can monitor and gather together all the scarce natural resources and keep development going in the same direction? Sustainable development, too, becomes a question of managerial and technical skills. It becomes an idea that enables new areas of intervention by the State and so on. 'Sustainable' development assumes that the consumerist and capital-intensive lifestyles of western societies are the models to which the rest of the world should aspire. But in order to keep this model going, natural resources have to be carefully managed, rationed and planned.

Of course, in this understanding of sustainable development, the biggest threat to natural resources, to the environment, is seen to come from the poor. So we find that the poor are targeted as the biggest destroyers of the environment. You'll have to set up national parks to preserve the environment and throw out the traditional forest communities who have lived there. The original reason why the forest would have been depleted is that forest contractors and the State took control over forest resources, but the understanding is that the forest communities who have used the forests for centuries without depleting them -- they are the real enemies. The poor are the real enemies of the environment: this is the understanding with which this model works.

Look at Delhi, at the way in which it is being cleaned up of the poor. You remove so-called polluting industries to, let's say, Himachal Pradesh. Let Himachal deal with the pollution. This is the way in which an unbridled notion of development works. You have to remove slums because slums are dirty, and they are using up water. Despite innumerable data, which shows us that the amount of water consumed by the rich is 50 times as much as that consumed by an entire slum. One house in an upmarket part of Delhi would consume more water than an entire so-called slum. Yet it would be the slum that would have to be removed.

So there is a way in which every critique of development is harnessed and marshalled back to attack the people again. You have the so-called 'green judgements' by the Supreme Court in the last few years, which have continuously pushed the working people out of the city in order to make the city cleaner and greener. For whom? For the middle classes. But who is going to keep the city running, if those working people are not there?

You must have read reports in the papers, which talk about the 'hawker menace'. The 'hawker menace'? That is, people who sell things that the ordinary person needs, the person who does not shop in the malls of

Gurgaon, are a menace. What is not a menace to society are cars. So the first thing that the municipal government does, when it introduces traffic restrictions -- the first thing it stops are two-wheelers from entering Connaught Place, not cars. If you want to make it a pedestrian zone, you don't start with cars, you start with what the less wealthy people might use.

Now all this, if you saw it in a street play, you would say, "How crass! Real life is not like this." But real life works exactly like this. I think the saddest truth is that the crassest street plays are in fact less crass than real life; increasingly so. I think the whole way in which even environmental concerns, which are after all the most democratic, because pollution affects you whether you are rich or poor, how even these concerns get used to protect only the rich, is actually what the World Social Forum should help us to contest.

Let me just read out to you a small passage by Ivan Illich. He is one of the people who have been talking about these issues for decades. He says, "Development is defined by the rich: rich nations now benevolently impose a straitjacket of traffic jams, hospitals, confinements and classrooms on the poor nations." What is interesting is the terms he uses. 'Hospitals' and 'classrooms' are not what we associate with lack of development, but he does. And we'll see why.

> By international agreement they call this development. The rich and schooled and old of the world try to share their dubious blessings by foisting their pre-packaged solutions on to the Third World. Traffic jams develop in Sao Paulo, while almost a million northeastern Brazilians flee the drought by walking 500 miles. Latin American doctors get training at the hospital for special surgery at New York, which they apply to only a few, while amoebic dysentery remains endemic in slums where 90 per cent of the population lives.

In India, what is the operation that is considered the most crucial one today? Heart bypass surgery. Do you know that heart bypass surgery is given as a package to corporate executives just before they retire? They are encouraged to go in for this whether they need it or not, the company will pay for it because they might need one in the future. And you might as well do it while you are still covered by the company. So bypass surgeries have become the kind of thing you just get done in case you might need it in the future, while tuberculosis, the most curable of all diseases, kills a large part of our population.

He then says, Each car that Brazil puts on the road denies 50 people good transportation by bus. Each merchandise refrigerator reduces the chance of building a community freezer. Every dollar spent in Latin America on doctors and hospitals costs a hundred lives. Had each dollar been spent on providing safe drinking water, a hundred lives could have been saved. Each dollar spent

> "We have to learn to work with people who will walk with us even two steps of the way. If people will walk with us even two steps of the way, we have to walk with them. We can't say, "If you don't walk with us the entire mile, drop out in the first step.""

on schooling means privileges for a few at the cost of many. At best, it increases the number of those who have been taught, that those who stay longer have earned the right to more power, wealth and prestige. What such schooling does is to teach the schooled the superiority of the better schooled.

**THE CHALLENGES BEFORE US**

What I was trying to bring before you is the idea that the notion of development has to be challenged, and has been challenged in ways that pose radical alternatives to development. And what the World Social Forum opens up is the possibility of a continuous questioning and the framing of radically different alternative visions. And this is not at all comfortable really, because the questioning can never end. The World Social Forum has to be open to further challenges and it will be continuously challenged. And more and more exclusions will seek a voice. For example, in Hyderabad, which had the Asian Social Forum as a run-up to the World Social Forum, non-heterosexual groups wanted a forum in order to discuss issues that circulate around the politics of gay, lesbian and bisexual groups. They had to fight for it, and so much so that their slogan became: 'Another exclusion is impossible'. (This is a take-off from the WSF's slogan, 'Another World is Possible!') In other words, even within the World Social Forum, there were voices that had to fight to seek space.

Take the idea of disability as another example; it is another issue that we need to recognise. I remember a line from a very significant book, the first feminist work on disability in India, by Anita Ghai (a teacher in a Delhi University College), where she quotes an activist, who is disabled herself, saying, "A friend of mine once told me that you are very brave, very intrepid. And I said to her I am only as brave as I need to be. I don't want to have to

be this brave."

Really, we don't want a world in which people need to be brave to be themselves. We want a world in which to be yourself is something you don't have to make a statement about each time. I would like to think of the World Social Forum as a space with enormous diversity and alternative visions. The whole point is that we should not, any longer, look for that one blueprint. We have to live with the messy diversity of the world, the messy heterogeneity of

the world. And we may well find that it's not that all the bad people are in the five Empires and all the good people are outside the five Empires.

Take a paper like the *Indian Express*. It is most resolutely secular, most resolutely anti-communal. It has conducted the most important campaigns exposing communal politics, but at the same time, it is equally resolutely pro-globalisation and anti-poor. Completely anti-poor. So what do we do with a position like that? We have to learn to work with people who will walk with us even two steps of the way. If people will walk with us even thus far, we have to walk with them. We can't say, "If you don't walk with us the entire mile, drop out in the first step." I think the purity of the Left — and many of us come from Left traditions — the purity that we demand of our allies is our greatest weakness. We are ourselves impure and we have to take that impurity and we have to work with it, understanding that there is no point at which all contradictions will be resolved and we will all live in one happy unified way. If diversity is the name of the game, then it's a very messy diversity. It has its songs and its poetry but it also has its quarrels and unpleasantness. I think that's what the World Social Forum should represent. ■

> My own sense is that the West-versus-the-rest dichotomy has become more dangerous than ever. We are not likely to find moral resources of non-violence, or the readiness to defend freedoms and dissent, in societies that have been eroded of these capabilities. Thus, it is important for global alliances to act to stop genocide.

# redefining the world

**Veena Das**

*Veena Das is Krieger-Eisenhower Professor at the Johns Hopkins Univerisity and a member of the Executive Board of Institute for Socio-economic Research on Development and Democracy in Delhi. She taught for nearly thirty years at the Delhi School of Economics. She has published widely on the themes of violence, social suffering and everyday life. She is currently engaged in a longitudinal study of urban health and poverty. Veena Das is Foreign Fellow of the American Academy of Arts and Sciences and has received an honorary degree from the University of Chicago.*

In his paper, 'Other Worlds Are (Already) Possible', the anthropologist Arturo Escobar made a compelling case for attentiveness to the tight connection between social reality, the theoretical framework for interpreting it, and the sense of politics. His argument was an important one: that the sense of hope needs to be located in an understanding of a social reality that is fast changing. The point, I take it, is that a failure to diagnose the nature of the present can be fatal if our fight is located more in the power structures of the past than in attentiveness to the present.

Escobar's contribution in this paper was to point to the changing models of power and resistance. He argues that over the last few hundred years, economic and social life has been organised on the logic of order, centralisation and hierarchy building; but paradoxically, alternative systems — including socialism and organisations of the Left — have been animated by the same logic. What has gone unnoticed, he argues, is that a different logic of social organisation has emerged that is most explicit in the domains of molecular biology and cybernetics. This logic, based upon the complexity theory, privileges potential and actual networks, in some ways replicating the logic of sub-cellular molecular structures — it assumes that in networked society, resistance is not mobilised through centralised command structures — but rather, like the proverbial fluttering of the butterfly's wings, small events happening in local worlds can affect the course of larger events. I believe this is an important observation. Power does not make itself present

only through regimes of visual technologies and staging of spectacles, nor is it only a matter of disciplinary societies — but rather, that the nature and form of control itself needs to be reconsidered. The reason why so many see a great possibility in the World Social Forum is because it is a new kind of social movement; because new forms of control can be sensed in it.

## A NEW ORDER OF BELONGING

Nevertheless, as an anthropologist, I believe my best contribution might lie in highlighting some of the issues around forms of domination that I see as typical to the notion of the globe as an interconnected one. Obviously the world is not simply a larger place than, say, a city or a country — it refers to new orders of belonging. I hope the old-fashioned idea of the world might be an effective place from which to confront this newly configured globe.

Many scholars think of globalisation primarily in terms of a number of intersecting flows. Arjun Appadurai famously offered the idea of different 'scapes' — ethnoscapes, mediascapes, technoscapes — to suggest both the threats and possibilities of the way that local worlds were encompassed within these cross-cutting flows. I want to take, instead, the question of how something like a 'global good' is put together to institute new regimes of power.

I would suggest that there are two points that are integral to this imaginary situation. First, is the idea of a bio-political state in which life becomes an object of management and control. Underlying this notion of life, however, is a basic hierarchy in terms of whose life is considered worth enhancing and who can be allowed in Michel Foucault's famous formulation to 'let die'.

Second, I want to suggest that new configurations of power do depend upon various kinds of networks as Escobar argues — but networks are a resource for both the Empire and those who wish to resist it. These places of power and resistance are not located in distinct spaces — they are connected through intricate webs and nodes. Instead of arguing this point generally, I will demonstrate it by a brief reflection on how the current Iraq war provides a challenge to think this. It is important to remember that all the terms used

by the protagonists of this war to describe it — 'global terrorism', 'war', 'security', 'exception' — belong to a field of emergent terms, and that it is not a single centralised hierarchy. Rather, it is the circulation of these terms and the techniques of governance and warfare that have emerged around these that constitute the global condition now. I suggest that the World Social Forum, as the prime example of global civil society and as a manifestation of new movement and new meaning, would need to confront these questions in the coming years.

## GLOBAL SECURITY

The idea that we are living in a state of 'exception' because terrorism has become a global problem — in other words, that the times we live in are 'unusual' or 'exceptional', therefore requiring and justifying 'unusual' and 'exceptional' measures — brings the idea of 'global good' to the fore. It generates the effect that normal procedures can stand suspended while this State of Emergency is brought into control — and that this suspension is a global good.

At the same time, it has to be remembered that this is not an entirely new idea. Earlier formulations of a war on smallpox, or a war on drugs, had used this particular repertoire of actions and effects. For instance, the eradication of smallpox is generally regarded as a great public health success story, but as the tireless labour of the historian Paul Greenough has shown, the notion of a State of Emergency was used to suspend all normal rights to privacy, or rights of consent to medical procedures — because the eradication of smallpox was defined as a 'global good' to be accomplished within a time frame that embodied ideas of emergency, exception and urgency.

Similarly, the concept of exceptional circumstances in the application of law is not new, although its relevance for understanding the conduct of normal politics is now beginning to press on scholars and activists alike.

The rhetoric of 'the world' has changed after September 11. By regarding the experience of North Americans as unique, it assumes that forms of terrorism with which other countries, such as Sri Lanka, have lived for more than 30 years, were relevant for those societies but not for humankind in general. The attack on the US, on the other hand, has been portrayed as nothing less than an attack on civilisation itself. Thus, September 11 brought about a state of exception in which nothing less than a global Civil War was at stake; it has made domestic security the overarching discourse within which claims of human rights are now framed.

Some people take it as self-evident that the rhetoric of human rights used with increasing frequency by the Bush administration to justify the war on Iraq was nothing more than an obfuscation to divert attention — it is increasingly clear that there were no stockpiles of chemical, biological or

nuclear weapons in Iraq that could have justified the war; and secondly, there was no clear plan for securing the peace.

It does not matter any more that most sober observers have concluded that the frequently voiced concern with human rights is simply a pretext for other motives. The rhetoric of fear has succeeded in creating a scenario in which the most powerful country in the world lives in a generalised sense of panic and that it is under a constant threat of terrorist attacks. No doubt, there are continuities between the present sense of an invisible enemy that surrounds us and the earlier wars — such as the war on communism or the war on drugs. Yet, it would be interesting to look at the differences and ask what is new in the present situation.

It is as well to remember that there were four military interventions in the past year in Africa even after the announcement of the global war on terrorism. Further, in some places such as Liberia there was an expectation that the US would intervene to stop the slaughter of civilians — many took the war in Iraq as a promise that the US would step in more decisively to stop human rights abuses in Liberia. The United States did briefly intervene, but the small number of troops it deployed had little effect. It was openly acknowledged by both President Bush and Senator Kerry in their debate on foreign policy that with the massive deployment of troops in Iraq, there was no prospect of committing the armed forces to stop the genocide in other places, such as Sudan. Clearly, the question of whether international interventions will

> “The idea that we are living in a state of ‘exception’ because terrorism has become a global problem – in other words, that the times we live in are ‘unusual’ or ‘exceptional’, therefore requiring and justifying ‘unusual’ and ‘exceptional’ measures - brings the idea of ‘global good’ to the fore. It generates the effect that normal procedures can stand suspended while this state of emergency is brought into control, and that this suspension is a global good.”

be possible even in the face of genocide depends very much now on whether a particular conflict is seen as affecting American security or not.

And finally, the nature of the enemy as perceived by the policy makers in the US has changed. The enemy is now seen as not only highly mobile but also highly unpredictable, since he follows some logic other than that of a rational pursuit of self-interest.

## HUMAN RIGHTS IN THE WEST

In the light of this reading, one of the most important tasks before us is to understand what is happening to democracy in the West. What is the fate of human rights there? The power of the metaphor that 'civilisation was under threat' allowed President Bush to gather the support of more than half the population of the US, and simultaneously, to present the war on Iraq as a means to protect US citizens against terrorism and to bring democracy to Iraq. I will not rehearse the arguments about the fact that the US foreign policy had itself supported the regime of Saddam Hussein, because these arguments are well-known.

My aim, instead, is to ask how the new perceptions of global threats are likely to influence the legitimacy of human rights discourses in the changed configurations of war and peace. The issue was earlier one of cultural relativism versus universal values — but this, I think, is not what is at stake now. Instead, the question is about the practices through which intervention in grievous circumstances of human rights violations is likely to happen, and what effect this will have in countries where a violation of human rights has become enmeshed within ordinary life, either through protracted warfare or through endemic violence.

In a recent paper, Deborah Poole and others examine the implications of a new conception of warfare — this includes a generalised sense of panic — for understanding how populations might themselves become complicit in the erosion of their rights, including fundamental rights to due process. Quoting from the writings of Brian Jenkins who was consultant to RAND as a military expert, they point to the significance of the idea that the threshold between conventional warfare, guerrilla warfare and international terrorism has become vague with "governments, sub-national entities employing them individually, interchangeably, sequentially, or simultaneously — and having to defend against them."

The prediction that warfare will cease to be finite, and that the distinction between war and peace will be more ambiguous and complex, means that there is a proliferation of both State and non-State actors who can claim that they are acting within states of exception. This is the common terminology deployed by groups defined as freedom fighters, insurgents or terrorists – the term depending

distinguish between assessments based on reasonable evidence and those that are put into circulation within a climate of generalised panic?

The second example is from the new landscape in which restrictions of freedom of information operate. Again, the relation between research in universities, that addresses special needs of the government such as defence needs, and that which serves the public interest, has been the subject of discussion and debate since the 1960s. However, the well-established distinction between classified research and unclassified research is now put into jeopardy by the emergence of new categories such as 'sensitive' research. The agreements reached in most research universities in the 1960s stated clearly that classified research should not be carried out on campus; that no student, graduate or undergraduate should be asked to get security clearance for thesis research; and that thesis research should not be carried out in areas that require access to classified material. This was consistent with the idea that universities serve public interest and that such an entity as a 'classified Ph.D. dissertation' would be a contradiction in terms.

It is salutary that while the war in Iraq is presented as one in which democracy and freedom can be brought to Iraqi people, the State of Emergency it has spawned is leading to new restrictions on circulation of ideas and knowledge in the universities in North America. The USA Patriot Act has defined restricted persons as those who are prohibited from possessing, transporting or shipping a number of biological agents and equipment for research. Under the expansion of agents listed under this Act, administrative orders continue to restrict access to many biological agents and equipment even in the laboratories located in the campuses in the country. The Secretary of Health and Human Services has been given special powers to expand the list of restricted items. Further, it is now being proposed that research results that are generated in the course of a programme could be designated as 'sensitive' and even discussion of these results could be deemed a criminal offence. It remains to be seen whether major research universities will be able to resist this -- especially if federal grants are at stake.

## RECLAIMING KNOWLEDGE

Two different trends are evident here. It is salutary that more than 150 universities in the USA have rushed in to introduce certificates in Homeland Security. A perusal of course-structures reveals such titles as 'American Security in a Dangerous World', but none that talk of 'Civil Liberties under Homeland Security'. On the other hand, the first meticulously planned survey of mortality in Iraq that concluded that more than 100,000 Iraqis had died since the occupation was conducted jointly by two universities in the USA and one Medical College in Baghdad. It shows that the battle for reclaiming

knowledge has to be engaged in every available institutional space.

My own sense is that the West-versus-the-rest dichotomy has become more dangerous than ever. We are not likely to find moral resources of non-violence, or the readiness to defend freedoms and dissent, in societies that have been eroded of these capabilities. Thus, it is important for global alliances to act to stop genocide, as in Darfur today; but it is equally important to see that questions on proliferation of small weapons that feed most of the regional wars today are addressed. It is time that the scholarly community stopped framing these issues in terms of cultural relativism versus universalism, and concentrated instead on the institutional mechanisms for addressing the kinds of problems that have emerged.

Perhaps the first step would be to reframe the questions of terrorism itself, not as a war on terrorism but a 'commitment to strengthen regional systems of democracy', even if this is at the cost of giving up the idea of American exceptionalism; the concept which diminishes the suffering of others and magnifies America as the motor of history — just as God or the proletariat once occupied that empty signifier.

## CONCLUDING THOUGHTS

When I posited a dichotomy between the globe and the world, I wanted to suggest that the answer to the ills of globalisation, some of which have become tragically manifest in the occupation of Iraq by the United States, cannot be countered by nostalgic renderings of the local. The great promise of the World Social Forum is that it is ready to use the resources that forms of domination have themselves produced, such as cyberspace.The new networks allow horizontal solidarities to be forged, even in the absence of solid structures of solidarity. The challenge to those of us working in traditional places, such as universities, is to be as attentive as possible to the new emergent forms of life.

I took my example from war, but could also have shown how anthropologists continue to think of health as a critique of medicalisation, whereas in the South medicalisation has already been replaced by pharmaceuticalisation; we often think that the problem of human rights is that of universalism versus cultural relativism whereas the problem has already shifted to that of granting cultural autonomy in order to subvert any serious use of available international resources to counter genocide; or to criticise universities, when many centres of knowledge/power axes have already moved to think-tanks. These forms ask for new ways of thinking of resistance, consent, solidarity and refusal. I believe that the opportunity of a global civil society is an important one to grasp, and that different people in their variegated efforts will help to turn the globe into the world. ■

# open forum

*I get a very confused picture of the New World Order or the New International Order that the WSF represents. it is said that the WSF is bringing together dalits, tribals, environment-artists and people against imperialism. But this is not new. Earlier movements have done the same — even if they have not been able to fulfil their aspirations. Now, there is this international movement. Are you optimistic about solving everybody's problems?*

**JAI SEN:** I have been studying world politics for the last ten years, trying to understand how movements grow from local areas, how they internationalise and how they struggle. But there are two things here: one is the actual participation and the ground reality; and the other, the theories provided to us by various thinkers, which are linear — they are determinate — there is cause and effect. We now realise that we are at the beginning of a cusp of knowledge that, in a deeper, organic, biological sense, is not the way the world works. It is not a set of linear movements which have led to emancipation. There are certain conditions – let's say, of blacks in North America, which are much different today from what they were, or of dalits here. But elsewhere history is very mixed.

I think one of the issues is the acceptance that transformation of conditions is possible. I think there is a need to accept that life is messy, that it is not clear. Even people you deal with, who are participants in the movements with you, may not behave predictably. We have to be able to see the world in all its glory and try and understand that it is messy, and not try to come up with clear conclusions in every situation.

It is a question of engaging, trying to understand that if you change one person's mind, that can help change another's, and so on. Our problem is that we have become eager for rapid resolution and revolution, and that is not the only way in which things take place. I think there is a need to recognise that we have multiple identities, we have multiple possibilities in life. At the time of the Forum, you should leave your ideologies behind, leave your mobiles behind, leave your arms behind, come

in and talk and share. You are not going to get polluted by doing that. I think this is what the Forum offers and that is partly why we want to discuss whether the university can be an 'open space', although, here too, there are dogmas which rule.

All institutions have dogmas. We need to explore the limits of this openness. The Forum is already showing it has limits. One of the questions that comes up is: How can you confront power? I think partly power is a construct in itself. We attribute, we ascribe power to people. I think we need to delegitimise power. We need to appropriate space from those who have the power. This is part of the struggle for democracy in a broader sense, of openness and freedom, which we need to think out. We have a long way to go, to rethink these concepts. The Forum offers us the opportunity to do so. It is neither the end of history, nor the end of the world; it is a useful continuation. But let's try to open up space, let's try to open up boundaries.

*At times it looks like as if it is only 'the representatives' of people involved in struggles who attended these meetings. For example, a representative of Adivasis rather than the Adivasis themselves, and this connects with the kind of politics and ideologies we talk about. How far are we ready to get into dialogue with representatives of politics? In a sense, we end up using our own set of principles. How does the WSF give space for this kind of dialogue?*

**VEENA DAS:** It is theoretically correct that if I talk on behalf of the urban poor, I cannot say that I have their experiences. The question of a political community is, "Do you learn to recognise, or to allow your voice to be represented by someone else, and recognise your concern in another's voice?" When is it that you can say, "Yes, I can, in fact, speak on behalf of someone else because I think, otherwise, political community is impossible."

Having said that, it does seem to me that there are ways in which this confrontation itself produces something much more interesting than if you did not have that confrontation. In other words, if you go by the notion that an Adivasi can only be represented by an Adivasi, then of

course you are into a problem of infinite regress. Because how can I represent you even when we are both Adivasis, if I am a woman you are a man, I am a child you are not a child? It would be impossible to have political community. In the end, how do I know that although at this moment I am representing myself, that I may not change my view in the next ten minutes?

From my own experience, I can to give you an example: the entire design of scientific research on AIDS has completely changed because AIDS activists began to say, "Sorry, we are not going to allow you to represent us." That would never have happened if scientists were representing the AIDS patient. There is something very interesting in what you are saying.

**NIVEDITA MENON:** There are two levels at which the question of representation can be answered. The simpler level is that the WSF has, in a sense, bureaucratised the mechanism of representation. You may be an Adivasi, but you cannot have 100 Adivasi groups at the WSF. So the Adivasi groups have to form a national network. That is what is happening to autonomous women's groups who have formed a network in order to be represented at the WSF. That is the question of the actual mechanism, a bureaucratised mechanism of representation.

I think that is the level at which the question of representation is far easier to handle. That is, in principle, there is no reason why we cannot evolve ways of physical representation in forums, that do not necessarily end up being bureaucratic. Of course, the philosophical questions remain. I don't think we have resolved them and nor can we resolve them very easily. Because, on the one hand, there is a way in which I have to be able to speak about dalits, although I am not a dalit. But on the other hand, there has to be a way in which I cannot represent them. There is infinite regression if you say, "Ultimately, I cannot speak of anybody but myself".

On the other hand, there are ways in which representation is made possible, through building a collective, political vision. I think that is where I would go back to the question of a normative principle of criticism.

Because then we are not referring to the truth, but something that lies outside our experience. We must recognise that our political work is about continuously trying to hegemonise political meaning around a particular notion.

So, if I am going to make a feminist critique of housework, for example, and I want to make that critique accessible and acceptable to more people, I cannot simply claim it as a truth that is visible even from outside the feminist framework. Rather, I will have to bring more and more people into that framework. It means that at a political level, we are continuously trying to make people share our common sense. I think that is what I would say produces a normative principle of criticism, which I can claim from within my framework.

*How much scope is there really to have a dialogue with the people who are not 'the converted' within the Social Forum?*

**NIVEDITA MENON:** How do we calibrate our responses to things happening around us? I think this acquires great importance in the context of globalisation. We all agree that certain kinds of coercive actions taken by the State are wrong: we say that on the street, when we are marching, we say that among our friends; but sometimes our response cloaks what we are actually saying.

There are certain kinds of actions that the State takes which are just wrong, where its policies are absolutely in contravention of things we hold so dear. Then we do have a responsibility to react. The question is: if we do have a responsibility, then how do we fashion a response, which on the one hand affirms democratic principles of justice and says, for example, 'no war', but which also manages the situation for the benefit of the people whose lives and interests are actually at stake? I don't know how to do that. So often, our responses can actually be read as pro-establishment stances when that is the last thing one wants to be saying.

In cases of violence, for example, we have to ask the State to intervene in very many cases, which might appear to be pro-establishment. For example, Gujarat is burning: intervene. A woman is raped: go to the police station. I

think that is something we have to be able to do. I don't think any of us would deny that. But, I think, possibly what the WSF could open to us is a question of radical alternatives. These are fire-fighting exercises which we have to conduct on a daily basis. But surely a radical politics cannot be limited to how do we deal with situations as they are 'right now'. Let's do a little tinkering. Let's get the State working, because we don't have an alternative or a radical vision. That is where I would disagree with what Veena said, that the old debate about development is over. I still hold to the idea of posing of radical alternatives that are completely outside the framework of existing ideas, whether they go back to the anarchism of the 19th century, or Gandhi, or whatever, all of which are political and intellectual resources of our people. I think we need to draw on those ideas of complete radical alternatives and go beyond mere fire-fighting.

# OPEN SPACE TWO

# OLD POLITICS NEW POLITICS

NEW ENERGIES, NEW IMAGINATION

FORM AND CONTENT

THE POLITICS OF ENGAGEMENT

FEMINIST INTERVENTIONS

> My own instinct tells me that the days of the nation-state as any resource for democratic or radical politics are probably over; although that is not to say that the nation-state is over. It is very much there, in all its repressive form and essence.

# new energies new imagination

**Aditya Nigam**

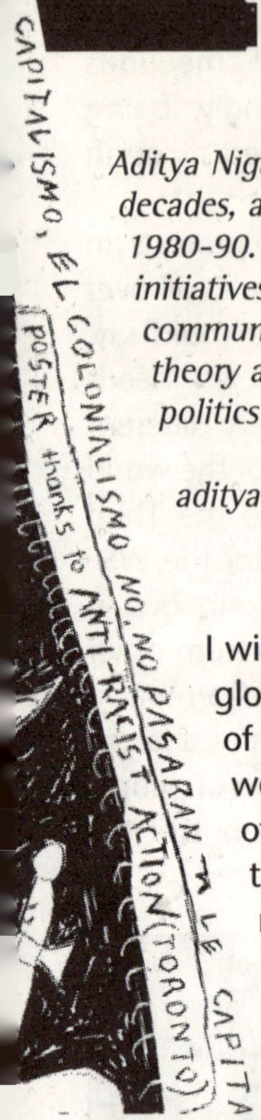

POSTER thanks to ANTI-RACIST ACTION (TORONTO)

*Aditya Nigam has been active in the Left movement for two decades, and was a full time activist with the CPI(M) from 1980-90. Since 1992, he has been part of various citizens' initiatives, particularly on workers' rights and in anti-communal forums. His interests include political and social theory and questions of identity, nationalism and radical politics on which he has written and published widely.*

*aditya@sarai.net*

I will not go into issues that we are all familiar with — the context of globalisation, the cannibalism of capitalism, particularly the new face of global capital and the ecological disaster it has brought to the world. What I'd like to discuss here is the question of the new kind of politics that we see emerging, the kinds of crises we have seen in the old politics and the issues that come out of these. I will just make a few remarks about some things that appear crucial to me.

The WSF has primarily been a product of recent western experience, in the sense that it brings together a diverse range of movements that have gathered strength around issues of environment, labour, minority rights, and racism. Organisations involved in these issues have come together on the WSF platform, to give a voice to their concerns outside the traditional fold of party structures. But what was it that actually brought this whole thing about? What were the kinds of anxieties or questions that were being aired through these movements?

One of the key points is that these movements represented a widespread dissatisfaction with existing forms of political mobilisation. Even prior to the Seattle demonstrations, on June 18, 1999, the first indication of what was bubbling came at the anti-capitalist carnival in London, when thousands of people came out on the streets in a show of protest. There was violence — the demonstrations manifested different expressions of anger against the new forces of corporate globalisation. But there was an air of carnival about these demonstrations: in that sense this was a very new kind of protest.

When the WSF process began, the inital gathering comprised some

20,000-25,000 people in Porto Alegre. The meeting was positioned to counter the World Economic Forum where the captains of the corporate world meet anually at Davos to discuss the fate of the world, since they are the people who 'determine' the future of humanity. The WSF meetings attempted to refocus on social issues, which were increasingly being marginalised. Many people felt that these could only be articulated through a separate platform.

Yet, what actually gave the WSF strength were the gathering protests in Europe and more generally in the West, as well as the massive struggles all over South (Latin) America, against the neo-liberal order. The story, one could say, probably began with the Zapatista revolt in the Chiapas region. But it also needs to be underlined that the European and US struggles expressed a very different set of anxieties from the ones that animated struggles in other parts of the world — for instance the relocation of higher paid jobs from the First to the Third World. The experience of Brazil — from where the initial initiative for the WSF started – was quite unique. A New Age Left-wing party, the PT, was engaged in a novel experiment with participatory democracy, almost in isolation from other regimes in the rest of the world. Opposition to corporate globalisation was a common factor and that is probably why, once it acquired the form of a larger platform, its slogan 'Another world is possible', caught the imagination of people across the world. It enabled people everywhere to gradually break out of the deep cynicism that had set in after the Soviet collapse.

## THE CRISIS OF REPRESENTATIONAL POLITICS

We need to note that the emergence of this new movement was enabled by two very different circumstances. One is the crisis of representational politics, of which we have been seeing a fair amount in India. Non-party political formations have been theorised and discussed in our context for about two decades now, but it is the Gujarat episode that comes to mind when we talk of the crisis of representational politics.

Months of continued violence in Gujarat shook all those who value democracy and pluralism. This was made worse by the part that followed on the violence, the party of murderers was returned to power, this time with a democratic mandate and the legitimacy of having gained power through elections. It is also interesting that when this was happening, especially during the peak of the violence, from February 27 to March 27, 2002 — one full month of mayhem and massacre — not a single voice of protest was heard on the streets all over India, except from non-party sectors. Most electoral parties were busy calculating their gains and losses. It was only after the Delhi Municipal Corporation elections that the impact of the events in Gujarat was felt — the BJP was trounced in a way it has never been in Delhi before. It was then that some of the parties started coming out in protest; although the protest was still mostly confined to the parliamentary arena.

New social and political struggles are now seeking different modes of expression. These include a wide array of initiatives ranging from middle-class citizens' groups to more grass-root struggles around questions of immediate concern. Because of their local character, they do not often figure in the electoral calculus, for they may not add up to large numbers in terms of votes. Therefore, there is a way in which the 'new' — the new popular — shows a kind of disjunction with the levels of representational politics that operate at the parliamentary level. We will leave the task of elaboration of what it means; how it manifests itself; and what is the way out for the discussion. For the present, I am just marking it as a possible point of interest.

## HORIZONTAL COMMUNICATION

The second point around which we can think of these new, emerging movements relates to the new possibilities of horizontal communication across different sectors of activities and movements. Many possibilities of building new solidarities across different movements and regions have opened up in the recent past. Movements that worked with different issues have been able to exchange ideas and information today, facilitated primarily though the open structure of the Internet. This is an important development. In an earlier time, communication between movements was mediated primarily through the leaders of those movements. Now many more people

are involved in sharing experiences and ideas; although in India the potential of this medium has still not been exploited as much as it should be because of the limited Internet access.

Despite this shortcoming, there are positive fallouts — after the Pokhran blasts the nuclear tests carried out by India in 1998, a great deal of information became available, precisely because of the Internet. The information was of both kinds: that is, information relating to the actual problems with nuclear energy and arms, which served as campaign material; as well as information on anti-nuclear protests and groups in different parts of India, which eventually helped build up an all-India coalition for nuclear disarmament. Information flow and communication was also taking place between Pakistan, Bangladesh and India on this issue, but it soon became available for sharing a wider range of concerns more generally, across the sub-continent. For the first time, spaces of dialogue have opened up between citizens of the countries in this region. As a result, new energies have come together to create a new imaginary of South Asia, beyond specific nation-states. In that sense, the very possibility of imagining South Asia as a post-national entity has been tremendously facilitated by these new forms of communication.

## RADICAL POLITICS AND THE NATION-STATE

I'll conclude with just one point, which seems to me to mark this moment of post-national politics in a way that is fundamentally different from the old internationalism, where the 'good guys' were supposed to be aligned with all the 'good guys' across the world. Today, we find ourselves in not-very-happy situations of alliance. The so-called humanitarian intervention in Serbia by NATO forces actually came as a relief for Kosovo Muslims and the Kosovo population, which was being practically eliminated, at the receiving end of Milosevic's ethnic cleansing programme. Nearer home, when US forces were preparing to bomb Iraq, the western media beamed images of Kurdish men and women, preparing to fight with the American forces to overthrow Saddam Hussein. Or, there are examples from Afghanistan after the fall of the Taliban regime. In the course of that war, all of us, including hundreds of students from Delhi University participated in the massive protests that followed. We were against the war. Yet there are two images that have stayed in my mind from that time and they have to do with the fall of the Taliban. The first one is that of a painter who used to cover all human forms in his painting with extra colours. Immediately after the collapse of the Taliban, he wiped away all the colours, revealing the human forms beneath, which he had concealed, because painting human forms was sacrilegous under Taliban rule.

The second image was of burqa-clad women playing football, taking off their hijab. These were probably young college students: their expressions of everyday pleasure and enjoyment, a taboo during the Taliban days, became possible with the help of US power. So these are actually complicated pictures that we have to deal with.

What does this mean for a new politics of struggle against Empire? Understandably, the western media made use of such expressions, as they did of RAWA's (Revolutionary Afghan Women's Association) critiques of the Taliban regime. But that cannot detract from the fact that all these voices are repressed by the nation-states that are struggling to find expression. How do we relate to them even as we fight US power? These are questions that a new post-national politics will have to increasingly deal with.

I end with a brief reference to another kind of experience that we have had in India, and are continuing to have today — the experience of the dalits during the national movement. They were always seen as betrayers — even leaders like Dr. Ambedkar — as people collaborating with imperialism and colonialism. There was no space for them in the nationalist struggle, except on the terms set by the nationalist leadership. Their attempts to negotiate a space for themselves were considered anti-national. Today, we have the minority Muslim community facing the brunt of the nation-State's attack. They are always 'outsiders', 'Pakistani agents', and 'never to be trusted'.

In the end, then, my question is this: Does the nation-state offer any ground today, on which a radical politics of the future can be erected? My own instinct tells me that the days of the nation-state as any resource for democratic or radical politics are probably over; although that is not to say that the nation-state is over. It is very much there, in all its repressive form and essence. ■

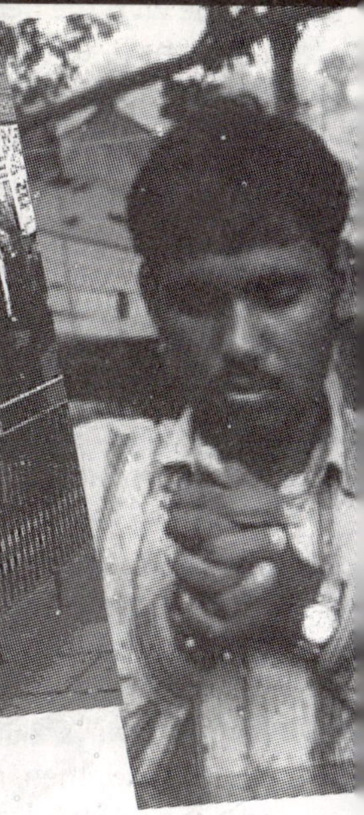

> Anti-globalisation is a spreading phenomenon and security agencies will have to be lightweight just as these movements are.

# form and content

**Vinod Raina**

*Vinod Raina is a member of Eklavya, Bharat Gyan Vigyan Samiti, Jubilee South, and All India People's Science Network, New Delhi and Bhopal. He has also been associated with the Bhopal Gas Victims' movement and the Narmada Dam movement. His published works include several essays in academic journals and activist volumes and a co-edited volume,* Victims of Development *(Hong Kong, 2002).*

*vinod.raina@vsnl.com*

We are talking of the new politics and the international dimension. The WSF is a part of this new politics. Both in terms of form and content.

**FORM: AN UNCONVENTIONAL ORGANISATION**

As far as form is concerned, the WSF is a part of the new politics because it is not a traditional organisation. We are used to certain institutions — societies or NGOs — or larger confederations, which have some kind of a registration, office-bearers and a governing structure; what you may call a conventional way of organising. The WSF has a different way of doing all that because, to begin with, it doesn't have office-bearers. There is no president, chairman, secretary, executive committee and so on. What is the WSF then?

It is a coming together of eight organisations of Brazil. There are major movements in this — MST (Movimento dos Trabalhadores Rural's Sem Terra or Landless Workers Movement), and CUT (The Unified Trade Union Federation of Brazil). Of the six civil society organisations, five are funded NGOs: Brazilian Association of NGOs (ABONG); ATTAC (The Association for the Taxation of Financial Transactions for the Aid of Citizens), Justice and

Peace Brazilian Committee; Global Justice Centre; and Brazilian Institute of Social and Economic Analysis (IBASE). There is also the Brazilian Justice and Peace Commission (CBJP). These eight organisations are held together by a secretariat, without any normal organisational structure.

After the first WSF in 2001, the Brazilians suggested that an International Council (IC) was all that was needed to make the structure an international one. Today, the IC is composed of representatives from over 95 international movements. It is without any office-bearers or chairperson; and the Council and the Brazilian Secretariat have held the World Social Forum process together. I am on the International Council representing a very large international movement called Jubilee South, which works mainly on issues related to debt. My specific work in this movement is on ecological debt.

## CONTENT: ANTI-GLOBALISATION AND REFORMS

In terms of content, one has to go back in history. The World Social Forum certainly has roots in the anti-globalisation demonstrations that you are already familiar with — Seattle, Nice, Genoa, Quebec, Melbourne and Florence. But if you try to look for a causal link between them — that these demonstrations added up, then people held a meeting to set up a World Social Forum — it is difficult to trace. It becomes very difficult to say how one thing led to another, except that what preceded the World Social Forum was the parallel meeting with the World Economic Forum at Davos, called the World Forum for Alternatives, in which people like Samir Amin and Francois Houtart were involved. Apart from the Brazilian groups, there were other

groups at the forefront of the WSF movement, like Jubilee South and ATTAC.

ATTAC originated from an article in *Le Monde Diplomatique* about reforms in the neo-liberal stock market-based economy, through a proposal to levy a tax on stock market transactions. The Tobin Tax, proposed by the economist James Tobin would be used for the welfare of people all over the world. A remarkable movement sprang up in Europe around this proposal, called ATTAC, a French acronym. ATTAC is now a worldwide movement, basically to reform the market-based economy. It has played a very major role at the World Forum for Alternatives. That, plus the Brazilian groups, set up what is now called the World Social Forum.

### A NEW PLATFORM

I would call the WSF a platform rather than an organisation. This means that any movement, any civil society group, can be a participant at this platform. There is a charter for the World Social Forum, a Charter of Principles. [It can be read at the end of this book along with the WSF backgrounder.] The major restriction on inclusion is that organisations must not uphold the neo-liberal paradigm. You can't be espousing the cause of neo-liberalism and be a part of the process or events of the WSF. The other restriction on which there continues to be considerable debate relates to groups espousing violence as a form of resistance. As of now, such groups are also excluded from the WSF. For the World Social Forum, 2004, in Mumbai, the Indian committee added one more dimension for exclusion: the platform would also exclude groups and organisations espousing communalism and casteism. So, if a group is opposed to neo-liberal economy, but espouses fundamentalist religious, ethnic or caste politics, it can't participate in the World Social Forum in India.

Apart from these restrictions, anyone else can be on that platform. This makes for a bewildering variety. Let me tell you about the kind of people and issues you can see at the Forum. You can see movements or members who espouse labour rights, environmentalism, feminism, freedom of migration, preservation of the cultures of indigenous peoples, bio-diversity, cultural diversity, food safety, organic farming, opposition to the Green Revolution and genetic engineering, sexual rights, opposition to war, ending or reforming capitalism and so on. Protesters could identify themselves as revolutionary, anarchists, socialists, Gaians, communists, feminists, humanists or reformists. Others agree, ideologically, but don't exactly identify themselves in any category. There are still others, who want to reform capitalism, like the Democratic Greens. Now, given this variety of movements and the causes they espouse, the platform seems chaotic and directionless to many. How do you put all of them together? What do you get out of it? This is exactly what happened in Seattle, Genoa and Prague,

because if you look at the millions of people who came to the streets, they were composed of all these different interest groups. There were also single-issue groups like anti-dam movements, anti-sweatshop workers, and ideological groups of trade issues. So, it was a very broad platform.

Allied to the World Social Forum are the anti-war demonstrations. There were those who protested against the Afghanistan and Iraq wars, with millions marching in London, other European cities and in the United States. Since the WSF cannot issue calls to action, or come out with common declarations, these rallies are not formally mandated by the WSF. However, one can trace links to the World Social Forum process.

One of the constant questions is this: What will it end up in? Can it create a new politics if it is so diverse? Where is the cohesiveness? I will leave that as a question, since there is no definite answer. The important point is that the WSF has emerged as a common platform where ideologies and groups that would otherwise never be seen together, let alone engage with each other, rub shoulders at the Forum. For many, that is the beginning of a new politics. I have heard many die-hard socialists say, "Oh, it's a new fashion. It's something that is local, and small communities are foregrounded in it; a post-modernist notion that has no future. It will just go away." At the same time, even the traditional political Left is really perplexed by the numbers involved. At the World Social Forum in Porte Alegre in 2003, there were 100,000 people. That is enormous — 100,000 people for seven days, on the streets!

At a time when even labour unions are hard pressed to get these kinds of crowds, you cannot dismiss such a show of strength. What is intriguing is the sociology of this resistance. There is no democratic centralism, there is no leader giving directions and issuing party lines, no trucks going to fetch the working class. It is spontaneous. The criticism is that funds are funnelled, from even dubious sources, mainly through NGOs, to facilitate travel and other expenses. If that is true, traditional 'conspiracy' theories — like, it is the conspiracy of the imperialists executed through their private foundations — would seem inadequate to explain the motivation for such funding, and the motivation of the majority to participate without any such funding support.

A creative commentary of the street demonstrations and the World Social Forum comes from an unexpected source — the Canadian Security and Intelligence Services — which has produced a comprehensive dossier. In an illuminating analysis, it says, "Anti-globalisation is a spreading phenomenon and security agencies will have to be lightweight just as these movements are." It goes on to say, "We admit that the leaderlessness of these movements is a nightmare for security services." The security agencies may not know how to deal with it, but the question is: despite its show of strength, how will it go forward without the traditional notion of leadership, traditional directives and

> "There is no democratic centralism, there is no leader giving directions and issuing party lines, no trucks going to fetch the working class: it is spontaneous."

final declarations? In India, where we continue to remain far more sectarian in forging alliances between NGOs, movements and mass organisations, the challenge of the World Social Forum is whether it is possible for diverse groups to share the same platform. The WSF process in India gives hope that indeed that may be possible to some extent, and that is a major step forward. I think the most important challenge in India is whether such an inclusive process will sustain itself beyond the event. Of course, there is a tremendous amount of tension involved in it, but it is heartening to see an emerging group of persons being attracted to undertake such a challenge. What else is hope? ■

# the politics of engagement

"Although as feminists we frequently used and understood the phrase "the personal is political" and the fact that the political had to become personal, we had a fear of what we saw as "politics"."

## Kavita Srivastava

*Kavita Srivastava is a practising lawyer and has for long been associated with the women's and human rights movements in Rajasthan and nationally. She is a member of the People's Union for Civil Liberties (PUCL) and works with PUCL and other groups on human rights law. For many years now she has also been involved in several key campaigns such as the Right to Work, the Right to Food, and the Right to Information and campaigns against communalism and fundamentalism.*

*kavisriv@yahoo.com*

I would like to begin on a personal note. I am 41 years old. My first political engagement was with feminist politics in the early 80s. For many of us, that was the moment when we began to see the world through the eyes of women, and for me specifically this meant rural women from Rajasthan, where I had made my home. The process meant translating our individual and collective experiences into knowledge, creating spaces within institutions, including the government, and fighting for our voices to be heard. Control over our sexuality and fertility were important questions too, and all of us, whether rich or poor, rural or urban, literate or illiterate, discussed these at length. We questioned undemocratic family structures, and developed our understanding of the links between women being deprived of their rights within the family, and within public institutions, as well as by the State.

A number of us associated ourselves with a government-sponsored programme called the Women's Development Programme (WDP), and this at a time when development was not called empowerment, when the notion of women's agency was not known at all. This programme was also different as it combined government and voluntary participation. Some of us were full timers in this programme while others were associated with it for short periods. In those days, the development sector was not divided into government organisations (GOs) and non-government organisations (NGOs).

The space for voluntary organisations was a distinct one and it was where experiments in development and social change were taking place. These were conducted by committed people, who worked with little or no funding.

While we were 'doing' politics, we never called it that. Many of us just did not perceive it that way. Although as feminists we frequently used and understood the phrase 'the personal is political' and the fact that the political had to become personal, we had a fear of what we saw as 'politics'. We never really used the word. It seemed to us that this was a dirty word, associated with party and electoral politics, and that it pointed to a world that was murky, manipulative and corrupt. Also, politics was associated with power, and as feminists, we wanted to have nothing to do with this. For us, power carried the connotation of something domineering, individualistic and, worse still, male.

At the time, I was associated with the women's studies and women's movements and was located in a research institute. In the field of academics, it was considered 'anti-intellectual' to address women's issues, and if we had defined ourselves as doing political work, then there would have been no space at all for us; 'politics' in the common perception was also considered to be anti-scholarly.

Our battles consisted of attempting to centre-stage issues of women's dignity and identity, their right to property, to work and equal wages, their right of access to water, to good education, to health and also the issue of choice, including sexual choice. We addressed everything that challenged the patriarchal foundations of our social structure, which are all pervasive not only

in the community, but also in the administration, in government and in the field of politics.

In 1987, a young woman, Roop Kanwar, was burnt alive in Deorala, in Rajasthan. She was said to have committed 'sati', that is, taken her own life because her husband had died, and for a true, devoted wife, this was the 'natural' thing to do. By doing this, she would attain sainthood. When women's groups protested Roop Kanwar's murder, they were told that they were making an attack on 'religion', that religion and custom needed to be protected from attacks by 'modern', 'western' feminists and by the Indian courts and Parliament, which had no business to interfere in people's right to worship. Large marches were taken out by particular caste and religious groups in defence of the act of widow immolation or sati. In these, young men armed themselves with swords, they were joined by religious leaders and also by women, many who had been in seclusion till now, and the 'right' to practise religion was defended vociferously. Attempts to silence the voices of women activists were followed by attempts to discredit activists, who were labelled 'western' and 'promiscuous', and who were told that they did not understand Indian culture, or what it was to die for the man you love.

When Bhanwri Devi, a grassroots worker in the government-sponsored development programme which I mentioned, broke the silence on her gang rape in 1992, and bravely challenged the powerful nexus between the upper castes, the police and the administration in her village, an attempt was made to silence her by ostracising her from the community, calling her a liar, labelling her as promiscuous, and denying the fact of rape in Indian society. However, women's groups were equally forceful in their defence of her, and gradually this led to the building up of the campaigns against rape and later, violence against women, in Rajasthan. This broke the silence on sexual violence and rape in Rajasthani society in a major way, and in the decades that followed it forced both the police and the government to change the way they looked at women's issues, particularly the issue of violence against women. This is evident even today.

Like many other trends, this too had its genesis in the late 70s and early 80s, and this is what I would like to call the new politics, as it gave birth to non-party, issue-based and community-based politics. Importantly, this initiative came from a group of people who located themselves outside the context of the mainstream, within a community space that was mostly rural, and among activists who did not necessarily see their roles as connected only in the macro context. People's concerns were articulated in a new language after this time. There was an attempt to search for a language in which the people who were involved in particular campaigns would find themselves at ease, rather than to receive a language imposed from above. The modes of

protest that were used were creative and interactive. There was an understanding that the spaces of engagement should be culturally appropriate, for only then could such spaces be comfortable ones to inhabit and work in, and only then could they be democratic. What was most significant about this new political intervention was that those who practised it, believed that the poor, uneducated and the illiterate also had something substantial to say and that there was infinite potential for change. There was no single leader or a political line imposed from above, something that was particularly important for women and dalits who were normally maginalised by the 'old' politics.

This phenomenon was similar to what was happening in the rest of the country. But what was different in Rajasthan was that it was not connected to mainstream electoral politics. For instance, in Bihar, a student group called the Chhatra Yuva Sangharsh Vahini, emerged as a leader in the anti-corruption movement, with the veteran leader, Jayaprakash Narayan at its head. Their protests were targeted at the Congress party, then in power under Indira Gandhi. From this, the movement developed into one that addressed the issue of inequitable distribution of land, and that continuously engaged with mainstream politics. At the time, although the potential did exist to do so in Rajasthan, there was no attempt to connect our practice to mainstream politics. Today, the situation is very different.

For us at the time, the old politics was something that was electoral, centralised and located within the party as an organisation. I want to look here only at parties that defined themselves as 'people's' parties, which means mainly the Left and Socialist parties, though we may say that they do not necessarily represent the voices of poor people. Then, and even today, their space of action remains centred around workers and peasants, but has increasingly moved towards representing middle peasantry and workers within the organised sector. The voices and concerns of the unorganised sector, especially rural workers who are in government-sponsored

> "Attempts to silence the voices of women activists were followed by attempts to discredit activists, who were labelled 'western' and 'promiscuous', and who were told that they did not understand Indian culture."

employment works or on farm employment, do not necessarily find a space here. Also, the language used by these parties to articulate what they saw as 'people's concerns' was very jaded. At this point, it is important to say that the front organisations of these parties were still more flexible and did get involved in issues that other organisations took up. For example, the All India Democratic Women's Association (AIDWA) was in the forefront of the movement against widow immolation.

The non-party political space, which fashioned the new politics, had split into two clear streams by the mid-90s. One of these called itself the NGO sector; it was funded and much of its activity was defined by this funding. Therefore its broader intervention space had been narrowed down to a sectoral intervention. Ideologically, this stream had nothing to offer, except that it gave birth to a large number of jobs in the development sector. The other stream gained maturity over time, and learnt to connect its local politics to the larger context. Their ideology was pro-people and they called themselves political.

Many of us who were part of the latter stream kept our distance from the first in a very clear way. We stated publicly that we were not funded groups, that we wanted to give a public platform to women's voices, and to do so in an informed way. Sometimes, our attempts at stating our difference almost became like practising untouchability towards the NGO sector. Our aggression also had another reason: we wanted ourselves to be seen differently, but the government and the older political groups refused to recognise us as different from the NGO sector. It is this latter grouping that I wish to focus on.

## CREATING NEW POLITICAL SPACES

By the mid-90s, most of us who were part of the Women's Development Programme, had moved out of the institutions we were located in. The contradictions of our situation had become too stark – being within a government programme, being part of certain institutions that were independent, and yet finding that none of these was willing to respond to the needs that were being articulated by women. For example, we wanted to challenge caste domination, or to assert our opposition to the government's anti-women policies, or to work towards making workers' unions within the WDP, but this was not something that was 'allowed'. So, along with our institutions, we also moved out of the WDP.

We realised that the struggle for justice in the Bhanwri Devi case required a political space that could not be carved out from within a government structure, or even from within an independent institution – several of these institutions were also meant to be part of the support structure of the programme. By moving out, some of us initiated this new public space for

women that then built upon the work that had been done by other groups in the 80s. Today, this space is being strengthened by every activity we take on. This public space was initially built with the support of groups in Delhi, particularly during the Bhanwri Devi case, but gradually, it became a space for all women's groups, including those belonging to political parties, as well as human rights groups. It was also open for participation by other groups, such as trade unions and associations of writers, lawyers, etc.

In fact, the movement against rape, which we called the People's Movement Against Violence Against Women (Mahila Atyachar Virodhi Jan Andolan, MAVJA) became the loudest voice in Rajasthan against atrocities against women. Its work had an impact inside government institutions, within the media, the non-government sector and some political parties, including those of the far Right. MAVJA became the first body to start monitoring crimes against women and to build a database on this issue. We – for I was also a part of this initiative – would prepare regular factfinding reports on this issue, collect data, compile it, then present it to the government and the media. The issue of violence against women thus received a fair amount of attention for the data were self-evident. We also learnt a valuable lesson: struggles that were based on solid information could not easily be ignored.

During 1997-98 this movement played an important role in making violence against women an issue in the parliamentary and State Assembly

elections. MAVJA undertook a campaign against three candidates who had supported rapists and had adopted an anti-woman stance in public. All three lost the elections. In the 1998 state elections we took up the question of what women could expect under the rule of the far Right, what we called the saffron-rule, and the Congress party also picked this up. When Ashok Gehlot, who was Chief Minister of Rajasthan, and a Congress party member, was interviewed by the media on the defeat of the Bharatiya Janata Party (BJP, or the Hindu right wing party), and asked what his priorities were going to be, he lost no time in mentioning the issue of violence against women. He also wanted to set up a state human rights commission and a state women's commission. Interestingly, the third issue that he put on his agenda also came out of our campaigns and this was the bringing in of the Right to Information Act, an act which handed power and information to the poor and underprivileged, to whom it rightfully belonged. Our pressure on government had therefore resulted in building several platforms where women could not only demand information about issues but also hold public officials accountable to the people whom they were meant to serve. Gradually, the government and the police also became more open to working with us, particularly in setting up redressal centres for women, which would be run by women's organisations, and located inside police stations. These centres have been conceptualised as an attempt to create women's spaces within the police and the administration. This did not mean that we had compromised our adversarial position vis-a-vis the police generally, but we remained open to raising issues with the government and the police through the media and on the streets.

It is important to say here that the Right to Information movement was pioneered by a group called the Mazdoor Kisan Shakti Sangathan (MKSS). In Rajasthan, MKSS has played a major role in changing the non-party political space in the state, and also in the country as a whole, for the movement has now spread beyond Rajasthan. Defining the right to information as an issue connected to the right to life, and connecting freedom of speech and expression as defined in the Indian Constitution in Article 19, to the right to life as defined in Article 21, was a path breaking conceptual shift. It was the MKSS and the movement that was responsible for making this shift. This was the most important dimension of this new politics and it generated a movement for the collective exercise of the right to information through a number of public hearings, a strategy that was hitherto unknown in our region. The demand that the State be accountable to the people in various forums for democratic rights forced bureaucrats to reconsider their roles, for now they had to come into people's platforms and were answerable to them.

The most significant dimension of this struggle was the creative way in

which issues were articulated. For instance, slogans such as '*hamara paisa, hamara hisab*' (since the money is ours, it needs to be accounted to us), or '*chodiwado ghano hogyo re, koi tomunde bolo*' (corruption is on the increase, it's time to speak up), and songs that established that what was being asked for was not gold, silver or magnificent houses, but a simple account and information, became very popular. These, and the MKSS's obvious commitment to the issue, helped to bring large sections of society into this campaign, and this included people from the working and middle classes as well as poor people.

The BJP government that was then in power refused to accept the people's demand for information relating to their panchayats. In response, the protestors and campaigners staged long sitins and demonstrations in Jaipur and central Rajasthan which forced the government to pass an order for revealing information to the public. The Congress government which rode to victory on people's struggles (even though they were not really connected to them) had to bring in an enactment on this issue within a year and a half of its being in power. The continuing pressure from the people then ensured that the drafting of the new legislation became a widespread public exercise. Although the government later rejected the people's draft and brought in a diluted version of the legislation, we still felt we had gained from the public debate and discussion, and the awareness that had been raised on the issue. Today, ensuring that agencies comply with the government order and implement the law remains a big issue around which people continue to mobilise.

> "Our battles consisted of attempting to centre-stage issues of women's dignity and identity, their right to property, to work and equal wages, their right of access to water, to good education, to health and also the issue of choice, including sexual choice. We addressed everything that challenged the patriarchal foundation of our social structure."

## CHANGING THE POLITICAL SPHERE

The campaigns on the Right to Information and Violence against Women built support for another key campaign for the Right to Food, in which many groups took part. The umbrella organisation was called the Akal Sangharsh Samiti, Rajasthan. Drought is a regular feature in Rajasthan, so protests built around it are not so well known. In the year 2001, however, those of us who were in this campaign, were surprised to see the kind of support we had. On reflection, there were some important things that helped in better mobilisation and effective intervention. These were:

- The support of experts such as Jean Dréze who gave us the symbol of overflowing food warehouses (such as the ones run by the Food Corporation of India). That year, food stocks were estimated to be 40 million metric tons and by the next year this figure had gone up to 60 million. The slogan we coined was: '*bhukhe peth, bhare godaam, nahin challenge, nahin chalenge*' (empty stomachs, and overflowing warehouses, this will not do, this will not do).
- Earlier campaigns which had helped to build trust among groups and which then helped to sustain the loose grouping that was formed around the campaign for the Right to Food. This also helped us to effectively bargain with the government and to maintain a joint front.

The way the issue was articulated caught the people's imagination and suddenly, there was an explosion of cultural activity – songs, plays, drama – around it. Rajasthan is a land of dance and music, and even the most feudal of its women find expression through dance and music. All of this helped to keep up people's spirits when long sit-ins and demonstrations were being held.

Lessons learnt through the other campaigns came in very useful. For example, apart from raising their demands through public action, activists also took up research on issues relating to food and water security, as well as distress and drought conditions. We also moved the Supreme Court on this issue in 2001 through a Public Interest Litigation (PIL). This PIL became a sort of symbol for the whole country, wherever there were agitations relating to the right to food and the right to work. Through the Supreme Court we managed to get a mechanism of making the state accountable to the people. A Commissioner of the Supreme Court was appointed who had powers to use the office and support of any individual and institution to set up a system of accountability for the state and central governments. So that, apart from strengthening gram sabhas, a system was put in place which could bring pressure to bear on the government from above as well. These results give us important insights into the scope and range of methods that can be used by people to raise issues within a democratic framework.

## MOBILISING AGAINST IDENTITY POLITICS

The momentum built up by these campaigns was, however, difficult to sustain when it came to issues of communalism, and when the pogroms against Muslims took place in Gujarat in 2002, under a Hindu right wing government. Both the old and the new politics in Rajasthan could not provide solutions to this issue, and mobilisation on this proved very difficult. As far as the non-party groups were concerned, it was difficult to get a consensus on how to address the problem. Some people felt that those who were working with a human rights perspective, had an agenda that was mainly reactive, and they did not like this, for jumping into action after sectarian/communal violence had actually taken place was not the right approach, and would not help mobilise people. After a while it became clear that the methods we had evolved in the course of mobilising people on the other campaigns, could not be replicated when we were dealing with fascist, communal agendas. People from within the communities we had been working with, were not easily inclined to supporting this particular struggle – for many this was not an everyday agenda, and for others, the subject needed much more discussion. Perhaps the only people with whom we found it possible to build alliances at the time, were those within Left parties.

## MOBILISING YOUNG PEOPLE

Mobilising the young proved to be another limitation of our new politics. While we had always tried to include young people in our discussions, and as a result had managed to build a cadre of young activists, once again it was difficult to mobilise people on this particular issue. This is not to say mobilisation is impossible on questions of the divisions created by religious identities, but the question is how to sustain the enthusiasm of the young, and how to make them believe that they can make a difference.

> "We realised that the struggle for justice in the Bhanwri Devi case required a political space that could not be carved out from within a government structure, or even from within an independent institution. By moving out, some of us initiated this new public space for women that then built upon the work that had been done by other groups in the 80s. Today, this space is being strengthened by every activity we take on."

Unfortunately, the non-party political space was not, and has not been able to respond to issues such as unemployment, which deeply affect young people. While there is a growing movement that addresses issues such as the Employment Guarantee Act, the issue of the right to work still remains virtually untouched and there is hardly any thought among groups on how it can be addressed. In what we called the old politics, there was little space for young people, so it is important we make this space.

## BY WAY OF A CONCLUSION

Perhaps we can then say that the non-party political space that emerged in the 70s has struck roots but that it still has a long way to go if it is to move out of issuebased politics and towards building comprehensive strategies for social change. As far as the old politics of the Left goes, there is some reflection that they have made connections with new movements, and new platforms, but they too still have a long road to travel if they are to break with their old modes. As far as the challenge of mobilising against State-support for the agenda of the Right wing is concerned, both the old and the new politics have not found any real solutions to this, nor have they managed to bring in young people into the struggle to fashion a new and better world for everyone. ■

*Mary E. John is Associate Professor of Women's Studies at the Jawaharlal Nehru University, New Delhi. She has published widely in the fields of feminist theory and women's studies. Her works include* Discrepant Dislocations: Feminism, Theory and Postcolonial Histories (Delhi, 1996), A Question of Silence? The Sexual Economies of Modern India, (Delhi, 1998), *co-edited with Janaki Nair,* French Feminism: An Indian Anthology, (Delhi, 2002), Enjeux Contemporains du Feminisme Indienne (2002). *Her current interests include questions of sexuality, feminist theory and politics, and comparative feminisms across the South.*

*mas01@vsnl.net*

"The fact that the movement has always ebbed and flowed in so many different ways fills me with a sense of hope, not despair."

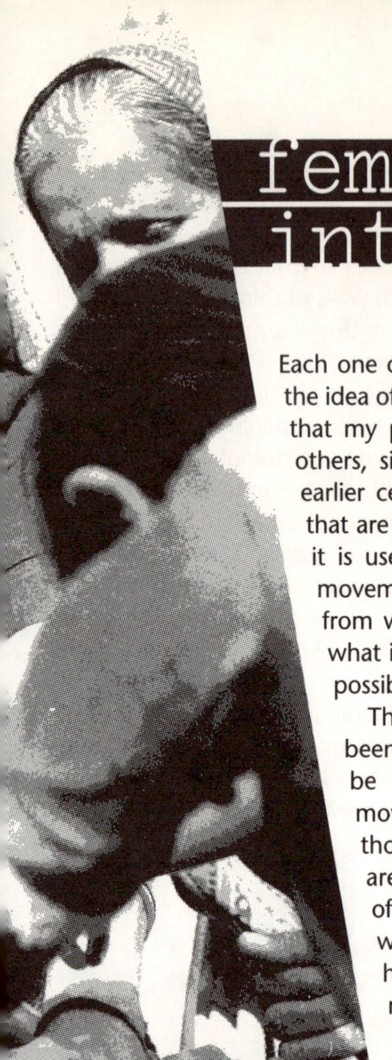

# feminist interventions

**Mary E. John**

Each one of us on this panel has attempted to interpret the idea of old and new politics in different ways, I realise that my presentation may be more idiosyncratic than others, since I'm going to take you back to an even earlier century. During times of deep transformations that are difficult to grasp -- such as the present time -- it is useful to have an understanding of past social movements. Obtaining a perspective on the history from which we have emerged gives us clues about what is different about the current moment and the possibilities that lie ahead.

The public face of women's movements has been visible for two hundred years. Today it would be quite uncontroversial to claim that social movements which have addressed women, and those that have claimed the name of feminism, are amongst the most significant developments of the 19th and 20th centuries. The impact of women's movements has been as extensive as it has been profound. Feminists have produced remarkable new insights that have restructured our lives at different levels. No institution has been spared -- be it the judiciary, the workplace, the family, the field of education, the academy -- social sciences and humanities, or, for that matter, the worlds of popular culture. Certainly, that is the claim I would like to make about the cumulative effect of a history spanning two centuries of feminist interventions.

When we consider 'older' and 'newer' forms of politics, women's movements are of particular historical interest precisely because they bridge the old and the new in different ways. From the mid-19th century, women began to organise themselves around a whole range of issues that prompted social and political change in hundreds of locations across the world. These have included the right to vote, promoting women's education, marriage

reform, legal rights and better working conditions. Women took to the streets and invented new forms of public protest, women's magazines and newsletters were published in a myriad of languages.

As these protests by women (and sometimes men) became a force to reckon with, they provided the ground for fresh ways of thinking, writing and analysis. While there were very few places where this was not happening, it is nonetheless instructive for us to think about some of the ways in which there were regional variations. Given the unequal nature of the globe we inhabit, much more information is available on what was happening in First World locations. Even here, it is telling to see what we do and do not know. Though the Proclamation of Universal Rights of 1799, at the time of the French Revolution may be well-known, many people may not be aware that it was in 1848, half a century later, that the franchise was realised for men without property, as well. The origins of terms such as 'feminism' are also surprising: the term 'feminism' is, in fact, French, and was first deployed as a form of abuse by the famous writer Alexandre Dumas Jr. in 1872, for those misguided partisans of sexual equality.

Yet another century had to elapse before French women actually gained voting rights in 1944, and the franchise became genuinely universal in that country. In the case of the United States when the 'woman movement' (as it was called) first emerged in the 19th century, few people knew how deeply

women's demands were intertwined with the abolition of slavery. Women's rights and the question of abolition sometimes converged and found mutual supporters; but equally often they came to be pitted in complex, and sometimes, opposing ways.

In other words, relations between movements and the demands for rights of different oppressed peoples, such as around gender and race, are not new problems. They go back to the very beginnings of modern social movements, as do differences in perspective and understanding. Profound differences and bitter conflicts arose, especially in countries like Germany, between early socialist and communist women and those with liberal orientations. Indeed, feminist interventions have been plural and conflicted since their very birth.

### ASIA: MULTIPLE HISTORIES

Let us move from First World locations to what we think of as Third World countries, or some countries in Asia -- Turkey, Iran, India, Japan, Korea and China. Here too, there have been rich legacies of organising around women's issues from the 19th century onwards, which we are still in the process of discovering through the efforts of feminist scholarship. This needs to be emphasised, because the frequent response we hear today is this: Asian women's movements are simply a western import, some kind of foreign ideology. Instead, it would be more productive to see how women's rights emerged in these locations, at times in the context of other movements – such as those of social reform – as part of the making of multiple modernities. Frequently such movements became part of political struggles over nationalism, as well as people's liberation of various kinds.

An extremely interesting example would be the case of China. China's modernity in the late 19th and early 20th centuries, and its sense of a renaissance were not simply the products of westernisation, but of complex regional and local developments. Against the backdrop of tremendous social and political upheaval, when Confucian ideology was being questioned, women's organisations were formed and women's armies were coming out in full force, Mao Zedong came forward as a young student. Not yet a member of any communist party, his first public statements in 1918 were around women's rights. His first efforts at political writing, including the creation of slogans and catch-phrases for which he was to become so famous, centred on the theme of the tragic death of a young woman, Miss Chao, who committed suicide because she had been forced into marriage by her parents. Mao wrote at least nine impassioned articles in 1919 on this theme, a non-issue at that time. Apparently such suicides were quite common in early 20th century society in China, though no one had paid them any public attention. But the mode in which Mao questioned this private tragedy, and wrote about

the 'three iron nets' that bound Miss Chao (her family, her in-laws, and Chinese society) was such that it became the biggest news item of the year.

In the Indian subcontinent, a whole of range of issues – involving violence, marriage and motherhood, education and political rights emerged. While in Bengal and Maharashtra, the period of social reform of the 19th century was subsequently muted by the growing force of nationalism against colonial rule in the early 20th century; in Kerala, social reform and nationalism worked together in complex ways to bring 'women' into the public sphere, and transform gender, sexual relations and caste in fundamental ways.

In conceptualising women's movements, it has become commonplace to think in terms of waves, or phases. Thus in a number of western locations, such as Britain, France or the United States (but not, for instance, in the Scandinavian countries) a common tendency was that, once fundamental political rights such as the vote were won, often after long-standing struggles encompassing a whole century, a kind of 'dying-off' took place in terms of political organising and public visibility. Similarly, when considering pre-independence struggles in a number of Third World countries, there seems to be a kind of retreat with independence, as women's organisations and leaders placed their trust in the newly formed nation-State and withdrew (or were marginalised) as a pressure group.

## A NEW PHASE

A new phase of organising emerged -- interestingly at roughly the same time in many countries across the globe -- from the 1960s onwards. 'Women's liberation' was the battle cry, especially by a young generation who knew little of the gains of earlier generations, or took them for granted. In Europe and North America, voting and public political issues were not on the agenda. Instead questions of violence, birth control, better working conditions and so on took centre stage.

'The personal is political' was a major slogan of the 1960s and 70s. And yet, remembering Mao, one realises that the personal was political in some

> "We have had to learn how to grow, while at the same time learning how to debate on issues."

parts of the world even 70 years earlier. Moreover, cases of domestic violence, rape and marriage rights had been sites for debate and public protest in colonial India, so that, once again the sense of 'the new' and 'the old' needs to be looked at with care. In India, what was interesting about this fresh phase of organising, was that it emerged from a number of different locations. It developed out of people's movements of various kinds — student movements, land struggles, and anti pricerise struggles in the 1960s and 70s. It emerged out of anti-State protest (especially, but not only, at the time of the Emergency and suspension of democratic rights under Indira Gandhi between 1975-77), but also from the State itself.

The state, along with the UN, actually initiated the publication in 1974, of the 'Status of Women Committee Report (Towards Equality)', that was brought out for the UN Year for Women in 1975. This report brought together government and field-based data for the first time after independence. It sent out shock waves. It showed that from the turn of the 20th century, and even post-independence, right into the development era, the status of a majority of women had been steadily deteriorating. These findings, too, were a major impetus for organising and raising awareness around women's issues.

## PROBLEMS OF MODERNITY

During the pre-independence era, in the first phase of thinking about women's issues, the prominent frame for politicising and bringing 'women' to the forefront was in relation to traditional cultural practices, such as the lack of widows' rights, the prevalence of child marriages and so on. Post-independence, however, what was so disturbing for feminists and women's organisations in the 1970s, and after, was the realisation that the problem was not simply that of 'tradition', but one of modernity.

Modern development itself was part of the problem, in the form of industrialisation -- the spread of a consumer culture, the structure of the State and its patriarchal power. The difficult lesson -- that modern processes could be disempowering -- was being learnt, for the first time, in the 1970s and 80s.

It would be impossible to summarise, in a short essay, how the women's movement has been growing from the 1980s onwards. But I should say that in recent years, possibly the most hotly debated issue, in India and elsewhere, concerns the question of universality. First World feminists have had to bear the brunt of the strongest critiques: that equality and sameness have been deeply entangled with each other, on the one hand, and that the co-construction of different forms of oppression make the notion of 'woman' or a single model of 'feminism' untenable, even oppressive in its own right.

In India, too, we are at a point in the women's movement where we have

had to learn to live with different positions on a range of issues. Even though we may all oppose women's subordination as a kind of common cause, we may disagree deeply, for instance, on whether we should have a uniform civil code concerning matters of marriage, divorce, inheritance, guardianship and so on (which, as the result of a complex colonial history, are presently dealt with under separate religious laws). Again, we may not agree on how we should understand the new demand for political reservations for women in parliament or in local political bodies. I think this is one of the few movements, at least that I'm aware of, where practically every issue has been a subject of debate and critique. There are also very few issues that feminists have not been forced to take on board — communal questions, caste divisions, questions of sexuality, to name a few.

## LOOKING AHEAD

When I think of the 21st century, and what might be 'new' forms of the political today, I'm struck by a number of things. First, fresh challenges continue even as older ones have not been settled, producing deeply disorienting effects. One of these is globalisation, a central theme of the World Social Forum, and which has been debated extensively in the movement. But we have also had to take on other challenges, which may not

> "I think this is one of the few movements, at least that I'm aware of, where practically every issue has been a subject of debate and critique."

appear to be significant to some, for example, the rights of gays and lesbians and those of sex workers. Today it is not enough to simply talk about violence against women in the women's movement, but also about sexual norms that have been fundamentally exclusionary. The list keeps growing.

On the other hand, and this is a source of some concern, as the women's movement grows and develops, it also seems to be getting institutionalised and professionalised. This is another side of the current moment that we need to take on board. That is to say, to what extent are we all intervening as experts, or professionals, through various institutions? These institutions could be universities, research centres, NGOs, or State organisations. They could be local, but increasingly, they are also international, with powerful agendas and funding, in the name of 'gender'. Should we be reminded of some of the ways in which colonial States used 'women' as part of their 'civilising mission'? What new dangers and new possibilities does this conjuncture reveal?

Often, one is overwhelmed by ambivalence: the women's movement has had a history of possibilities, on the one hand, with an ability to reinvent itself, to take on new challenges. On the other, and equally pressing today, are the tendencies of co-option, of stagnation. Where do we go from here? Where is the newness? Perhaps that is a question that the newer generation will have to address. The energies, the conflicts, the desires of a younger generation of women and men will carry the future of this movement. The young have been the source of new energy and new directions over the last 200 years.

The fact that the movement has always ebbed and flowed in so many different ways provides us with a sense of hope, not despair. ■

# open forum

*It is difficult not to be overwhelmed by this initiative – so many exciting things are coming up with it. But at another level, there is also this sense of déjà vu – as old limitations persist. In academics we are familiar with this, we carry the deliberations at a certain level of sophistication and have a certain vocabulary. This is probably a problem of the institutionalised teaching of these disciplines of social sciences. The vocabulary of history fails you there.*

*Also, I noticed that when we talk about a movement, whether the labour movement or the feminist movement, they have made commendable strides. But there are serious limitations. We tend to believe that women's rights movements, for example, have reached a certain stage in terms of their accomplishments. We tend to often ignore the fact that these accomplishments have an extremely limited reach – to the urban, literate, even English-educated, elite if you like. In a majority of Indian villages, women's rights stay where they were in the 19th century. That's my personal experience. One can differ, but not with the general spirit of what I'm saying.*

**VINOD RAINA:** I think a very significant question has been raised -- I am not making any answers or assertions -- but I will give my opinion, about how I see it. I don't think we can just sit here and count the number of examples of 'something new' from the so-called social movements, or civil society. They have been there for almost 35 years -- and one can count movement after movement, and action after action, which has something significantly new to offer. I think the question that we are confronted

with internationally, as people of the world, is that of a certain tyranny of governance by nation-States.

A basic question about a reason for transforming the very notion of governance remains. And, to that extent, how can non-party examples, or civil society, help in transforming forms of governance? This is a very critical matter to me. It is also a major issue that has been debated in many forums including the WSF, with people of differing viewpoints.

I must clarify, the World Social Forum is not a programme set up by some 30 people, to which you have to be invited. Rather, it is a platform where you can say, "We want to do a workshop to discuss contradictory notions of governance." For that, you can register at any time, and call whom you want, but you have to take responsibility for doing it. That is how some 2,000 events took place last year. You don't have to wait for someone to give you the clearance to do that.

Now, coming back to the question: Mary talked about the great event when women got the right to vote. Today you look at it with such cynicism, *"Kya vote dena hai? Bekaar ki cheez hai"*. (Why bother to vote? It is a waste of time). But you realise its importance when she talks about what a big event this was historically. I think somewhere in this discussion we also have to have a sense of balance about what we consider new or old. My feeling is that cynicism can overtake anything, blurring the lines between new and old. Unless the degree of cynicism is changed, this line cannot be seen very easily.

I would like to take up the question that has been raised: Doesn't the feminist movement articulate mostly urban viewpoints? I think that the 33 per cent reservation for women in panchayat elections has transformed many things in this country. If you were to ask me what are the most significant political changes that have happened in the last ten years, my assertion is that this is one of them. It shows significant qualitative changes in the countryside.

I'm not saying that it has happened evenly all over the country, but it is significant. From the places that I work in – Bihar, Madhya Pradesh, Orissa -- I can tell you not just stories, but significant policy changes that have happened. I could give you more examples of how these so-called 'non-metropolis urban changes' have taken place, particularly with respect to gender.

You must all be aware of the anti-arrack movement of Andhra Pradesh which was led spontaneously by women. That was a display of rural women power which is unprecedented in this country. There were something like 15 lakh women, walking, protesting. They would not allow arrack auctions. They surrounded the police stations in ten districts and made sure they were heard. This led to the state government eventually being toppled.

These are not middle-class women's movements — but they are rural movements. Now, these raise other questions: Were they sustained? What form did they take? How have they continued? But the point is that from the so-called non-party world there are an enormous number of examples that give us clues about a different form of governance.

It's not just that. That old man, Gandhi, when he rejected the British parliamentary system, he had a vision of a different kind of governance. The president of Brazil, Lula De Silva, has a very different vision of governance. So there are visions available to us, and if there is an Andhra women's movement, if there is a Gandhi, if there is a Lula, it can show us that it is possible to break the barriers of sectarian movements. Then they have to become horizontally linked, so you have to break national barriers.

*When we talk about student politics, it seems to come up only in the metropolises. I come from Bhubaneswar, where I did my graduation. There is hardly anything resembling student politics there. Is it that the concerns are different in smaller places, or that they are more focused on academics?*

**MARY JOHN:** I was really taken by Kavita's initial plea when she said, "What about the students in Rajasthan? They are nowhere, they are not doing anything." That has now been echoed by one of the speakers in the audience. It is something we really need to take on board.

Historically, students have been one of the most significant political forces of change and we have always assumed that it would be progressive if they would actually raise questions that would in some sense break existing patterns of power, to move towards greater democratisation.

If that is not the case, or your politics is not being echoed by a resounding response from students, I think we need to retool ourselves, in terms of the issues that face students. Are we saying that their understanding of the political is blocked in some fundamental way? Or that their understanding of the political clashes with ours? We need to explore this more deeply. I think it's not enough for us to simply step back and reinforce our notion of the political, vis-à-vis their notions of the political that are not measuring up, or are not visible to us and have therefore somehow degenerated.

In fact, if you look back in time, yesterday's generation would have said the same about yesterday's students. Right? So I think we do need to think about the younger generation who are going through anxieties, struggles and conflicts of the most profound kind as they try and build their lives in the current scenario. If they don't echo our language, then I think we need to ask ourselves, "What language are they speaking?" I get the sense that perhaps we do not risk our own frameworks enough in terms of recognising what new forms may be out there.

Another part of the issue that I brought up towards the end of my presentation was about institutions. I really appreciate what Vinod has said about the potentially revolutionary aspect of one-third reservation for women in panchayats, in municipalities. My concern here is that we may have also inherited a certain understanding of reform, of revolution that inhibits us from exploring what happens when those who have been excluded from certain institutions actually get a space within them. What happens when women, who have been outside institutions of power, actually gain a foothold in power? What happens when Dalits, and others, who have been largely excluded, gain entrance?

Furthermore, I can no longer assume that when women get access to power, it would automatically be 'my kind' of empowerment, the feminist kind. I am not so sure that there is a naturally progressive way in which those who have been subaltern, those who have been excluded, gain space. This too requires more exploration.

Another question that strikes me is the need for debate on issues – we shouldn't just have a lowest common denominator type of agenda, but actually look at issues. For

me, one of the most bewildering things, at least in the women's movement, is that every possible position on the spectrum is covered by someone or the other. You can be a feminist and quite pro-globalisation. You can be a feminist and pragmatically anti-globalisation, or completely anti-globalisation. This range of positions is quite remarkable. The person who is pro-globalisation may actually be doing so in the interest of feminism, not because she is a neo-liberal, and not because she wants to serve the interest of MNCs, but because she actually thinks that women will gain a space in these new industries to raise issues which was not available so far.

So, I think we need to grapple more fully with the kind of profound uncertainty of the moment -- such a range of positions is actually arguable. People can occupy positions from progressive locations -- not simply from 'pro' and 'anti' positions.

*When we talk about the old political parties as against the new social movements or NGOs, where does this 'new politics' stand? One finds that the old parties are the ones occupying most of the spaces. So, what categories do they represent?*

**KAVITA SRIVASTAVA:** I really want to respond to a few things: the impact of this whole non-party political space, electoral politics; the nature of leadership; to bring in the rural-urban issue; and some aspects about the media.

As far as the whole rural-urban divide is concerned, a lot of things have changed. There is increasing access to information: we are really shocked and surprised by the effects of the Internet. I am part of a huge network of 400 organisations. Of these, some 250 organisations are on email. That is amazing. I am not saying that it is representative, but there seems to be a shift. TV and electronic channels are changing things on the media front, and in addition the two main newspapers have something like 17 editions. We have 32 districts, so you get your local news completely. At the same time, we also have a lot of small newspapers that are coming up. We also run a feature service ourselves, which we started with some 60-70 newspapers whom we knew as friends. That has grown to around 150 such associations -- so somewhere there seems

to be increasing access, and a desire, to receive information out of metros. Frankly, there seems to be less energy in metros. We find maximum energy in smaller towns, not in villages -- that is my experience in Rajasthan. The Right to Information campaign emerged from a town like Beawar which you probably have never even heard about. When the Iraq war happened, we did a listing of the number of protests from outside the six main cities. There were some 180 protests that happened at the *tehsil* (district) level.

All this indicates that there is some change in situations. People seem to be taking an initiative and finding a platform; they are now expressing themselves. But are processes able to carry forward and add some inputs to such initiatives? Are they able to give them an ideology? Are they able to give it a framework? Even though there are a lot of citizens' initiatives, there is a new politics unlike the old one which could not take things forward, the question is whether the new politics will be able to sustain itself. Will it be able to be more organised? That is one concern.

I love this open space concept, but to carry initiatives forward, you have to have a structure. I disagree that structures have to be like they were in old times, that you have to have president and secretary, with centralised decision-making. All that has to undergo a change. But there has to be a structure in place.

Then, as far as electoral politics is concerned, I still feel that this non-party political space is keeping itself outside electoral politics. And that is really a matter of concern. You see, for us, Congress is a secular BJP and BJP is a saffron Congress; they are the same, their character is the same, they fight in the same way, their issues are the same. If there is one politics that unites them both, it is caste.

But this new non-party space has not been able to address this new politics of caste. This is a major challenge, apart from globalisation and communalism, which is, of course, very deep. The non-party political space has some extremely charismatic leaders, but very often these initiatives are short-lived, and they tend to get very individualistic. These are just some of the ills that we have to take into consideration. I'm not saying they are good or bad: all I'm saying is this new politics has more than a toehold and it can play a very important role.

While I agree that the World Social Forum can be a place to meet and exchange ideas and not have an agenda beyond that, the whole scenario cannot be a World Social Forum. The World Social Forum has its space, but you have got to rise to the challenge, to have your own leadership with a clear vision resulting in concrete action. The initiative should impact resistance movements on the ground.

The WSF is a process that gives space to small initiatives, but that does not mean that proper organisational politics does not get its act together -- to impact electoral politics, to impact issues like accountability, and to impact issues like caste and communalism which are really facing us.

# BOUNDARIES OF VIOLENCE

A HIERARCHY OF VIOLENCE

VIOLENCE AND THE NATION-STATE

RESISTANCE, DEFENCE OR VIOLENCE?

A THOUSAND VOICES

REVENGE AND COLLECTIVE GUILT

# a hierarchy of violence

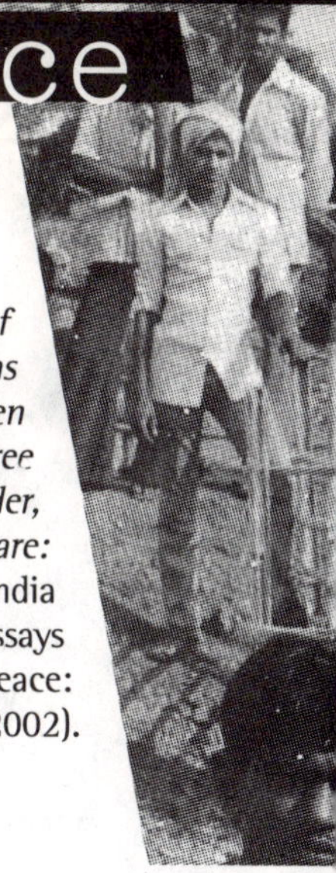

**URVASHI BUTALIA**

*Urvashi Butalia is a publisher and writer. She is co-founder of Kali for Women, India's first feminist publishing house and has recently set up a new feminist imprint,* Zubaan. *She has been actively involved in the women's movement for over three decades. She writes on issues relating to women, gender, religion, fundamentalism, identity. Among her publications are:* The Other Side of Silence: Voices from the Partition of India (Delhi, 1998), Women and the Hindu Right: A Collection of Essays (co-edited with Tanika Sarkar, Delhi, 1995), Speaking Peace: Women's Voices from Kashmir (edited, Delhi, 2002).

I don't see any document about the WSF that describes its attitude to those individuals who beat their wives and children at home. You may, for example, have an organisation that espouses non-violence, but individuals within that organisation may be extremely violent within their homes. This isn't an unlikely scenario, but while one kind of violence is easier to name, the other is not. While one kind of violence is easier to identify, the other is not. In some ways, there is a hierarchy we set up between what can be called 'external' forms of violence and 'internal' ones.

I would like to address the question of gender violence. It's important that the WFS charter explains and lays down some boundaries about inclusion and exclusion, boundaries that attempt to define, without making it too rigid, the Forum's spirit of inclusiveness. While technically, the Forum is open to anyone who wishes to participate individually, there seems to be a conditionality attached to group or organizational participation. I find this both important and intriguing. Important because no matter how open you are, how inclusive you wish to be, there are some boundaries that get defined even if you don't necessarily deliberately define them. Intriguing because the way in which the WSF has defined at least one of its boundaries in terms of inclusion, leaves room for a lot of questions. I don't know the exact terminology, but I believe it is something that describes the fact that participation in the Forum is open to all organizations except those that espouse violence as political action. As a statement, this is very important, but also very problematic, and it leads me to the issue of gender violence. But let me explain.

It's a truism to say that the world today is becoming increasingly violent. Both at the global and local levels, we see much more violence, we see it coming ever closer to us, entering the spaces that we inhabit, such that battles and wars today do not necessarily take place somewhere far away, but it is the community tap, the village well, the neighbourhood space, the shopping centre, even places of worship and of death such as churches,

mosques, temples, graveyards and cremation grounds, it is these that form the sites of violence. And it's a matter of much concern internationally that such violence is spreading. I won't go into the causes here, they're familiar ground to all of us: things such as the end of the Cold War, the change in the 'balance of power', the rise of unilateralism, neo-liberal and market economies, the growth of the arms trade and its links with crime, the exploitation of resources, the failure of given development models, and many more.

But while it is interesting that we are actually able to acknowledge – indeed we can no longer ignore – this kind of violence, there is another kind of violence that has always existed in our lives and that we still do not acknowledge, that we are perhaps even afraid to acknowledge. I don't see any document about the WSF that describes its attitude to those individuals who beat their wives and children at home. You may, for example, have an organisation that espouses non violence, but individuals within that organisation may be extremely violent within their homes. This isn't an unlikely scenario, but while one kind of violence is easier to name, the other is not. While one kind of violence is easier to identify, the other is not. In some ways, there is a hierarchy we set up between what can be called 'external' forms of violence and 'internal' ones. These are not entirely satisfactory descriptions, but I am using them for the sake of convenience. Another way – also problematic, but also convenient – could be to describe these as public and private violence.

It's well known today that violence within the home takes hundreds of lives and statistically, is a crime that involves much larger numbers than the crime of murder, but it is seldom addressed with the same kind of seriousness. I believe there needs to be a strong concern about it. I believe that there are strong links between what happens inside the home and the violence that we see outside, and that the fact that certain kinds of violence are seen as private

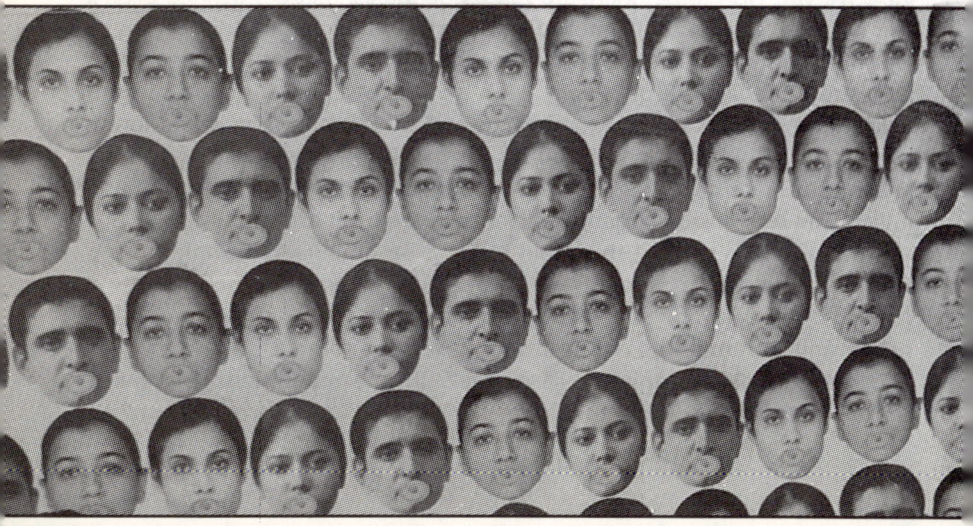

is no reason for us to be ignoring them. It's interesting also that neither the perpetrators nor the victims speak about this kind of violence, the former because they see it as so naturalised, that it does not seem to them that it merits any consideration at all, and the latter because they know that even if they shout about what they face inside the four walls of the home, there is no one to hear, no one to listen. I have wondered, since I heard about this particular inclusion/exclusion (of organisations who espouse violence) that if it had been expressed differently, that if the WSF had sought to exclude those who practise violence within the home, the numbers of people attending (and I don't only mean men here ) would have been drastically reduced !

The issue of violence within the home is a difficult one, and as you begin to look at it more closely, the boundaries between what we may call 'private' and 'public' violence, begin to blur, and at times to connect so closely that you wonder what it is that is being talked about. In the last few years, as you may know, there has been considerable pressure, by women's groups on the government to bring in a law on domestic violence. Such a law is not yet in place, but the actual Bill (now a much watered down and distorted version of the kind of legislation women's groups were demanding, and therefore the subject of considerable debate) is expected to be put on the table in every session of Parliament, and each time it gets deferred. This is indicative of the importance the State gives to the issue, but it is also something that women's groups are not necessarily complaining enough about.

You might ask why, since it is these very groups who fought for this legislation to be brought in in the first place. Well, it's like this: women put together a draft for this legislation, the lawmakers then examined it, added, amended, "improved", changed and so on, and the final document that ended up on the table in Parliament, bore little resemblance to the original. Its very definition of domestic violence, for example, is faulty: only if a man beats his wife or is violent towards her "habitually" does it count as domestic violence. More, if he is violent in defence of his property (whatever that means) then it does not count as domestic violence. So, the question arises, what makes something habitual ? A beating once a week ? Once a day ? Once a month ? What is "defence of property" ? If someone wishes to hold on to family property and deny the woman her rightful share, and beats her into submission – not an unlikely scenario at all – does that make it all right ?

It doesn't take much to see the thinking and logic, or lack of it, behind this. Women simply don't count, and violence within the home is a man's business, "private" business, there are some things (such as property, or if it is only sporadic) that justify it. Most of our laws are made by men, and it would be easy enough to blame this lack of attention to this most pervasive of crimes, this most widespread of human rights violations, on men. But the

truth of the matter is, that many women also sanction this kind of relegation of domestic violence to a "private matter", something that is outside the realm of law. And precisely because it receives so much social sanction, it becomes difficult to talk about, particularly for those who are at its receiving end. Clearly, the question is a complex one.

Let me now turn briefly to the history of a few campaigns in the women's movement to take this point a bit further. I'd like to examine the trajectory of some campaigns on violence against women within the movement. Many of us who came into political consciousness of feminism in the seventies and eighties, cut our political teeth in these campaigns and movements, so their failures, successes and lessons – and there are plenty of these – remain very close to our hearts.

The first example I want to use is of the campaign against rape which began, as some of you may know, in the late seventies. This was one of the key campaigns of the women's movement. I know that there has been considerable debate about whether or not we can call the activism of the last three decades a movement, or whether we should refer to it as a set of quite different campaigns. But I don't want to go into that particular debate at the moment. The fact is that there are some campaigns within the movement that have acquired a sort of pan Indian character and the campaign against rape was one of those. It's always difficult to put a starting point to a particular series of actions because it's not as if the issue we are talking about did not exist before those actions began. Rape, for example, is not only among the most common of crimes against women, it is also one that is the least reported, and in recent years it has acquired new dimensions by being used as a weapon of humiliation and ethnic cleansing in the battles between different communities that have so marked our societies. In India, the campaign against rape is usually dated from a particular incident of rape that took place in March 1978, that of a woman called Rameeza Bee, in Hyderabad. Rameeza Bee, the wife a rickshaw puller, was out at night with her husband to see a film. As often happens with the poor and marginalised in our country, Rameeza Bee and her husband were picked up by the police — clearly the poor have no right to leisure — accused of drug running and prostitution for after all, why should a poor man and woman be walking along the street at night except if they are involved in some illegal activity, this is how the police reason all the time, and the poor are much

> If we are to expand our vision of violence, to make it more and more inclusive, we have to begin to address the silence around the issue of violence against women.

more vulnerable than those who have wealth and class behind them. The husband and wife were then taken to the police station, questioned and beaten, and Rameeza Bee was gang raped. When her husband tried to protest, the police beat him to death, presumably in order to teach him a lesson. When this news spread, it infuriated people, and thousands came together to protest – the figure is usually put at over 20,000. These were poor people, who protested in different ways. They laid her husband's dead body in the police station verandah in full view, held demonstrations, stoned the police station, demanded justice. As an aside, I want to say that one of the accusations that is often directed at the women's movement in India is that it is a largely urban, middle class movement, peopled by urban women, but actually, virtually every campaign that you look at, has been initiated by people who are directly affected by a particular issue, and often this means they are not necessarily middle class, although middle class activists have formed an important part of such campaigns as the campaigns have grown. But this is another debate, and I'll not get into it here.

Protests over Rameeza Bee's rape escalated over the next few days, with the police being beaten by protestors, and very quickly, the issue reached parliament. In Delhi, a number of women members of parliament decided to take up the issue, and some even travelled to Hyderabad. So volatile did the situation become, that President's rule had to be imposed on Hyderabad, and eventually, a Commission of Enquiry was set up. In all of this, however, the woman, as always happens, was lost sight of.

Several other incidents of rape came to light at the time as the issue began to come to public attention. I'd like to mention the case of Mathura, which was the one that actually led to a nationwide campaign. Mathura, a young woman, was raped by two policemen, the incident took piace in or around 1975. The two men were acquitted at the Sessions, or lower, court, convicted at the High Court and then acquitted again at the Supreme Court. Four senior lawyers protested this acquittal by writing an open letter to the Supreme Court, and the letter acted as a catalyst to spark off a campaign, initiated in Bombay and then spreading to different parts of the country. As the issue was joined, support came from Nagpur, Ahmedabad, Bangalore, Hyderabad, Delhi, Bombay and other places. Rape became a national issue, and as other cases began to come to light (in particular one that came to be known as the Maya Tyagi case which took place in June of 1980) politicians stepped in. In one instance, a politician called Raj Narain, known more for the ample girth of his body than for anything else, decided to go on an indefinite hunger strike, supposedly in protest against the government's failure to protect the lives, property and honour of women !

For feminists, however, the issues were different, and remain so. As a result of the concerted campaign against rape, the law on rape was changed in

1983, and at the time, many feminists saw this as a victory. But now, several years later, as rape statistics continue to mount, and the problem to become worse, the victory seems rather hollow, and the law that was then drafted with the assistance of feminist groups, seems woefully inadequate. But what were the questions for us at the time (I say "us" because I was very much part of these campaigns): the first of these was that not until the Mathura case took place, did we even begin to think of working with the victim of such violations. Yes, we took up cases on their behalf, but it was only when the Mathura case became so important, that feminists thought to ask the woman herself what she felt. And a further question arose: if Mathura herself, or any other victim, was opposed to her case being taken up, and being made into a flag for the movement, where would feminist activists stand ?

And that wasn't the end, as you can see, in those years and even much later, many of the cases that have become landmark cases in the anti-rape campaign, have come to be known by the name of the woman: thus Rameeza Bee, Mathura, Maya Tyagi, Suman Rani, Bhanwri Devi. And yet, isn't this another violation of the woman, another kind of violence towards her, for after all, she has to continue to live in her social milieu, and by making her name public, aren't activists treading that fine line between support and exploitation ? It took many years for feminists to begin to question their own contribution, albeit unknowing, to a kind of violence against women, and that then led to a further questioning of what justice meant for women who had been thus violated through acts of rape. Was it enough, as happened in Rameeza Bee's case for example, to have an enquiry commission set up ? Or

to ask for a retrial ? To succeed in changing the law ? To have the rapist imprisoned ? How could we deal with the issue of stigma, with the fact that our social mores are such that often it is the victim of rape who gets blamed for it, and that this too is a kind of violence?

### THE BURDEN OF PROOF

But there were lessons too. One of the key changes in the new – at the time – law on rape was that in cases of what is known as custodial rape, that is, when a person in a position of authority or responsibility, such as a police person, or the head of a government office, is accused of raping a woman, if the fact of rape can be proved (say, by medical evidence) then the accused is held guilty until he can be proved innocent. In other words, the burden of proof shifts to the accused. Now this was a historic reversal of the very principle of law which assumes that the accused is innocent until proved guilty . There were differences among women activists on the advantages and disadvantages of this provision. But we probably should have saved our breath, for the first time this was ever tested, in a case known as the Suman Rani case where two policemen were found guilty of custodial rape by both the lower and the high courts, it was the Supreme Court that decided that by the time their appeal came up for hearing, they had served enough time (only half the mandatory minimum sentence) and that they should be let off. The argument was that because the woman had not reported the rape for four days (but to whom should she have reported ? The same men who raped her ?), therefore her character was suspect, and the men were young and had families, so they needed to be out of jail. Such was the violence of the system.

But this lesson – not to trust the system for it remains largely male biased – stood women's groups in good stead in the Bhanwri rape case (the rape took place in 1987, the case still continues) where they demanded that because Bhanwri was raped in the course of performing her duty, i.e. doing government work, the State owed her compensation, and with this move, already the whole notion of what is justice, especially in cases of violence against women where you are not dealing only with a crime, but also with a whole cultural baggage that accompanies the way those involved are perceived, began to broaden out. First, justice was owed not only as punishment, but also as compensation, and second, an acceptance that the State's laws and practices could be quite violent towards women. But, despite these major developments, the real extent of rape remains unknown, the number of cases vastly under-reported, and justice largely elusive, for convictions take place in only 3 per cent of the cases that are brought to court. So, I want to come back to the question: what if the WSF had decided to rule out those who have ever raped a woman/girl (or man), sexually

assaulted her/him, forced violent sex on their wives against their consent... how many participants would that leave us with ?

In many ways, and I am just thinking aloud here, notions of violence are very patriarchal. The violence of men towards other men is violence, the violence of other men towards "our" women is violence, but the violence of men of one community towards women of the same community, the violence of men of a family towards women in that family, does not count as violence. The most glaring example of this is that shocking thing called "honour killing" . You kill to save your honour, and the person you kill is the woman, the person whose honour is saved is the man. But my question is: can there ever be honour in killing ? This takes us back to the same debate: are some kinds of violence (i.e. the "privatel" forms, usually directed against women and children) more acceptable than others (i.e. the "public" forms, the violence of men towards men, the violence of war) ? These are questions we might ask ourselves as we pursue the path of creating a new politics, for these are deeply political questions, and without taking them into account, there will be little that is "new" about our politics.

Of course, having said this, it's necessary also to say that while we may critique people (particularly men) for not recognizing gender based violence within the home, it is also important to understand that these are not easy problems to address. For example, it has taken women activists long to understand and admit that women too can be violent towards other women. Many activists have equated nonviolence with women, believing that women are essentially non-violent, and over the years, as issues of violence against women enter the public arena and begin to get discussed, it is also becoming clearer that such a belief is not quite warranted. Yes, women may not go out and attack others, or be as violent towards people as men often are, they do not have the burden of masculinity upon them, but that they can be complicit in violence is widely accepted. The fate of a woman being battered within a marriage or a home is often well known to other women, but they prefer to keep silent about it. This too is a sort of violence.

But also, recent years have provided ample evidence that women can and

> Violence within the homes takes more lives and statistically is a crime that involves much larger numbers than the crime of murder in any given place, but it is seldom addressed with the same kind of seriousness. I believe there needs to be a strong concern about it.

do participate in violence and the most glaring example of this that we have is of their participation in sectarian, community based violence, against women and men of the other community. The most recent example is in the carnage in Gujarat where Hindu women actively participated in violence, and even encouraged rape of Muslim women. In Bombay in early 1993, after the destruction of the Babri Masjid and in the communal pogrom that took place, women assisted their men, prevented help from reaching other women and children. And for activists, this posed another problem: if you see women being violent towards others in sectarian violence, and if those same women come to you then, seeking help in cases of domestic violence, how do you react ? How do you deal with the issues and dilemmas thrown up by this kind of all-too real experience ?

Finally, I want to bring this discussion back to the links between what we have loosely been calling internal and external violence. I will only briefly mention I would have liked to have elaborated, and this is best said by using an example. I'll turn, for this, to Kashmir. In Kashmir, as in every conflict zone in the world, it is now becoming clear that in recent years, the levels of domestic violence have risen sharply. What is happening here ? If other parts of the world can provide any pointers, I think we might speculate, and we wouldn't be far from the truth, that situations of external violence almost inevitably impact on the home, that the "external" violence of war and conflict inevitably enters the domestic space, and here, much of it takes the form of domestic or "internal" violence. But we hear a lot about violence in Kashmir, very little about violence within the home in Kashmir. Because here too, the State, or the media, are doing what, in an odd kind of way, the WSF organizers can also be held guilty of, which is to build up a hierarchy of violence, in which certain kinds of violence are seen as more important, more dangerous and more deserving of attention than others. If women were to start making a noise about domestic violence in Kashmir right now, do you think anyone would listen ? If they don't listen to them in times of peace, why should they when there is a 'national crisis' ? The argument is that the nation and its security, its interests, are more important than what goes on inside the home. Do you remember that case of the woman police officer in Punjab, Rupan Deol Bajaj, who was brave enough to accuse her senior officer, K.P.S. Gill, the hero of Punjab, credited with having got rid of the problem of militancy, and what happened to her ? If we were to take a poll of how many people felt she was justified, and how many thought she was making a mountain out of a molehill, I suspect the numbers subscribing to the latter point of view would be many more. That is the tragedy of our limited vision of the new politics. If we are to expand this vision, to make it more and more inclusive, we have to begin to address the silence around the issue of violence against women. ■

On the one side, the State is in the business of killing, and on the other it is in the business of providing compensation like this. It is the ability of violence to transit between these two that really begins to show to you complexity of this phenomena.

# understanding violence

**Deepak Mehta**

*Deepak Mehta is a Reader in the Department of Sociology, Delhi University. He is the author of* Work, Ritual, Biography: A Muslim Community in North India *(Delhi, 1997). He has been exploring the Mumbai riots of 1992-93 and has published several academic papers on this theme.*

At the outset, let me state my position on collective violence. The problem of violence is not merely one of behaviour; it is also of trying to find meaning – of its force and its effects.

Second, violence is not something that merely happens to people: it is a dimension of living, a brute fact that has to be acknowledged. This is the initial step towards understanding it better.

Third, there is an important methodological thrust to understanding violence: you must arrive at a frame by which you are able to understand the violence between States and within States simultaneously. This 'one frame' should be able to explain both together. For example, violence between India and Pakistan is of course an armed conflict, but also communal violence at home. An anthropology of violence, as with anthropology in general, must be able to bring people and places to life. It must also follow the idea of displacement or place-less-ness, the circulation of goods and ideas connected to military cultures, machismo, jingoism and so on, to show how displacement is conditioned by associations that have little to do with actual sites of violence. In effect, ethnography reveals the shadowy world of violence. In this way ethnography is in a privileged position to study the invisibilities of power.

As far as representations of violence are concerned, I'm not sure there is a direct and referential relationship between violence and those who talk of how they have been violated. It is very difficult to assume that there is a one-

to-one relationship between people who talk of violence and the violence that was actually inflicted on their bodies. I say this because there are a number of case-studies of rape and torture survivors which suggest that when words stop, terror begins; that the precondition of terror is the absence of communicability and language. I think this is an important insight but we must also recognise that words themselves have the capacity to wound — this is the terrain of hate-speech, although I'm not going to develop this argument here.

What I present to you is unfinished work, which I have been exploring since 1994. I don't have a set of conclusions; much less do I have answers to the questions that I seek to address. This is related to the Mumbai riots of 1992-93 that began a day after the demolition of the Babri Masjid, on December 6, which was very well documented. Less than 24 hours later, large parts of India were engulfed in communal violence.

I started my fieldwork in Mumbai in 1994, in a slum called Dharavi, trying to understand the effects of violence; the way people talked of the riots; and the various ways in which it became part of the everyday life of Dharavi residents. Typically, when you look at the effects of such large, collective incidents of violence, you find that when people and communities begin to remember such violence, this talk turns into a kind of memorialisation. In the western world they create monuments and museums: you will find a number of western state capitals with Holocaust museums, which try and show you what actually happened during the Second World War. That kind of thing doesn't happen in India. We are unable to create monuments to violence here

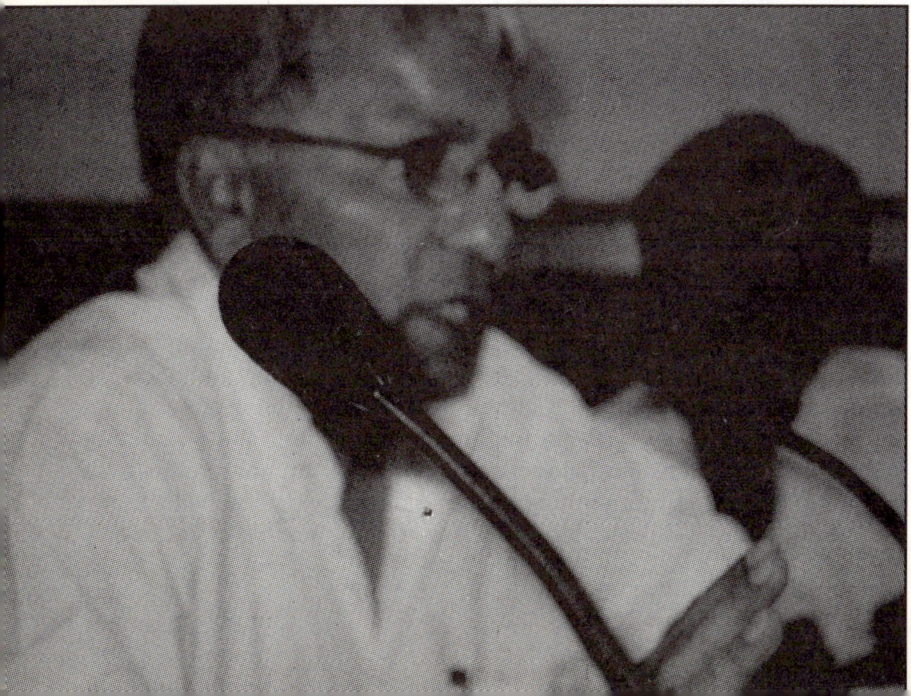

because it is not something that is distant from us; it is part of everyday life. I am talking specifically of violence between Hindus and Muslims. It is difficult to put this away in museums, precisely because it has not ended; it is a continuing negotiation, and an attempt to understand which negotiations might work.

## THE EFFECTS OF VIOLENCE

For this reason my concern is to try to understand the modalities of violence, the procedures and techniques by which it enters into the everyday life of people. But at the same time, I am wary of trying to arrive at universalities about violence — I do not have a generalisable view of it.

From my conversations with people who have been affected in communal riots, it seems to me that both emotions of and about such violence, and an understanding of violence, change over a period of time. For example, what was represented to us in 1994 is not what was represented to us in 1999 or 2000, even when we talked to the same people, or had the same debate. It seems to me that violence has this capacity to break established orthodoxies; it moves across boundaries. In this sense it is literally transgressive, being marked always by an excess.

The literature on communal violence has until recently rested on a few assumptions. There is a peculiar way by which people are able to talk of 'communalism' and 'communal riots'. The latter is a law and order category, while the former is its authorising ideology; the literature on both of these is enormous.

Communalism is a concept, and the practice of this concept is the riot. It seems to me that this is a neat and unfortunately static way by which one begins to talk of violence. For example, when commentators of the violence in Mumbai talk of the violence in Dharavi in December, '92 and January, '93, most, in fact all, begin by saying that actually these were two riots. The first began on December 7 and lasted for about two weeks or ten days and the second began during the first week of January and lasted about three weeks.

## VIOLENCE REVOKES TIME

Now, you have it in two parts — the first is generated by spontaneous Muslim anger over the demolition of the mosque, and the second is really the backlash of majority communalism. These two seem to be separated; one is spontaneous, the other aided by the police force. It is really the rallying of the Shiv Sena that allows this sort of violence to occur. But when you talk to those who experienced this violence (as victims, perpetrators, witnesses, voyeurs, etc.) for them December 1992 and January 1993 present a seamless whole, and a number of them say that the violence really ended with the bomb blasts of March 1993 when high profile political and financial establishments were targeted, apparently by Muslim extremists. From our narratives we find

that the six weeks or so of violence (December 1992-January 1993) revoked normal time – of work, production, leisure – and instead positioned violence as an absolute in the lives of the people. Once violence revokes time, you cannot go back to the resources of your tradition to make sense of what has happened: that is what comes out repeatedly. I think collective violence has the capacity to break the sense of 'belongingness'.

How does one understand violence, then?

Perhaps the most sustained work on violence has been introduced by historians writing on communalism and riots. Broadly, historians use two themes with a number of sub-themes. The first theme they pick up is that violence is actually what is called a 'residue'. It is the outcome of socio-economic conditions that include poverty, criminalisation of politics, illiteracy, unemployment and, especially over the last decade, the disintegration of the labour force. The second theme, made most famous by Gyan Pandey (Professor of Anthropology, The John Hopkins University, USA), is that the riot is traced to the colonial administrators, or apparatus of governance. That it is the British who actually did it to us; colonial administrators deliberately instituted and sustained an artificial divide between Hindus and Muslims. Here, communalism, or the fundamental Hindu-Muslim divide is the primordial signature of Indian civilisation.

Anyone who works on the communal riot must take into account the historians' telling of it; but what this literature does not give us is how communal violence affects local areas. Nor does it explain the capacity of local spaces to use the resources of communal ideology to mobilise its own interests. This is where – and I am making a plea for my discipline – the sociology of violence can make productive interventions in trying to understand the communal riot.

## SUSTAINING NEW COLLECTIVITIES

Broadly, there are four basic areas of inquiry. First, I argue that violence is capable of forging new solidarities. It is unfortunate that these solidarities become violent in turn, but this is important, because once you have collective violence in place, it divides people like nothing before. This division

> Communalism is a concept, and the practice of this concept is the riot.

is ordained on the basis of certain symbols, which constitute you as being a member of this nation or outside it.

Dharavi, which is known as the largest slum in Asia, is estimated to have between six to ten lakh (1 lakh = 100,000) people spread over 430 acres (or 1.74 square kilometres) of land and a population density of 1.87 lakh people per square kilometre. You will find that people are organised on the basis of language, religion, region and very centrally, on the basis of occupation. Once the violence of December, '92 - January, '93 happened, these divisions were effaced; they were replaced and subsumed by the division of Hindus and Muslims.

Muslims living in Hindu settlements or *chawls*, as they are known in Dharavi, migrated to Muslims chawls and vice-versa. During the violence, Muslim majority areas are called Pakistan and their inhabitants treated as belonging to an enemy country. In like fashion, Muslim women are treated as the property of Pakistan, and if captured are treated as spoils of war. We have a number of narratives which mention that when women are attacked the crowd chants, *'Dekho hum tumhara Pakistan cheen rahe hain'* (Look, we are snatching away your Pakistan). Just as women become the mark of Pakistan, circumcision for men becomes the mark of belonging to it and the location where men are stripped so that their religion can be determined is called the *'majlis-e-Pakistan'* (the Parliament of Pakistan).

In this way, communalism or communal riots, or violence — whatever you call it — actually institutes a system of apartheid on the ground. Once this system is in place, it becomes difficult to bridge. In this sense, violence — in Dharavi at least — has infused new solidarities on the basis of religion, aligned to nationality. After the violence runs its course one does not return to a prior everyday life. Neighbourhoods and bodies are forever coloured by this vision of the nation. Violence, thus, is capable of sustaining new collectivities.

Second, when you begin to look at the way in which this one event of violence affected residents of Dharavi, and continues to affect people ten years down the line, you find that far from being a historical event removed to a past, it has become part of one's 'here and now'. It is on the basis of this that people can make claims to certain kinds of housing facilities; that they are eligible or ineligible for electoral and identity cards; that they can access certain institutions of the State; and the type of work they can do. It is through this process of local apartheid that you can see how notions of citizenship are formulated on the ground.

You will find that before 1992-93, between 40 to 50 per cent of the working population in Dharavi was engaged in textile manufacture, which was almost entirely controlled by Muslims. After this time, there was almost no textile industry available in Dharavi. All the textile workers had left: either

for Coimbatore or for north India. You will see that there is a way in which violence begins to infect daily life; it begins to infect the 'here and now' of people. This violence has a peculiar quality of determining who is a citizen of India, the kind of work that is allowed to them and where will they stay. In this way violence moves in to daily life.

The third dimension of violence that sociology elaborates is the relation of violence to gender. I would like to present vignettes of how residents of Dharavi began to think of gendered violence. The traditional view has been that the first victims of communal violence are women and children, and that is indeed true. But we do not really have an understanding of how communal violence is also directed at men. Communal violence unmakes you as a man.

I would like to read you a couple of excerpts from a conversation we had with two Muslim brothers in 1995 who were textile entrepreneurs in Dharavi. We asked them what happened during the riots of 1992-93, and this is what the younger one, Shameem, said: "The roads were under constant threat. Groups of boys from outside would wait on the roads. If they found anyone, they would strip him to discover his identity. They would not spare anyone who was *katua.*"

Katua, is a term for circumcision. Katua is used interchangeably with *landya.* Both terms think of the Muslim male body as less than human. In fact the body is made bestial and is to be treated as you would the body of a dangerous animal.

Shameem said: "Some of them were knifed. Others, who were more fortunate, were made to stand in a sewer and shout 'Jai Sri Ram'. If they didn't shout, they were beaten. When they came in to attack, you could hear them shouting, "*Katua kahan hai, katua pakdo. Kat do usko*". ("Where are the circumcised men, catch them. Cut it off").

Later in 1999, I met Shameem again. His older brother had left Dharavi and migrated back to his hometown. Shameem talked of how the violence of 1992-93 had affected his working life, how he had schooled his children to be careful in public. What this conversation revealed was that the public space of his neighbourhood did not allow the previous kind of co-existence; it was no longer a place of congregation or socialising. Instead this public space, having been emptied of heterogeneity, was now a zone of transition and passing through it necessitated a series of interdictions by which one tried to efface any indication of Muslim religiosity. In Shameem's view the public space of his neighbourhood was coloured by a culture of fear and impunity.

Shameem and I talked over a beer at a pub and returned to this violence they had faced. He said that workers were unreliable, and you had to be careful what you said to them in the *maidan* (his house adjoins a park referred to as the maidan). Initially he used to get workers from there – his job is dyeing cloth – and the clothes were dyed in the park. "But now I give my orders by the day," he says, "and I pay them by the day. I have stopped buying on credit even from the cigarette shop, where I had an account earlier. One gets respect by being silent and in control. The Muslim dye-workers have all left – Maharashtrian service people have taken their place."

"Was there any violence in the maidan?" I asked.

"During the disturbance, Muslims were brought here and stripped. Even now I find it difficult to talk about what they did. The maidan was called the majlis-e-Pakistan (Parliament of Pakistan, the parliament of the castrated). As if all us motherfuckers are castrated." I don't see any reason to not include it in its original form.The anger is essential; we cannot denude – castrate – it... "What happened after Muslims were stripped?"

"Whatever you can imagine — I can only say it was worse."

## THE BODY IS A MARK OF THE NATION-STATE

It is not only the male body but specific parts of the body that were being violated. The attempt was to emasculate the male and this was very deliberate. It was not done in one incident but across the board. You get a number of accounts of how this kind of violence affects the body. But what is the signature by which this violence is organised?

Clearly, this violence is framed under the sign of the nation-state. The body becomes the mark of the nation-state. We were talking to a woman, who said, "We went out during the *danga* (violence). The men were afraid to go out because of the curfew. While coming back, the crowd pounced on us, took three women away and while taking these women they said, "Look, we are taking away your Pakistan". So, there is a way in which the Muslim body becomes available for a certain kind of mark that is generated through the boundaries of the nation-state.

It is not only the body that becomes available for this mark; you also find that this mark travels to certain neighbourhoods that are thought of as belonging to Pakistan, and others that are thought of as belonging to Hindustan. If a particular neighbourhood is considered a territory of Pakistan, it invites a certain kind of action over there. This kind of action is ordained. You find that the same mark that works itself out on the body, works itself out on neighbourhoods, and then becomes a replay of how the person or neighbourhood is able to conceive of the nation on its own terms.

I would like to put it in the words of one of the people we have been talking to since 1994 in Dharavi. Her name is Farida Behn. She has become fairly prosperous, and now exports mattresses to West Asia. She is the one who told us that they said, "Look, we are taking away your Pakistan."

We talked to her later and she said, "I understand things better now. In a riot they can cut up the body, but not the spirit. After all this had happened, we asked them, 'Why haven't you looted the Hindus in our neighbourhood? Is it written on my forehead that I am a Pakistani, and if I am a Pakistani, does that mean I should be raped'?"

"How did you organise yourself?"

"We made a committee. Relief was given; names were forwarded to the

> ...When words stop, terror begins ... the precondition of terror is the absence of communicability and language.

Srikrishna Commission Enquiry (constituted to investigate the Mumbai riots of 1992-93). But what about the fear in our hearts, how will you make a committee for that? The men here, the Muslims, are called the progeny of Dawood (a mafia leader) and told that they are pimps. Every day their honour is under attack. Whenever there are riots anywhere in the country or even when India plays cricket against any country, the Muslim men heap abuses on Pakistan. But look at them. (She points to her son). In India, you make us impotent and we abuse Pakistan."

How does one negotiate with this culture of fear and impunity? It raises the problem of how one negotiates your status anew, not merely in the public domain, but also in the domestic where Muslim men have to hear these harsh truths.

The last conversation is about the consequences of this kind of violence. We had been having a conversation with a man whose son was killed on December 7 — he was shot in the head by the police. For three days, the body lay in the house, because this man was unable to arrange a burial. Eventually, with the help of a Shiv Sainik, presumably one of the members of a community that organised the violence against them, and the intercession of a local policeman, he was able to take his son's body to the police station. Those responsible for the violence also arranged for the burial. Once this man had taken his son's body to the police station he insisted that his son's post-mortem be done in one hospital while the police insisted on another. Eventually this man had his way. During the course of the negotiations one of the policemen said to him, "Should we send you to Pakistan as well?"

"Why did you want a post-mortem?" I asked him.

He said, "Don't you see, it is with the post-mortem that the State will not only give compensation, but also acknowledge that wrong was done to me."

Then I said, "But what effect does this have?"

He stopped and said — he later provided evidence to the Srikrishna Commission — "You will find the history of Akhand Bharat (Greater India) in documents such as these."

So, the history of greater India is going to be counted in the letters of compensation. On the one side, the State is in the business of killing, and on the other it is in the business of providing compensation. It is the ability of violence to transit between these two that really begins to show you the complexity of this phenomenon. ■

# resistance, defence or violence ?

**SWAPAN MUKHERJEE**

*Swapan Mukherjee, born and brought up in Delhi, joined the working class movement while studying in Delhi University and left his studies to join the CPI (ML), popularly known as the Naxalite movement, in the early 1970s. He worked underground till the State of Emergency was lifted in 1977. He was involved in the formation and development of Indian Peoples' Front (IPF), a mass political platform initiated by CPI (ML). He worked in Delhi and adjoining states, particularly Punjab and Rajasthan among unorganised labour in agriculture, brick kilns, textiles, construction etc. At present, he is General Secretary of All India Central Council of Trade Unions (AICCTU) and Central Committee Member of CPI(M-L) Liberation. He is also President of Coal Mine Workers' Union (CMWU), based in Jharkhand and West Bengal.*

*aicctu@rediffmail.com*

> "The right to strike has been taken away; dalits have not been given the right to vote; women are raped inside the police stations. Then we are told: "It is wrong to resist all this." Will you say this is wrong?"

The world has changed a lot in recent years. Ten years ago, the Soviet Union still existed: but after the collapse of the Soviets, America rules the world, unchallenged. There have been many rallies as a reaction to this around the world, especially on February 15, 2003, when millions of people took to the streets against the planned American attack on Iraq — it was a worldwide collective assertion. Basically, as some people say, the consciousness for this was developed somewhere in the process of the WSF. I believe the global anti-war rallies can help form another superpower, and are a demonstration of 'people power' against American power. From this point of view, the WSF should be looked at in a new way -- although it is not the only alternative.

In the past decade or so, there have been anti-globalisation and anti-capitalist movements and now people have found their place against USA – the lone superpower. As Michael Hardt and others have said, the Non Aligned Movement has now been replaced by the WSF. Some forces even consider the WSF as a Fifth International.

**KEEPING SPACES 'OPEN'**

Whether other worlds are possible or not is a question open to debate; but other fora are certainly possible. Because, on the basis of its Charter, the WSF excludes forces of resistance from Latin America – but those are powerful

forces. Such exclusions exist within the 'open space' where the WSF draws some boundary lines as well — I don't think that is a very 'open' thing to do. But even if it is not a completely open space, the WSF does provide an opportunity for interaction, to provide an exchange. In a changing world, we can learn many new things through such an experiment: this is the positive aspect of the WSF.

ATTAC, the Association for the Taxation of Financial Transaction for the Aid of Citizens, was among those who started the WSF, along with a Left organisation from Brazil: both are not really known as being against globalisation. But what was distinctive about them — what the world knew about them – was their grass-root experiments: their participatory budget-making and experiments with democracy; both of them took an initiative together. ATTAC, which is basically an international-level institution, took the initiative to lobby international-level institutions for taxation on transactions – this is called the Tobin tax, named after American economist James Tobin. It was his proposal that Third World countries be helped for social welfare through taxation. ATTAC is not so much against globalisation: it talks of globalisation as a process that needs reform. The WSF is unique because it has organisations like these — strong sections which want globalisation to have a human face. But there are other forces that maintain that globalisation should be totally rejected, that it is an imperialist globalisation. Both these forces interact in tandem at the WSF.

**THIRD WORLD CONCERNS**

When the WSF began in Brazil, there were 15,000 people, mostly from Latin America. The numbers grew, and are still growing. The European Social Forum, the Asian Social Forum and many other fora were started; and within these, many types of debates and opinions emerged. If the WSF does not pay attention to these opinions, there are likely to be problems in the coming days. Some of these might include typically Third World concerns, such as women's issues, which are described differently in Europe and America. There is a way in which the State machinery colludes with the way they are viewed.

In India, globalisation has brought starvation and a massive growth of the unorganised sector with it. You will find nothing in the Charter of the WSF on this. It is basically a Third World concern, and it is my understanding that by championing a Third World concern we can make it an issue of imperialist globalisation.

Another important point today is the issue of pensions: once it was a very ordinary issue, but now it has become a major problem. At one time, pension, healthcare and education were considered the best in Europe; but now even the governments of these welfare States have been reneging on these fronts.

Recently, France had one of the biggest rallies in Europe, to protest against the proposal to end social welfare. The rallies took place in Britain, France and Italy – all of which had social welfare schemes but wanted to end these as a part of their solidarity with the European Union. Some people in the European Social Forum advocate it; others oppose social welfare positions – 'dialogues' like these are possible under the aegis of 'open space', and came up at the European Social Forum.

Another growing debate within the WSF is about which financial institutions should be allowed to contribute. At the European Social Forum, an important minister from the French government was present. The question is: are some European governments sponsoring the European Social Forum's meetings in France? This, and other concerns, like those of the WSF disallowing some politicians – on another occasion, Lula, the Brazilian President was allowed to deliver a lecture, but the President of Venezuela was not allowed to speak – this is a discrepancy of policy. Concerns are surfacing about the political, economical, structural, ideological, and financial structures of the WSF.

**THE LAST RESORT**

Another important issue for the Third World is that of violence. The Indian Supreme Court recently gave a verdict banning strikes. Reading that judgement made you feel that people really like going on strike, as if people go on strike without any reason! Perhaps they do not know that employees

who go on strike face a salary deduction, and that they go on strike only if there is a real need.

Similarly, this talk about violence: nobody actually likes violence, or likes to resort to using arms. But like Gandhiji had to take his movement back after the Chauri Chaura incident, the same Gandhiji, in 1942 gave the slogan — '*Karo ya Maro*' – 'Do or Die'. Now is the slogan of 'Do or Die' a statement of non-violence?

We also have a movement with the working class, but we are not allowed to collect the masses; in most of the Third World countries collecting masses is illegal. The right to strike has been taken away; dalits have not been given the right to vote; women are raped inside police stations. Then we are told: "It is wrong to resist all this."

Will you say this is wrong?

This is resistance; in fact, this is defence which even the Indian Constitution allows. The Supreme Court has given judgements on this many times. But this sort of resistance is not allowed to be a part of the WSF.

In other parts of the world, in Bolivia for instance, the government, along with the US, exploits its reserves of natural gas. What happened there? Thousands of people surrounded the President's palace and removed him forcibly. Even though the WSF is in its initial stages, it is possible for it to play such a role in Teheran, Baghdad or Kabul. You could organise one lakh (100,000) people if you really want to root out imperialist globalisation, or take them in the midst of war. This is something that could be done through the WSF.

### THE WORLD SITUATION

What is new in terms of the world situation is that there is no Soviet Union to counter-balance America; and the UN is also weakened now. At this time, you will agree that America's authoritarianism has grown. It is not just the

> "In India, globalisation has brought starvation and a massive growth of the unorganised sector with it. You will find nothing in the charter of the WSF on this."

language of Narendra Modi here; look at Bush's language: in USA if anybody speaks against the war, the word 'un-American' is used to describe them.

This is a culture in which they have attacked Iraq militarily and say: "If you are not with us, you are against us." This is a form of authoritarianism, and with it a politics through which they loot and control Third World countries.

Many years ago, we saw a Charlie Chaplin film, in which Charlie Chaplin said: "The norms of the capitalist world will have to be broken." At this time the biggest power in the world is the American President, George Bush. His followers — the Third World countries — are creating an atmosphere of violence. This is true from Narendra Modi to Bush himself. The WSF should decide something about them: it is time for the norms of the capitalist world to be broken.

The WSF has its own Charter, according to which it works, but I don't feel it is the 'New Internationale'. The 'Internationale' has been there for a long time, it has not come about in a day. Basically, the WSF is a centre for interaction, which calls itself an open space. In that case, what is the reason for blocking out some people involved in resistance, even when they work in relation to people's movements? What is the point of keeping them out?

The Cancun talks failed basically because of two reasons. One was the Forum for South Korea and the African nations walked out at the last moment. The most backward regions, Asia, or the Third World, are the only ones who have the power to stop Bush — but the culture and agenda of these countries has to be put forth. We need to debate political and ideological questions, the financial implications and questions of the organisational set-up in regard to the WSF. The issue of imperialistic globalisation in the present times needs to be brought up, and through Forums like these we can bring these issues to the regional level as well. Now we are talking of bringing it to the local level: there have been many such new experiments the world over.

But these new experiments are necessary in the new world, and George Bush's declarations with regard to the New World Order show that he does not have regard for the world at all. The WSF will have to become the centre for those who choose to stand against all this. We cannot have a collective action through the WSF, because the WSF does not pass any collective resolution of its own; but there can be other ways of reflecting a collective will and collective action, which we should talk about. ■

> Do not classify violence as 'positive violence' and 'negative violence'. Violence just leads to more violence.

# A thousand voices

**P.V. Rajagopal**

*P V Rajagopal has championed the rights of the poor for the past 33 years. As a social reformer he has worked to uphold the rights of indigenous people, dalits and women, helping them realise their economic rights through land distribution and food production. He is a human rights activist who has adopted Mahatma Gandhi's style and values in his work; his most unique contribution has been to identify a different political culture based on 'sarvodaya' (well-being of all). He is the founder of many institutions, including* Ekta Parishad, *a land-based people's movement, and the Vice-Chair of the Gandhi Peace Foundation.*

*jillharris@now-india.net.in*

I am going to try and share the experience of practising non-violence. Non-violence is a tool that assists with conflict management and resolution. I believe that it is important to take the idea of non-violence down to the field, practise it and fine-tune it. It is vital to use these tools in your daily life and social interactions in a manner where they influence one's behaviour; it is insufficient just to describe non-violence as 'transformative' without the actual experience. People sometimes see this as a point of contention -- but how can one benefit from a debate that remains in the classroom and coffeehouses? For the last 30 years I have been endeavouring to take this debate on violence and non-violence from theory to practice, from classrooms and coffee houses to the field. I would like to share some of my experiences from different parts of the country with you, particularly from the Chambal valley.

## DACOITS IN THE CHAMBAL VALLEY

I went to the Chambal valley in 1970, because it was notorious for dacoits and gangsters. At that time, I had no idea that dacoits like Madho Singh, Maurya Singh, Makhan Singh and Lakhan Singh would ever listen to us, or for that matter consider surrendering – in fact, I did not even dream of it. I went into the area only with the hope and conviction for non-violence. Initially, there was heavy resistance from the dacoits and they assaulted and beat me up, expecting that I would run away. But I did not run away. I stood my ground, and worked with the youth and children, with a genuine conviction for peace and harmony. I found that villagers were getting the message – and in the end, with the help of Jai Prakash Narayan and other Sarvodaya leaders, more than one thousand dreaded dacoits surrendered before the photograph of Mahatma Gandhi.

In the course of that non-violent struggle, I began to understand the problems of dacoits in the Chambal valley. These were related to the fact that there were no schools, no support for farming, and no industry. The adivasis were upset, so were farmers and shopkeepers. To help the situation, we decided to start an ashram, in a modest way; though not really believing that we would be able to end this violence. But through consistent work with young people and children, and the support of the villagers, we were able to find a solution.

Slowly, the people there began to believe -- and so did we -- that non-violence is something practical, that in fact it can be done. While doing this, I also realised that violence is not merely a physical thing; it is not only someone physically attacking you with a bullet, rather it is deep-rooted and it is the very structure of violence that needs to be reviewed.

### HANDLING SYSTEMIC VIOLENCE

Systemic violence is the most dangerous: lakhs of people in this country are hungry; there is exploitation, corruption and injustice; there is oppression -- all these are different forms of violence. Many of those who perpetuate violence believe that they themselves are non-violent. Keeping people hungry, not giving them wages, beating them up, preventing people from wearing *chappals* when they walk around -- those who do these things spread corruption and injustice in society that ultimately leads to violence; in spite of all this, these perpetrators believe they are non-violent.

I believe that there is no point in fighting just one form of violence; rather there is a need to fight all forms of violence including injustice, exploitation and poverty, simultaneously. We understood this after working for ten years in the Chambal valley. We started training young people and sending them into the villages. These young people began fighting against systemic violence. They started questioning all forms of exploitation that could lead to violence. For instance, if people did not get their land, they asked: "What is the reason?" If someone created difficulties for the poor, they asked: "Why are they doing it?" If the government officials indulged in corruption, they asked: "Why are they doing it?" All these are big issues for poor people. We have destroyed the space in which they live their lives and we must help them get it back. We began fighting against structural violence; even though we knew that this would be very difficult. A boy would be deliberately embroiled in a legal case; another locked up at the police station, a third put away in jail and so on. But our message was clear. What we were saying was: "Bring unorganised people together; raise your voice to resist this injustice."

### SOLIDARITY

It is a difficult task to resist violence in our country. To make this happen, we started networking. If there was an injustice done against one person, then thousands raised their voices; they wrote letters and made their presence felt. By doing this, we understood that you can fight against structural violence. But you cannot fight it alone: you need to be united. And not at the level of one district or village: you need to be united at the national and international levels; so that this fight is about solidarity. We have learnt this lesson after a long time, and we know it is very important.

I often appeal to the people who propagate violence that it is easy to sit in a university campus, or in a coffee- house and say: "There is no other way to solve a problem than to pick up a gun." But those who say this do not know how much harm they are causing. Please note, that by glorifying violence you are contributing to violence, even if it is without your knowledge, and young people get a lot of encouragement to go this way. Therefore, I make a request: do not intensify violence by glorifying it. Instead, strengthen the possibilities of non-violence; add power to it.

I have another request: do not classify violence as 'positive violence' and 'negative violence'. Violence just leads to more violence. It is difficult to get mangoes from babul seeds: babul seeds will give you babul. So, please don't promote violence while sitting in Delhi, Mumbai, Hyderabad and Kolkata, because the ones who promote it don't have to pick up the gun; they don't even have to go to the targeted village; they just have a bit of fun, sitting here and saying, "There is no other way than using the gun." This is something I have understood once again during our discussions this morning.

## SOME EXAMPLES FROM BIHAR

I would like to tell you about Kamlesh, who is a journalist, and the president of the journalist's union in Bihar; he comes from the village of Banke Bazar in Bihar, 60 kilometres from Gaya. He was trying to sensitise journalists; to say that they should not write too much about violence and kidnappings, but rather report more positive things. That was his agenda -- to rebuild the image of Bihar and do only positive reporting. But this is what happened to him: his house was attacked twice, and a bomb was put there. The ones who did this said: "If you agree to report about us, we will let you go or else we will not spare you." This kind of demand for reporting violence is increasing, because there is a craving for publicity and communication among those who

> I believe that it is important to take the idea of non-violence down to the field, practise it and make it sharper: because if you don't use these tools they are of no use.

perpetuate violence. This desire in itself motivates more violence. Therefore, there is a need to check the violence done by people for whom it is a hobby, to let them know that nothing good will come of it.

The second example, also from Banke Bazar, is about the 19-day long hunger strike we had – we fasted – and there was a *dharna* and satyagraha before the government agreed to talk to us. It was about '*pattas*' (deeds) for land that had been given to the poor 25 years ago. For the last 25 years these people had papers showing possession, but they did not have any land. They had been saying: "We got this land from Vinoba Bhave, but where is our land?". Finally, the government agreed that they would go from village to village and give the land to the people. On the 19th day of the camp we got an agreement to solve this problem.

## SPACE FOR NON-VIOLENT ACTION

The land that belongs to the poor has been seized by the Forest Department, and they have been robbed by powerful, dominant people. Initially, violence was used in the interest of the poor and the exploited; now it is being used against them. The MCC started out with the intention of getting back land for the poor and the dalits; but now there is no difference between them and the Ranvir Sena; the people who had set out on the path of revolution once do not believe in it now. Many people joined the MCC, the Ranvir Sena, or the government to protect their property; they were prepared to do anything to achieve this goal. But now that all that ideology is finished, I believe that non-violence can also be used.

I would like to draw attention to this space, the space for non-violent action, where everyone can help. This space is challenged, because those in government positions believe that if people get organised and raise their voices against corruption, appropriation and exploitation, there will be trouble. So they try and sideline every non-violent agitation, saying that there is a potential for violence. They say that it is non-violent at the moment, but in some years it will become violent and a frontal organisation of the Naxalites -- so crush it now!

We need to use non-violence in an effective way: wherever there are non-violent movements, they must be brought together. Non-violence should be presented as a powerful tool to make governments bow in a non-violent way. This would promote 'people power' instead of 'party politics'. Through people's politics, we can put pressure on the State to act in the interest of the people, because in a globalised world the interest of the people is not the same as that of the party, or that of the State. The only way we can do this is by playing people's politics.

I think it is important to have an agenda of land reform to achieve this.

Whether it is in Brazil, Philippines or Thailand, land appropriation is a problem. In India, after Independence, the landed community came to power and did not allow the proper structuring of the Land Ceiling Act; they set a ceiling of 40 acres. But it was a ceiling of 40 acres, in a country where there were 460 million people! They were able to do this because the law was made by the 'big people'. But then, in spite of making the law, they did not allow it to be implemented. And today, they are trying to do away with the Land Ceiling Act. So, those who have money in a suitcase can buy thousands of acres of land. They can make farmhouses and plantations – they can control all the land.

If we don't stand our ground, how will we fight? A floating population cannot fight against globalisation. They need roots. A rooted population is needed. The landed community comes up with another solution: uproot them all; send all the Biharis to Punjab and Haryana to fill their stomachs, and send the Chhattisgarhis away; then all of their lands will be in our control. These people then run farmhouses to convert black money into white — that is how they are hard at work!

We need massive action at the national level for the tillers to get land; we need to unite the non-violent struggles across the country for land reform. That is why I am talking of a big conference, during the WSF, where

> I finally understood the problem of dacoits in the Chambal Valley: there were no schools, no support for farming, and no industry.

thousands of people will gather and if they say, 'Land First!' it will help to unite people fighting for land across the world. My request is this: let us strengthen this agenda in the World Social Forum and make a united effort.

We keep talking about employment generation; but the government does not have the means to give employment to even one per cent of the people! Even those who have jobs are being removed from them. If employment is to be generated, there is only one way – that is through land. Land will create employment and generate food security. Those who have kept 20 or 200 acres of land should give it back; those who have shops should run those; those who have jobs should work there; those who have factories should do that job. But those who till, those who work the land -- give them land because in a country like India, a billion people are looking for work. We cannot do without proper land reforms here.

If you want to fight on special issues of violence, migration and poverty, then a forum such as the World Social Forum must unite on these issues. I made a padayatra (a foot march), which is a big and effective medium for mass mobilisation, walking thousands of kilometres to strengthen the non-violent struggle, and to make governments bow to the need for land reform.

We mobilised people in a big way in Madhya Pradesh, Chhattisgarh and Bihar. Through the padayatras we put pressure on the state to bring about change at the policy level. You have to prepare people to benefit from changes in policy.

Once again, I would ask that the debate on violence/non-violence should not be limited to classrooms and coffee-houses, but put into action. A non-violent social movement can and must bring about a policy change and a revolutionary change in society. With such a request I want to move towards the WSF. ■

"When we indulge in violence, it is the dinosaur's brain that is actually operating in our heads. We do not really apply our minds when we do violence."

# revenge and collective guilt

**DILIP SIMEON**

*Dilip Simeon taught history at Delhi University for several years. He has been a research scholar at the Centre for Social Studies, Surat, the Institute of Development Studies in Brighton, the University of Chicago, and the Institute on Asian Studies in Leiden, Holland. In 1994-95 he was Visiting Fellow at the Department of History, Princeton University. His writings focus mainly on labour history, politics and violent conflict and his published works include a book:* The Role of Labour Under Late Colonialism *(Delhi, 1995). In 2001, he became Director of the Aman Trust which works to understand and reduce violent conflict.*

*dilip@amanpanchayat.org*

I am not going to address the question of what position the WSF takes on violence. However, it is very interesting to note that people and political parties with very ambivalent positions on violence are there in the WSF. I am sure Swapan (Mukherjee) would agree that he doesn't have an absolutist position on non-violence. I do. Frankly, it is good if people try to exclude violence from their political activity.

There are many communists in the WSF, who have an ambivalent position on violence; they believe that in certain circumstances political violence may be necessary; that one should not condemn violence outright. I am not going to address this issue, because there are numerous situations in which you may understand or excuse it; you may feel violence is inevitable; or sympathise with the victim who engages in it to defend herself or himself. There are situations -- particular encounters -- where one might have to defend a child, or someone who is being attacked.

I am not trying to preach a moral line for everybody to become a saint and go around being non-violent. That's not the position I am taking; nor is that the issue. Neither am I talking about a society in the future where there will be no conflict, no violence, and children will not be slapped occasionally to discipline them; I am not taking that type of position either. Nor am I talking about the past -- some people like to argue about what Cromwell should have done, what Bhagat Singh or Lenin could have done; I am not giving a moral prescription for dead people and what they should, or should not, have done.

I am not denying that violence achieves results; I am not arguing about whether it ought, or ought not to be used; or trying to make a moral judgment about people who use it. Nor am I condemning people who are fighting in the name of national liberation and adopt violent methods: I am not making an outright condemnation here.

I don't deny that violence leads to certain results; but as Hannah Arendt has said in *Reflections on Violence*: "The practice of violence, like all actions, does change the world. But the most probable change is a more violent world".

## UNDERSTANDING VIOLENCE

I am saying that it is necessary to address the question: 'What is violence?' What I am trying to deal with is the need to understand violence per-se. I find it very difficult to get this point across, even though it's fairly simple.

Also, I want to ask,what are the repercussions of a massive use of political violence? What are its innate tendencies? I am not ashamed to say that I am

a Marxist. I also mix this with Gandhiism, and many of my Marxist friends find this unpleasant. As far as I am concerned, each flows from the other.

I feel that the Marxist tradition has not addressed the issue of violence theoretically, but rather has addressed it tactically. I think this is erroneous: to deal with violence tactically, without understanding what it is, just as it is to deal with nationalism without understanding what it is. It is time we stopped doing that, because in order to understand a very complex world, it is necessary to address certain issues theoretically and philosophically. It is not just an esoteric pastime of philosophers, but something everybody has to think about very carefully.

Broadly speaking, there are three positions that go together to support a pragmatic approach to violence. First, it is presumed by those who use violence, or who have an ambivalent position on violence, that violence is a radical method. Violence infuses political action with radicalism. This position may be found across the political spectrum. Everybody from ultra Left to ultra Right believes that violence is the radical element to use.

Second, that violence brings about closure. Hence the phrase: 'final solution'. Once you do violence, that is the final card to play; it is the trump card. It brings about an end to the issue.

Third, that violence is capable of being ideologically controlled by processes of legitimacy. A legitimate exercise of violence means there are some institutions that channel violence; focus it on a particular end; achieve it; control it; and then stop it. So, there is a notion that violence is an instrument, and that violence is an instrument that may be controlled.

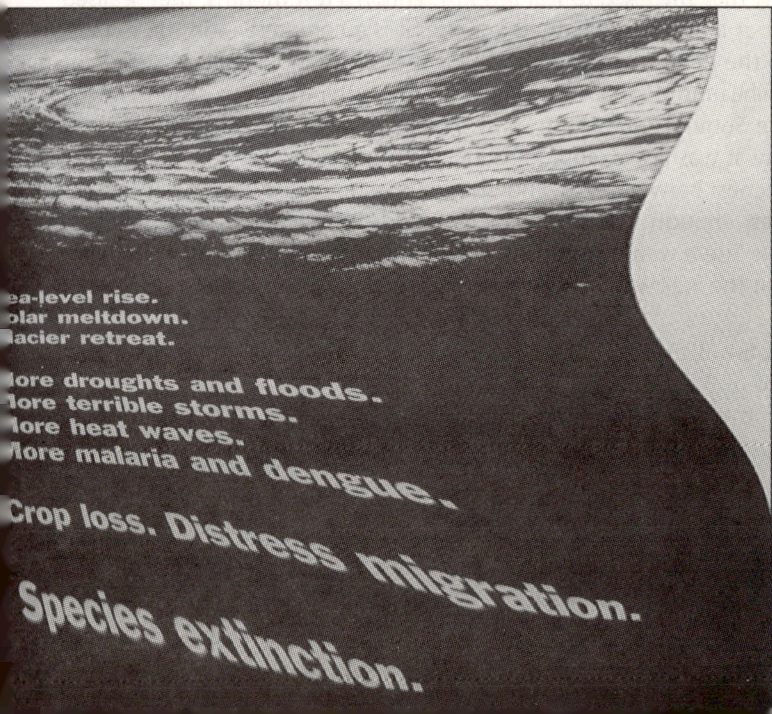

### A DIFFERENCE IN PERSPECTIVE

My position is exactly the opposite on all these three issues. First and foremost, I believe that violence is not radical at all — but rather it is pre-human — it goes back to the time of lizards. When we indulge in violence, it is the dinosaur's brain that is actually operating in our heads. We do not really apply our mind when we do violence. 'Violence' is a very sanitised and euphemistic word — using half of a blade to sever someone's jugular vein — that is how class enemies have been annihilated. But it's not a very pretty thing to do. When you do something like that, you are operating with a different part of your brain.

So, I believe that violence is not something radical, it comes from the lizard still inside us. Far from being radical, it is the most atavistic form of activity that unites human beings with other living creatures — across species.

Secondly, violence does not bring about closure. On the contrary, it brings about incessant duplication of violence. It never brings about closure; and there is no question of a final solution being achieved by violence. A violent revolution to overthrow the existing condition will not result in the end of violence; it will only lead to further problems. As a historian I can say this, and I would recommend you read Paul Fussell's *Great War in Modern Memory* (Penguin 1975, reprinted 2000), which provides the literary history of the First World War and its impact. This book makes a very interesting point: that the First World War shattered the innocence of modern humanity. Young men went into the First World War with celebrations, balloons, buntings and bands -- that is how they marched to war in 1914. Within a few months, they realised that this is not a circus, but something else: it is a complete nightmare. I will not go into the details, but this was the first effort of industrialised society at actually annihilating people. They achieved many things in this regard. In the battle of the Somme, the British army alone had a rate of attrition of 7,000 people a day. It was like a sausage-producing machine.

The trenches between the English Channel and the Swiss border ran 25,000 miles, enough to go around the world. People spent months inside the trenches. There were people who were writing mad poems 20 years later, thinking that the war was still on. There was a group of soldiers on the Allied

> "It is fashionable to jeer and sneer at Gandhi, but I think he had more physical courage than many revolutionaries put together."

side who constituted themselves into a group called the 'Never End-ians'. The meaning is clear — they believed that this war would never end. And if you look at the history of the 20th century, you will see that this is actually true: it never ended.

Historically, you can show links between the First World War and almost every other thing that has happened since then. The First World War led to the Wilsonian World Order. It also led to the Russian revolution; to the emergence of Hitlerism; and the repercussions of each of these.The Second World War was an extension of the First, and led to the problem of the Middle East, the Israel-Palestine conflict, and so on. In between the First and Second World Wars, there were several other wars: the Manchurian War, the Sino-Japanese war, the wars in Ethiopia and the Spanish Civil war. Immediately after the Second World War, there was the Korean War, then the Vietnamese war, and it has just carried on non-stop.

**WHERE IS THE "CLOSURE" HERE?**

In fact, it may be argued that there are certain economic-political systems that generate war. As a Marxist, I would argue that the capitalist system generates war; it needs war; it cannot do without war. As a Socialist I would argue that it is the foremost duty of Socialists to liberate humanity from violence — this should be on top of their agenda. Not the use of violence to liberate humanity from something else. I am arguing that violence should not be used as an instrument. Remove this word violence from the domain of instrumentality, it is not an instrument to heal a disease: it is a disease in itself. Stop talking and arguing whether it is justified — I want to first understand: "What is this thing, and what are its repercussions?"

I address this issue in a paper I've written, 'The Brains of the Living: A Discussion on Political Violence'. I will highlight certain aspects of it. One is that we have a blurring of violence, — I am not talking only about resistance groups, as a matter of fact, my entire argument in the paper is about the State. The only problem is that those people who were rebels against the State today, become the owners of the State tomorrow. Then they do exactly what they were railing against from the other side. I am claiming again that the notion that you can legitimately control violence by legitimating institutions is a pipe-dream.

**A NEW TREND IN VIOLENCE: KILLING INNOCENT PEOPLE**

We all sympathised with the Iraqi resistance, but what has happened is that they have started using bombs in which innocent people, like school-going children, are getting blown up. We may take a position of righteous indignation and say, "Iraqi people have a right to resist. People have a right to resist." But who are these people? Who is doing all these things? I might

sympathise with some of them, but what is happening is that this violence is developing a tendency to cross the boundaries of legitimate control. If you look at the history of the LTTE (Liberation Tigers of Tamil Elam) you will find the same. The notion that you can keep it under some kind of legitimising influence is nonsensical.

Now, what position do you take against people who are blowing up school children, and so on? This is what we call collateral damage. We condemn George Bush when he does collateral damage. His answer is always the same: "We went to do a good deed and a few people got killed -- it was an accident; we did not kill them intentionally." But when we do the same thing, is it all right? Exploding bombs, attacking the American presence in Iraq. I also feel it should be resisted. But in the process of resistance, you are killing 40 people who have nothing to do with it!

I have a friend who has just returned from Nepal: she took some photographs of villages that have been burnt down by the comrades. They did this because sons of some families in the villages had joined the army. In a poor country like Nepal, there are bound to be a lot of villagers who will join the police and the army, to earn a living. And you burn down their houses? Is this revolution? I am sorry to say, everything positive that is done by revolutionary forces gets tainted the minute you engage in this kind of thing. I state this as a theoretical point, that despite your best intentions, the violence you engage in will cross the boundary. The distinction between an innocent bystander and a combatant will disappear. This is the tendency of modern times.

In previous centuries, wars were fought between combatants; soldiers used to kill each other. But to deliberately target civilians is a new trend. Even in the case of the Vietnam War, the Vietnamese resistance fought against Americans in Vietnam, but they did not ask their supporters to blow bombs in the New York subway. They could have done it, they had a lot of sympathisers. We have all have been politicised through the Vietnam War, and I know how much anger we all felt at that point; but that did not happen. They never did it.

Now you have a situation where attacking civilians is considered an acceptable part of war strategy. The phenomenon of 'total war' , that is, a war that strategically targets civilians, is peculiar to the twentieth century. You blow a bomb somewhere and don't care who gets killed. I quite understand the agony with which young Palestinian teenagers are blowing themselves up. I support every single demand of the Palestinians, but one thing I would like to say is this: don't use violence.

People say that violence resolves everything; non-violence doesn't resolve anything. But what is violence really achieving? My own answer would be that in Palestine, the only answer is Gandhian Satyagraha; with the most radical demands. Because you are going to die anyway, you say they are

going to kill you. Maybe they are going to kill you: but in turn, by killing innocent people, are you actually going to achieve something? I would like to point out that 'do or die' is not the same thing as 'do and kill'.

## NON-VIOLENCE IS STRENGTH

I am saying that the traditional positions on violence are insufficient. It is our duty as thinking people to change that. But here (in India) people invest pride in violence; it is treated as a matter of preserving honour. Most men, especially younger men fall prey to this sort of rubbish; I have been a young man, so I know. They think that if they talk about non-violence it makes them look like some kind of a wimp; a person who has no strength. But if you look at it, the most powerful man was that old man who withstood five attacks on his life, but yet faced the revolver with courage. It is fashionable to jeer and sneer at Gandhi, but I think he had more physical courage than many revolutionaries put together.

This is the issue I would like to place before you here: we are actually too scared to face the truth about what violent politics means. We are more comfortable with engaging in practical and pragmatic discussions about whether it should or shouldn't be used; but are not comfortable actually addressing the issue, because this can take us to a place that is both dangerous and uncomfortable for us.

## JUSTIFICATIONS FOR VIOLENCE

You will find people taking a similar position on violence across the political spectrum – that, "If there is a war, then there will be retaliation". This is exactly what Narendra Modi says. You find this position with both the extreme Left and the extreme Right, and it is enthused by the notion of revenge. The concept of revenge is very strong here. Violence is being justified by these kinds of notions. The superpowers also function along these lines; they also want to take revenge. But what about some kind of liberatory politics? Can this function on the basis of revenge?

The notion of collective guilt, you know, is the notion with which Hitler functioned -- that an entire community is responsible for some crime. So Jews were held responsible for something or the other. This kind of notion of collective guilt is the basis -- sentimental or ideological basis -- for justifying violence. I feel that modern politics cannot function on this basis; we need to get past this somehow.

Another thing that occurs across the political spectrum is the whole issue of authoritarianism. I cannot say that this is a hard-and-fast rule, but I believe that the organisation of violence breeds authoritarianism. I am not referring to individual incidents, but rather the deliberate organising of violent political

activity -- this breeds authoritarianism. For example, if you want to construct an army or a paramilitary force, you will have to have authoritarian politics.

I also feel that the organisation of violence begins the process of degeneration of the Left. Further, the more organised violence that you indulge in, the more the tendency is for you to become very much like your enemy. Just like the Ranvir Sena and the PWG (People's War Group) are becoming like mirror images of each other. The CPI (ML) — the Communist Party of India (Marxist-Lennist) produced a pamphlet recently, which listed the number of people who had left the Ranvir Sena to join the PWG. What does it mean when people from the Ranvir Sena join the PWG? What does it tell us about the PWG and about the Ranvir Sena? I know that this is a very provocative statement, but I sincerely believe that this is what is going to happen.

## VIOLENCE AND PATRIARCHY

I believe that if you want look for the roots of violence in Indian society you should look at informal labour relations. Identifying the method by which labour is controlled and managed is the surest way of understanding the roots of violence in society. Here, of course, the issue of patriarchy comes in — it is inextricably linked to a capitalist society. We are seeing Indian capitalism here; Indian modernity, and this society is steeped in patriarchy; and patriarchal values make it possible for labour to be treated in a certain way. The whole structure of informality — of the informal sector — actually has a lot to do with the structure of domestic relations as well. One thing endemic in Indian labour relations is corporal punishment; and this is not something that is going to pass away in due course. It's going to remain, because it is structural.

Some people believe that after some years this informality will disappear. On the contrary, it is increasing. In 2003, more than 92 per cent of Indian labour forces have been found to be in informal labour relations. Most of the Indian women labour force is in this sector; many of them are subjected to physical punishment.

> "Violence is such a horrible thing that we have to take recourse to God to actually give us some strength to do it and therefore every religious tradition has got this: you will find some justification for violence across all religions."

I would suggest that one theoretical approach to try to understand the roots of violence is to understand labour relations: particularly the structure of informality.

### VIOLENCE AND RELIGION

Finally, the issue of religion and violence is very important. Very often, in anti-communal politics we go around saying that religion doesn't teach us to hate each other. I believe that this is not true. I believe that every single religious tradition has produced justifications and legitimisation of violence. Violence is such a horrible thing that we need to take recourse to God to actually give us some strength to do it, and therefore every religious tradition has got this: you will find some justification for violence across all religions. To keep on pretending — just to massage each other's egos — that your religion is very nice, my religion is very nice, mine doesn't teach violence, yours doesn't teach violence — this is all rubbish! We had all better start speaking the truth.

Young people today, who want to see a slightly better world in another decade or so, better realise that this is becoming a runaway issue. It is no longer sufficient just to hand over your brains to some political parties. I am appealing to you in public: don't do it. By all means approach political groups, and find out what they have to say. But groups that have already arrived at the complete version of truth: beware of them; please, be afraid of them; they are the most dangerous people. There should, at least, be a space for discussion. There are people who do not want to discuss any matter, even this issue.

### A BETTER UNDERSTANDING OF VIOLENCE

I feel that we are really coming to a phase where there is an increase of violence: violence in the name of ethnicity, violence in the name of sentiment; it is all structural. It appears to be in the name of religion and sentiment but it has a structural function. It is important for us intellectually to try to understand this structural function. The structural function of Hindutva violence is not the defence of Hindu sentiments and building temples; it has got a role to play in building and maintenance of Indian economic and social structure. That is really what it is.

We must try to understand these issues, and address violence as an issue that is very important for us to deal with, within the ongoing crisis in the world today: because violence is only going to increase. Every day that one opens the newspaper you find that this tendency is increasing.

In closing: I feel that the WSF also has only taken a tactical position on violence. I would prefer that it allow people who believe in violence to come in and have a public debate; that is what I think is necessary today — in every political movement — the WSF and all the others. ■

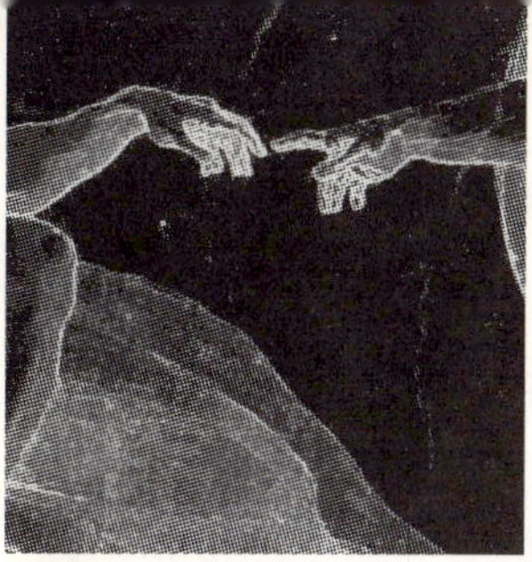

# open forum

*Can the issue of violence in rape be resolved if we have a death sentence for the culprit responsible for the rape?*

**DILIP SIMEON:** I am philosophically and politically opposed to giving a death sentence, to anybody. I don't think that the State has a right to accord that kind of punishment to a person. There are certain people who believe this, but I believe the only thing that emerges from this is more violence. I'm not in favour of giving death sentences to rapists — I'm in favour of implementing laws so that women are harassed less and the process of getting a conviction is improved. That is what is necessary.

**URVASHI BUTALIA:** If I can add to what Dilip is saying, putting forward the death sentence as a solution is not only philosophically and politically wrong but also strategically short-sighted. It does not address the root of the problem at all. Nothing will go away by imposing the death sentence in cases of rape. First of all, the harsher the punishment, the more reluctant courts are to impose it. Then, in any case, as we know, there are strong biases against women, which allow judges to deliver anti-women judgments, and to minimise on punishment, as in the Suman Rani case. If the punishment were of a much more serious nature, do you think they would see the crime as meriting it ? Very likely not.

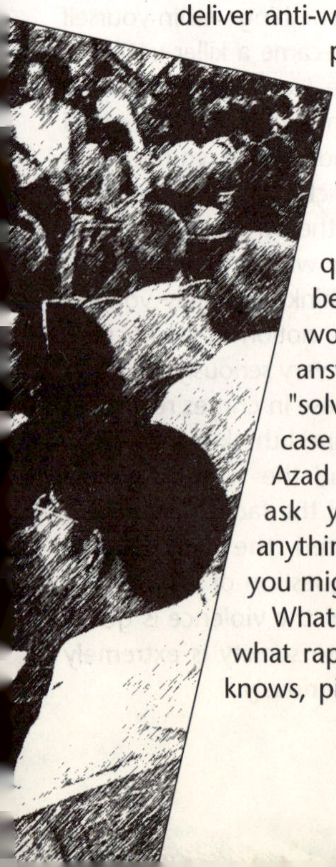

This is apart from the issue of the question of whether or not there should be a death sentence at all. Like Dilip, I would oppose this, but I am trying to answer your question of whether this will "solve" the problem or not. If you recall the case of the woman doctor from Maulana Azad who was raped by a young boy, and ask yourself the question of whether anything will be solved or learnt by his death, you might have your answer.

What does someone like him know about what rape does to a woman? All he probably knows, picked up in the streets, in the media,

from around him, is that you can be free with women's bodies. If you kill him, that knowledge that you can be free with women's bodies is not going to change. It is that knowledge, or lack of it, that you need to address. That is the only way the problem is going to be solved. So politicians like Mr. Advani, our Home Minister, coming in, and making these big announcements about bringing in the death sentence for rape, this is nothing but a load of nonsense, and designed not with the interests of women in mind, but with an eye to the main political chance. This is why women's organisations rejected this. Even worse was the other thing they came up with: a life insurance policy against rape, which basically meant that if every woman pays the insurance company Rs. 15 a month, she would have this money in the event of a rape; the Prime Minister inaugurated this thing ! It's not the death sentence that will solve the problem, it never has done, it's what's inside our heads.

**MUKUL MANGALIK (MODERATOR):** I want to add to what Dilip said earlier; that violence is not simply an attack against a person. It is not easy to go out slapping, boxing, hitting or killing somebody — you have to kill something within yourself as well. It is not possible for you to became a killer until you begin to brutalise yourself in some sense. I am talking about the individual instances where you might actually get out of control. But once you make it into a kind of habit, you begin to legitimise and justify it. It also makes a victim of the perpetrator, and finally, I think it is linked with the whole question of democracy. The greater the violence which is breaking in society — no matter the cause — I think ultimately you are hitting at the entire edifice, the entire notion of democracy. That is something we need to consider very seriously.

There has been a tremendous increase in crimes related to women over the last year and a half, and I think that to some extent the way the public rapes, and the way the whole situation in Gujarat was handled, and the fact that nothing happened to those who committed the crimes, has something to do with it. I think the question of violence for a particular cause, and the notion that the violence is going to stop there, and not come back into society is extremely problematic: we need to take it very seriously.

I agree with Dilip that one needs to understand what violence is, and what it does; then should come the discussions about whether it is right for an organisation, or institution, to indulge in violence. I am very glad that these questions were posed.

*You said it was a tactical position that WSF does not allow certain organisations to participate. I think it is not tactical, but sort of structural, because even if they can make it open for militant organisations, they will not be able to invite certain people in for discussions.*

**DILIP SIMEON:** Let me make it very clear: I am not a member of the WSF, I have never been to the WSF and am not part of the decision making process there. But what I am saying is that the issue of violence has not been given the theoretical and philosophical significance it deserves. It has only been treated in a tactical manner, and I feel that the WSF is continuing to treat it as such. But whether you call it instrumental, pragmatic or strategic – addressing this is essential, and I would like to see a really serious discussion on violence in the WSF.

It should be the place where such discussions take place — not whether Zaptista should or should not have taken to violence, but the whole question of 'what is violence?'. I have no objection to hearing different opinions, but the whole point is there should be a dialogue.

**SWAPAN MUKHERJEE:** I think when we are talking about violence in the context of WSF, we are not speaking of Osama Bin Laden, or about the inclusion of violent, militant groups: we are talking about those people in Mexico and Latin American countries who are fighting against American dominance. Their primary concern is to get rid of this dominance, and they use all sorts of tactics to reach this goal and win. We are talking of these forces, and not about terrorists.

*This question is for Swapan Mukherjee. When we talk about social security, pension, and labour rights, what have communists done in the era of globalisation? What stand have you taken? What was the situation before 1991?*

**SWAPAN MUKHERJEE:** I never said that before 1991 the world was a very good place; nor have I said that whatever was happening under the law was in favour of labourers. What I have said is that after globalisation, there has been an increase in the attack on labourers. We are fighting against that to the best of our abilities. There are many parties in this country, but do you actually know how much force they have? We are trying our best to fight against these forces. We are united -- all the unions are united on this matter, on a platform. WSF is an open space and we will look for solutions there. Strikes are not the main weapons, but the last resort.

Last time, before we went on strike, the Prime Minister assured us that there would be discussions and the problem would be solved. He said that the ceiling on gratuity and bonus would be removed. The next day, Yashwant Sinha, sitting in America, said that if the ceiling from the bonus was removed it would send the wrong signals to multinationals. Only after that we went on strike. Labourers don't go on strike regularly, in fact that is usually the last resort.

*Strikes are not only a national issue, they set off a chain reaction. In China, multinationals are being battered, and it is also the same in India. It is related to an international order so how can you only relate it to national politics? Your method of fighting is obsolete. You talk about social security, but I don't think communists are doing enough. I think all labour organisations should take a stand.*

**SWAPAN MUKHERJEE:** I agree that we should be united. Let me first say that whatever is happening in China is fine, but what inspires us is what is happening in India. We don't draw inspiration from China, nor from the US. We draw our inspiration from our own Indian people.

The second thing, is the unity of labour; if you compare it with 1991 then we are more united now. We are fighting with whatever resources we have; but I must admit, the situation is very bad. Ninety per cent of our labour is in the unorganised sector; our base of unions is also in the unorganised sector, which has its own problems. We provide full support to labour in agriculture and construction, and their numbers are increasing every day. In fact, a recent

report by the National Labour Commission describes the flow of rural labour to cities, and due to this phenomenon of globalisation, most agricultural work is done by women. Our job is to bring those women into the fold of trade unions, and to organise them to help to create the right policies. We cannot leave all the responsibility to our Communist Party: when that is weak, we cannot do that. This is the duty of all the members of civil society and parties who believe in democratic political values. If you think that the Communist Party has failed, let us accept it, but we must continue our fight. You must understand: we are communists not because of the communist party, but the Communist Party is there because we are communists.

**MUKUL MANGALIK:** I just want to clarify -- what he is saying is that the world is constantly changing; in a nutshell, globalisation has entered the world, and in our lives, where there is increasing mobility and freedom to move, to gather and to collaborate. The results are very disadvantageous for labour all over the world; organised labour is moving into a situation of complete disorganisation, or complete informalisation. There is a complete crisis of union strategy across the spectrum. The truth is, and not blaming communist parties 'I' or 'M' or 'ML', but I think that there is a serious crisis of union strategy all over the world.

Capital, on one hand, is being given an increasing freedom to move and to collaborate -- in terms of advanced national corporations and commercial corporations. So, capital has become organised on a world scale, but on the other hand, labour is getting more segmented and fragmented: it is a serious crisis, allowing capital to then do whatever it wishes to to do. Meanwhile, imposing labour issues within different nation-states needs the help of the structures of nation-states. The question is how can labour be globalised; and how do we respond to the question of international labour standards?

Why is it that when it comes to the question of actually re-orienting and re-working union strategies to be able to take on all the processes of labour, why is it that we keep working within national standards? I think it is a significant question he is trying to raise about how can labour union strategies,

be re-negotiated and re-worked. It is not a question of blaming this party or that party; it is a very serious question about what labour should do. We cannot simply say, 'We should organize', that is not the point. I think new ways of organisation have to be worked out, especially to deal with a globalising world where capital is free to move and create alliances. It is not a question of individual Communists from different nations, but in a sense how we organise internationally, in a concrete way.

*One thing is clear: violence has a language. Can that be traced back to a kind of pre-history, perhaps to partition? What is the formation of abuse, and sometimes certain forms of abuse that is actually directed inwards, not necessarily at another community? What is the role of language in these kinds of vandalising positions, in terms of actually describing a new sense of space?*

**DEEPAK MEHTA:** I don't think there is a referential relationship between the way people talk and what happens to them when they engage in violence. There is no direct one-to-one sort of relationship -- all too often you talk to forget. A person who loses his son, refers to his sons death as sahadat (martyrdom). This is a way by which a certain death becomes meaningful, and is orthodox, whereas from other people's accounts the boy who died — who was shot in the head — was actually demolishing a temple.

So there are ways in which you begin to understand that language is not always the basis to show you what actually occurred: language is also the basis of trying to hide what occurred, and in this sense it becomes therapeutic. I would suggest that this happens especially when you know that person who has violated your children, or your women; if for example he is your neighbour, how do you make sense of this? How do you begin to pick up the pieces of your life? I suggest that one of the very powerful ways of trying to negotiate it is the use of language, and the ways in which language allows you to forget those moments.

Now, in times of communal tensions these stereotypes become an invitation to action. Stereotypes are a way of moving from a didactical notion up to a practical notion, of

eliminating you. Sterotypes have a very powerful role to play in violence, just as rumours do. What happens with notions of abuse, is that it acknowledges the dehumanising tendency that is built into the heart of violence. So that it's not only something that you use to denigrate the other, but it confirms your relationship; for example if you refer to someone as a 'namard' (wimp), this can then be used in a series of contexts which have nothing to do with Muslim relations. So, if you say, "Shut up, you're a namard": you know exactly where it came from. That is the way in which abuse becomes a movement by which you are able to deny the other person his or her humanity.

Language is not only the business of recalling or remembering – it is also the business of forgetting. I think that this is another dimension of violence that we need to take into account and address.

OPEN SPACE FOUR

# RHYTHMS OF OTHER WORLDS

FORUM AS RAGA

THE IMPORTANCE OF SMALL THINGS

ELEMENTS OF NEW MOVEMENT

# forum as raga

CHLOÉ KERAGHEL

> "Let's see the World Social Forum as a raga, with a fixed structure, which allows a diversity of variations and improvisation."

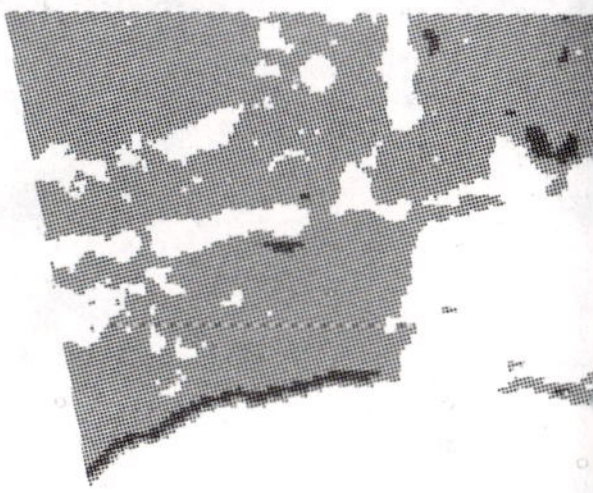

*Chloé Keraghel works with UNESCO where she co-ordinates projects on HIV/AIDS prevention and on the synergies between formal and non-formal education. She has worked on the World Social Forum for UNESCO, and has attended each of the World Social Forums since 2002. She is currently co-writing a book on the World Social Forum. She has also been Editorial Adviser, with Jai Sen, to the* International Social Science Journal *for its issue 182 on the theme 'Explorations in Open Space: The World Social Forum and Cultures of Politics'.*

*C.Keraghel@no-log.org*

Looking into Indian culture for something similar to the World Social Forum in both structure and process I have found some analogies with Indian classical music. Hilary Wainwright wrote a very relevant foreword to the book *Challenging Empires* in which she compared the Forum to jazz. I think we can extend that analogy and look at the Forum as *raga*. So, let's see the World Social Forum as a raga, with a fixed structure, which allows a diversity of variations and improvisation. Let's listen to the *alap*, the first part of a raga. The crescendo of this *alap* sounds like the growing global movement with which the different counter-summits in Seattle and then in Birmingham, Cologne, and Paris created the first World Social Forum in Porto Alegre in Brazil in 2001.

Let's take a *kaida*, any one:

*Dha ti dha ge na Te re ke te ta ka*
*Dha ti dha ge Thun na ke na*
*Ta ti ta ke na te re ke te ta ka*
*Dha ti dha ge Dhin na ge na*

And you have the fixed structure of the World Social Forum as an epiphenomenon, a global meeting once a year. The annual meeting is the part that is repeated; that we will return to every year.

You can then consider all the variations of this kaida as the profusion of all fora, which emerged at different levels: at the regional level, with the European Social Forum in Paris, or the Asian Social Forum, in Hyderabad in 2003. The forums also mushroomed at local and national levels, contributing to the extension of the process worldwide; these meetings focussed on specific themes, such as drugs during the Colombian Social Forum.

The Forum is not only this: it is also something different from a traditional raga. Have you ever heard someone in *teental* (16 beats), moving to *jhaptal* (7 beats) and coming back to *teental*? No, not in Indian classical music. But you can see this happening during the Forum: you can move from the World Social Forum to parallel events organised at the same time. For instance, you can attend a seminar at the World Social Forum in the morning; participate in the Parliamentary Forum in the afternoon; move to the youth camp by the end of the day; and spend your evening at a theatre, or participate in the Assembly of Social Movements.

Another difference is that, as a process, the WSF is a kind of never-ending raga today; no *tihai*. I would like, once, to listen to this tihai, this ending-sentence of a raga, which is repeated three times and say, '*Kya baat*'! This tihai would not mean the end of the World Social Forum, but that the Forum has overcome its challenges; not only by globalising its process, but also by concretely generating other ways of doing politics, other ways of conceiving partnerships between civil society and other actors; and by thinking about projects for new societies — societies that do not yet exist.

## A MORE HUMANE GLOBALISATION

Let's come back to the WSF, and underline its different challenges through its evolution. I will try to do this the through arguments developed during the last Forums in which I have participated.

The main debate I have found in the forums and one that interests both participants and delegates, relates the identity and strategies of what the French call the alter-globalisation movement. It is a movement which is not against globalisation, but which looks for alternatives to build a more humane globalisation. The European Social Forum in 2003 showed us the importance of deepening our analysis and discussing the nature of the movement itself, as a *sine qua non* condition to define better political strategies; to search for alliances; and for ways to transform global society.

Thus, we explored the nature and identity of the alter-globalisation movement, as well as the recent historical and political context that influenced the WSF process, and finally the political strategies within the evolution of the WSF. It seems to me that the alter-globalisation movement has gained in political maturity; the question of its identity was present during the debate about planning a second stage of the Forum process, of the extension of the WSF to other parts of the world. This happened in 2003 with the choice of Mumbai as a venue for the Forum.

## NATURE AND IDENTITY OF THE MOVEMENT

The aim of this movement is to fight against neo-liberalism and to exchange information on global political challenges. Activists introduce themselves as being part of an emancipation movement that is made up of great social and cultural diversity, and which is seen as a strength in the way it conceives and practises democracy. Even if the political orientations of participants (individuals as well as organisations) can be very divergent, their willingness to gather together is based on the conviction that 'rights' must prevail over 'profit'. At the same time, the political consensus defines that everyone recognises different visions of the world and the need for agreement on common strategic action. This political consensus is reflected in the Charter of Principles and underlines the fight against neo-liberalism and imperialism.

The Social Forums (the global, regional, local and thematic meetings) are said to be open space dialogues for meeting, debating and suggesting alternatives to neo-liberalism. Within these spaces, it is possible to discern three different kinds of participants: the anti-hegemonic; the anti-capitalist; and the anti neo-liberal. Convergences and contradictions exist among the three, but a question remains: What can be done and with whom? This question may either divide them, or contribute to building a new collective identity. These two questions (What can we do? With whom?) help change the movement

from a logic of anti-globalisation to a dynamic of alter-globalisation. The movement in its alter version can conceive and think about new propositions. When you look closely at the reactions of different actors during the debate however, there is one question that has received no answer: How and why do we move from an anti to an alter position? This question seems inscribed in the debate. For some actors, there is a need to build a new economic system on a non-capitalist basis. For others, it is important to conceive of political regulation mechanisms within the existing capitalist system. It seems to me, that the movement cannot avoid this essential question about its position regarding the capitalist economy. It is a fundamental question in the building process of the 'alter-globalisation identity', and it needs to be addressed.

**DIVERSITY AS AN ELEMENT**

There is another question, which is related to the previous one: How do we maintain diversity as an element that will not divide the actors? There is a need to keep in mind the capacity of action taken together to build a counter-power, but there is also a need to avoid conventional and traditional political power. The movement has to suggest alternatives to the practice of government as it exists in order to provide the seeds of a new democracy. But it also has to take pragmatic aspects seriously into consideration, and not get detached from the ground realities that local mass and social movements have to face, because if it gets detached, this may result in the splintering of the movement. In other words, diversity without the critical consciousness of the need for dialogue can generate political and strategic problems for the evolution of the movement. We can sum this up in the following question: How can we maintain unity within diversity, and at the same time contribute to transforming the system?

Everyone agrees that we want another world, or other worlds; but we still don't know which world for the moment, or how to build collective alternatives. I believe that this kind of meeting or process as we have today, which follows on one forum (Brazil) and precedes another (India) can help in maturing these questions. The alter-globalisation movement will also have to face the management of a non-technocratic time by respecting historical processes and by producing results.

"Diversity without the critical consciousness of the need for dialogue can generate political and strategic problems for the evolution of the movement."

### THE RECENT CONTEXT

The debate on identity is related to the current context of the movement's evolution. There were two important events in 2002-03 — the invasion of Iraq by the United States of America and the failure of the WTO negotiations in Cancun.

The big demonstrations organised all over the world on February 15, 2003 against the war in Iraq were the result of a common action between anti-war movements and alter-globalisation activists. The Trade Union movements partially joined these demonstrations, but we have to remind ourselves that this participation was not possible during the wars in the Balkans, nor in Afghanistan. With these demonstrations, peace is now being considered a *sine qua non* condition to build another world.

Second, during the WTO meeting in Cancun, governments were unable to come to any agreement because some large countries of the South, like Brazil, India and South Africa, managed to take advantage of the untenable positions taken by the USA and the European Union. But within this, the alter-globalisation movement also won, because there was an echo of its ideas in the positions taken by the representatives of some developing countries at the WTO. Thus 'Cancun', or what took place at Cancun, can be considered as a political microcosm of what the alter-globalisation movement strategy can become in the future, in its relation to the WTO and the multilateral system.

In conclusion, I would like to reiterate that we must think strategically. It is possible to say, in the words of activists, that the global movement has gained:

First, by constituting a global public space through the image of the World Social Forum. This space, being part of a more global movement, has a central role to play at the symbolic level.

Second, by the constitution of a movement that is linked to global public opinion.

Third, by gaining a moral and ethical victory on Davos.

Fourth, by its growing legitimacy even in traditional politics. In France, for instance, some political leaders say that they are for alter-globalisation themselves.

Fifth, by managing to arouse the interest of political parties in the process and the movement.

Sixth, through the popularity of the ideas put forward at the World Social Forum.

And finally, through the demystification of neo-liberalism.

There is a need to take these ideas further and this is what can be done through meetings, seminars, discussions. These help us to extend knowledge and experience on the World Social Forum at many different levels and to enlarge and expand this process and make it increasingly participatory. ■

In these workshops, lectures, discussions, young minds come together; intellectuals share ideas. There is space to walk around and think. The dancing and sharing of ideas generates a process of thinking.

# the importance of small things

**Lachlan Tan**

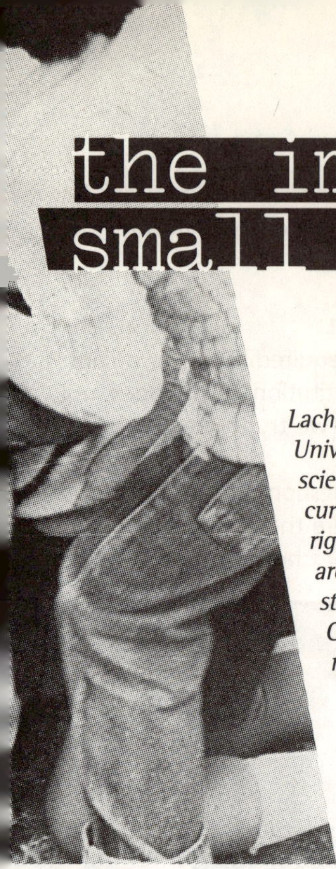

*Lachlan Tan is a law student at Melbourne University, Australia. He has studied political science at Sciences-Po, Paris and is currently working on intellectual property rights and traditional knowledge in the arena of International Trade Law. He has studied piano at the Melbourne Conservatory, and performs primarily music of the 20th century.*

*lachlant@yahoo.com*

At the World Social Forum, people from different parts of the world come together to share their ideas, sing, dance and at the end of each day, to share the sense of having learned so much. In these workshops, lectures and discussions, young minds come together and intellectuals share ideas. Asking questions, thinking critically; these are among the best things that come up, the WSF. This is how the World Social Forum is helping to make other worlds possible.

**CAN OUR PROBLEMS BE SOLVED?**

What we are doing here is to think, and analyse if our problems can ever be solved, and if another world can become possible for us. NGOs, activists and people with similar ideas stand on the same pedestal and share their thoughts. Other things, like exhibitions and bookshops, encourage a dialogue, where you can also sit down with children, talk to activists about their plans, and understand how to look ahead. Creating a new world is about understanding the differences that you think exist, then interacting with students and academics, and sharing ideas about how to make another world possible. In India, these seminars held in colleges have provided space for students. The special thing about the Forum is that these questions make you

think critically, in different directions. Are we organised knowledge-wise? Do we need to think otherwise? We get a chance to seriously challenge our basic assumptions.

**CREATING A NEW WORLD THROUGH THE 'SMALL'**

The rediscovery of the 'small' is something that is required. The war against neo-liberalism is about regaining control from institutions. This does not mean that we *become* those institutions, rather that we try to create a place where human beings can work with broad horizons.

I know of a couple of books that relate to this question of 'the small' and of the process – one is called *Small is Beautiful,* where the writer talks about economics and how it concerns people. He describes how profit should be

> "We should put development before government, individuals and everyone, to make the small act beautiful."

people-oriented and that we should put development before government, individuals and everyone, to make the small act beautiful. The other book I would like to mention is Arundhati Roy's *The God of Small Things*. We should try thinking how small things like money tend to control us: we think about our career in terms of money; we think about which goal will fetch more money; but not about the hold that material things have over our lives. The WSF makes us realise that the social struggle in life is not a personal struggle – it is a collective struggle.

I would like to make one more point -- the WSF makes the world a better place, even though it doesn't take responsibility for any task. Individuals go to the WSF, make their own decisions and take responsibility themselves. You can get back what you want from the Forum. It teaches you to be responsible for yourself. The WSF is a platform where people come and learn things and enjoy being with like-minded people. When we talk about social movements, we talk about new horizons. The WSF induces a level of critical thinking, and encourages staying connected with people through such thinking. ■

"The new social movements tend to believe that all the different groups that are oppressed by capitalism – the working class, women, Dalits – all need to come together and negotiate differences on an equal basis. None of them are supposed to lead the other, so this movement tends to value diversity much more than movements of the past."

# elements of new movement

**EZEQUIEL ADAMOVSKY**

*Ezequiel Adamovsky is a historian and anti-capitalist activist. He studied history at the University of Buenos Aires — where he also teaches — and has a PhD from University College London. As an activist, he has been involved in the students' movement and, more recently, in the Neighbours' Assemblies movement that emerged in the city of Buenos Aires after the rebellion of December 2001. A member of collectives and networks of global resistance, he also participates in the process of the World Social Forum. Apart from his academic publications — mainly in the field of intellectual history — he has written extensively on issues of globalisation, anti-capitalism and Left politics for websites and journals from several countries. He has recently published a book* Anti-capitalism for Beginners: The New Generation of Emancipatory Movements *(Buenos Aires, 2003).*

*eadamovs@mail.retina.ar*

I would like to talk about a new family of emancipatory movements — that is, the anti neo-liberal or anti-capitalist movements — that are emerging today. Also, I would like to examine whether the WSF is actually finding an answer to our question: is another world possible? For this, we need to understand the meaning of the WSF in historical perspective.

In the last four years, the WSF has been crucial for the development of a new family of social and political movements. To see why this is the case, we have to go back in history, and look at how the capitalist system has expanded throughout the world in the last couple of centuries. By 'world' I do not mean a geographical space alone, but also most areas of social life: now capitalism has even expanded into the private life of people. The effects of capitalism on our lives are very negative; that is why many different movements have opposed this system, and tried to create an alternative world — another world.

### REGAINING CONTROL OVER OUR LIVES

Neo-liberalism means the freedom for capital to move as it pleases those in power; to make money, to buy whatever they want, to please themselves without limitation. The WSF is about regaining control over our own lives,

about taking back the things that have been taken away from us by the market, by money, by companies and corporations, by powerful institutions like the IMF, WTO and by the State. In this respect, the WSF continues a long tradition of anti-capitalist struggles; although, it is also different from that tradition.

At the beginning of this struggle to change the world, in the 19th century, there was a big debate about what to do to achieve such change. Out of that debate, there emerged three families of social movements: one of these was the Social Democratic, or the Reformist movement. Their idea was to gain control over the State through elections, and then to use the control to implement measures to change society so that it gradually becomes socialist.

The other family was that of the communist or 'Leninist' movements: their idea was to take the State by revolutionary means, and then again, form the State to create a new society, with no market, and led by revolutionaries.

The third family emerged in post-colonial countries: National liberation movements that tried to mobilise the whole population against the colonial powers, to create a more egalitarian and free society. Again, in this case, the political strategy was based on seizing power, and on 'big leaders', who were to take the lead in this movement.

### THE COLLAPSE, AND AN ALTERNATIVE

For different reasons, all three political perspectives collapsed more or less at the same time in the 1980s. Take, for example, the communist model in Russia and in other countries: these were societies that were more oppressive than capitalism in many ways; and the people ended up rejecting them in the 1980s. The Soviet Union finally disappeared in 1991. Likewise, the Social Democrats had the chance to rule many of the European countries for a long

time, but even their moderate projects failed: they did not bring about a different kind of society. In the 1980s many of the Social Democratic countries implemented neo-liberal measures instead of what they had proposed in the beginning. Something very similar happened in Third World countries with the National Liberation Fronts and like-minded parties: they started to implement IMF and neo-liberal measures in the 1980s. So, by 1990, we had the unchallenged dominance of neo-liberal thinking throughout the world. Margaret Thatcher declared: "There is no alternative. It is neo-liberalism or nothing." Likewise, Francis Fukuyama announced 'the end of history'.

The aim of the neo-liberal measures in 1990 was to deregulate the market. This meant giving the powerful absolute freedom to move capital across the globe, with no restrictions or limitations whatsoever. As a result, people lost their jobs; most social security programmes were cut; and public services, health and education deteriorated. As these measures were taken, the lives of the vast majority of people got worse. Salaries were reduced, people had less social rights, and the environment deteriorated quickly. Due to the failure of all three families of radicals, there was no solid movement to resist this new advance of capitalism. But that was when, in the mid-90s, new families of social movements emerged, to resist neo-liberalism and create a new world.

### LEARNING FROM PAST MISTAKES: A NEW VOCABULARY

These were new types of movements. They had learned from past mistakes: they were different in many ways. It was the same struggle, but with different kinds of means and values. They had a different philosophy and strategy.

There is some disagreement about when this movement was really born. Some say it was in 1999, in the 'Battle of Seattle', others argue that it all begun in 1968, in France. As a turning point, I personally prefer the year 1994

— which was the year of the uprising of the indigenous peoples in Mexico, in the state of Chiapas. To me, the Zapatistas were the first to present a coherent set of new political ideas and values. And it was somewhere in the 90s that the new family of emancipatory movements became visible.

I want to talk about how these movements are different from the movements of the past. As these movements are only just being born, this will be a hypothetical exercise; at this point we only have a few clues to imagine what the new family will look like.

In my opinion, four new elements or mutations can be perceived in the new movements. First, there is a difference in the way they conceive power. For the three families of movements of the past, radical politics was more or less about taking the State via elections, revolution, or by whatever means, and then changing society from above.

The new emancipatory movements have realised that changing the world is not that easy; moreover, by trying to impose a new society from above, you often end up doing exactly the opposite. Thus, most Left wing parties ended up creating new forms of power, new hierarchies, inequality and oppression, reproducing the old, rather than building a new, emancipated world. That is why the strategy of the new family of movements is not so much about seizing power, but building a strong 'counter-power', a movement able to dis-empower the State. In other words, it is not about taking power, but rather about not being taken by power; it is about creating spaces of 'autonomy' for the people to live according to their own rules.

The second set of differences can be summarised by the word 'horizontality'. Horizontality means a type of organisation, but also a horizon, a value. It consists in striving to avoid the difference between those who make decisions, and those who 'follow' or 'obey'. It is contrary to traditional Left-

> "These were new types of movements. They had learned from past mistakes; they were different in many ways. It was the same struggle, but with different kinds of means and values. They had a different philosophy and strategy."

wing parties, which are based on the idea that a few 'professional' revolutionaries or politicians are to perform the role of a 'vanguard' or to be the leaders, while the rest are supposed to do as they are told. On the contrary, horizontality means that all those who participate in the movement decide its direction. There is no permanent difference between 'representatives' and 'rank-and-file'. This ideal also becomes evident in the field of strategy. The new anti-capitalist movements tend to prefer methods of 'direct action', rather than petitioning the authorities and waiting to see if they make this or that decision. Direct action means not depending on the State, not depending on representatives, but taking things in your own hands. These new movements tend to reject the idea of representation, that there will be certain leaders who will tell us what to do.

The third element is 'multiplicity' or 'plurality', that is, the idea that social change will not be created by one social class or group alone. For example, for the communist tradition, it was always the 'working class' that was going to lead the process to change the world; all other groups were 'secondary characters', and therefore needed to subordinate their interests to the aims of the workers. The new social movements tend to believe that all the different groups that are oppressed by capitalism — the working class, women, Dalits, the poor, aborigines, students, consumers, artists, etc. — all need to come together and negotiate differences on an equal basis. None of them is supposed to lead the other. For that very reason, this new movement tends to value diversity much more than movements of the past: diversity and difference is not something we need to 'overcome' for the sake of unity; on the contrary, this multiplicity adds to a richer notion of collective action. For that very reason, they are trying not to organise a hierarchical party with one programme that everyone must follow, but rather a network with voluntary, informal links, with no centre, and no 'secretariat' playing a leading role, but connectivity among people through different voices.

### EMPHASIS ON GLOBAL ACTION

Finally, another important element of these movements is the emphasis on global action. We can call this 'post-nationalist politics'. Again, it is not enough to get control over national governments, because there are many things that we simply cannot change from there. Since capitalism or neo-liberalism is global, the movement also needs to be global if it wants to change the world. So the new movements emphasise a coming-together of the global world. This is where the WSF has been an extraordinary experience, an extraordinary opportunity for the movement. It invites people from all over the world to come together, to share new ideas and experiences, and also to build networks for global, collective action.

Let me tell you one personal example of how this new family of movements is coming together globally. I participated in the WSF in Brazil (in 2003), where I met activists from other countries, including some amazing and experienced people from the UK. A few months later we had an Argentinean Social Forum, in which, again, we met people from all over the world. Some of the guys from the UK whom we had met in Brazil told us that the situation in Argentina was quite similar to the situation in South Africa, and that, therefore, we needed to meet South African activists and share experiences with them.They helped us get some funds, so we succeeded in inviting one activist from South Africa to the Argentinean Forum.

This person was from a social movement called the 'Anti-eviction campaign', based in Cape Town. The Anti-eviction campaign helps poor people who are victims of house evictions. As part of their struggle, they have developed effective ways of direct action, both to resist evictions and to relocate the people back in their own houses. In Buenos Aires, the experience that the South African activist shared with us became fundamental. I am a member of the Neighbours' Assemblies movement in Buenos Aires, which emerged spontaneously during the popular rebellion that we had in December 2001. Basically, it is a movement

of neighbours who gathered in local assemblies to reclaim the right to decide on different political issues. Just before the Argentinean Social Forum, several Neighbours' Assemblies in Buenos Aires — including my own — had decided to take over empty buildings in order to use them for the community (for cultural activities, soup kitchens, political meetings, etc.). So, with some 60 neighbours we squatted this amazing three-storey building, and we were in a difficult situation with the police. We faced the possibility of being evicted at any moment. It was very hard for us, and we really didn't know what to do; we were desperate. That was when we met this South African activist, an expert in resisting evictions. One day he came to our squat, and taught us everything about resisting eviction. Among other things, he taught us a simple thing: eviction is not the end of the story for a squat, because even if you cannot stop it, you can actually return to the place afterwards. All this was a revelation for us, and really helped us to deal with our situation in a more strategic way. And, by the way, we are still using the building!

After this South African activist left, we kept in touch. Next year, in the following World Social Forum, we met one of his comrades from the same movement. We learnt from him that the situation in South Africa was really bad. The police were repressing and imprisoning the members of the Anti-eviction campaign. They desperately needed some money to pay the bails in order to get their comrades out of prison. They asked if we could support them. As we also come from a poor country, we didn't have many resources to offer them. But what we did have, were our links with other movements in other countries: so we started to talk with all our contacts, and eventually some activists from the US got some funds to help our friends.

This simple example may help us visualise how the global network of movements is being built day-by-day.There are many other examples of such networking taking place, but we don't get to read about them in the newspapers. It is mostly a silent and invisible process, but grows stronger every day. By means of this network, we are learning from each other, and finding ways to co-operate internationally. At this very moment, we are collectively inventing a new radical and global politics of emancipation.

The WSF is really helping us to build these networks, to come together and to invent a new world. Will it continue to do so in the future? That depends on us. ■

# open forum

*What does an 'alternative world' really mean?*
*Can you tell us which New World we are struggling for?*

**EZEQUIEL ADAMOVSKY:** In the WSF, we are debating concrete alternatives to the existing world: there are thousands of people and movements who are designing new alternatives, which they bring to the WSF and discuss with others. It is a place to create and experiment with the idea of a new world. Whether it is the US bombing of Iraq, the destruction of the Amazonian forest, or offshore banking in secret accounts to save on taxes, these are actions being taken by a tiny minority but which affect the vast majority of us, common people. The problem is that we have no say in these issues. People perceive the WSF as "anti-globalisation", which in fact is not true; the WSF proposes an alternative globalisation, globalisation from below. The rich and powerful are always talking about globalisation, to which we say: "Fine, but we want globalisation all the way. Not just global rights for capital to move freely: we want global political and social rights. And we want the right to decide how we want every single aspect of our lives to be." While our political and social rights still remain constrained within national boundaries (and therefore become more and more empty and ineffective), the WSF and the global movements are inventing new forms of democracy, beyond the narrow limits of liberal democracy, and also beyond the limits of national borders.

**ANITA GHAI (MODERATOR):** The choices you make in your life will also help you to define the 'alternative world'. When I talk about creating an alternative world for disabled people, I often try and tell

them that they are 'temporarily abled' bodies. As we age, we lose so much of our ability. To understand this, there should be an alternative form of understanding. What I am trying to say is that the new world is not only for me, but also for many people around who share the world. The quality of life for many people improves when you become gender-sensitive, for example. You also become sensitive to many other forms of power structures.

It is not limited thinking, but thinking on a broader horizon. But, being part of such a big Forum, we have to be intensely motivated to take certain steps, and then think about implementation — which is easier said than done. We should not be sitting here and having conferences and talking about big things, and then doing nothing. Ultimately we are on ground zero, at least individually.

I also believe another thing: we can do a lot collectively, but that collectivity will only come when we do something individually. If we are part of the World Social Forum and think of an alternative world, I think we have got to do something at the individual level. We cannot expect others to do things, and not do anything ourselves.

*What does neo-liberalism mean?*

**EZEQUIEL ADAMOVSKY:** By neo-liberalism, we mean the unchallenged hegemony of capital, the US, MNCs and institutions like the IMF, the World Bank, and the WTO in particular. The best way to see it is in terms of a position of power, where a group of men get richer and richer by exploiting the rest of us, and by making all the decisions that affect our lives, thus excluding us from the decision-making processes of our society.

**ANITA GHAI:** I am a part of the WSF. As a disabled person, I have to fight at many levels, especially with the invisibility of disabled students. From that point, fighting from the level of the disabled is really a disadvantage. When I first wrote to the WSF to organise a panel on disability, the first question that was asked was: "What relation does disability have with globalisation?"

I said, "Disability is as much an outcome of the capitalist structure as anything else." I kept on insisting that the Forum

open forum

be made more environment-friendly for disabled people, before they finally decided to hold the panel. Accessibility had to be looked at before the talk was organised; ramps had to be set up so that wheelchairs could go on them, along with other alterations, like sign language for deaf people and Braille for the visually impaired.

When I reached the World Social Forum in Mumbai, I was horrified to see I could not reach the registration desk till the fourth day — accessibility was so bad. What I am trying to say is that many times, even while fighting a hegemonising structure, we establish a counter-hegemony. We are protesting against things like neo-liberalism. But even in that protest, there is some hegemony that comes about; there is a tendency towards universalisation. As a result, what becomes difficult is to understand how one oppressed group understands another oppressed group. This is very important from all angles. Do oppressed and marginalised groups get ample space? What do all of us have to say about this?

**EZEQUIEL ADAMOVSKY:** One of the main characteristics of neo-liberalism or capitalism is that it is not only an economic thing that happens in the factory, or in the marketplace, but is also a culture we have in our minds.

It is the culture in our minds that says: you are valuable or you are not; that you are successful only if you have money or power; that all other aspects of a human being are not valuable. If you can't spend energy generating money and being 'successful', if you are 'disabled', then you are not valuable.

In the WSF, we are trying to build a new culture, one that values all the different sides of human beings. But I think that, within the social movements, even the most radical ones, we still have many patterns of the capitalist culture. We discriminate against each other, we don't listen enough to each other, even in the WSF.

However, I have seen improvements in this field also. The horizontal 'open space' format of the WSF itself works towards this aim. When you are 'forced' to move and to interact on an equal basis with all fellow human beings, this makes you more ready to listen to each other and to respect each other.

# Searching for a new politics

## NOTES FROM THE FILM **A NIGHT OF PROPHECY**

**AMAR KANWAR**

*Amar Kanwar is an independent film maker. His films have been widely screened in film festivals, educational institutions, and non-governmental forums around the world, as well as in several museums and art galleries. He works on ecology, politics, sexuality and violence. His film* A Season Outside *received the Golden Conch award in 1998 at the Mumbai International Film Festival, and the Golden Gate Award a year later at the San Francisco International Film Festival. He was given the Jury's award for* King of Dreams *at Film South Asia in Kathmandu in 2002, and the Grand Prix at EnviroFilm 2002 in the Slovak Republic for* Freedom.

Like a huge wave that you cannot see there comes a period when time begins to roll downhill. Once frozen in mid-air, the wave slowly begins to come down in a million droplets. Invisible hands in no one's control hold other unseen hands and many lives slowly move in slow motion… change...so colossal … so large that you cannot see the other end. Only some can sense it.

Who can sense change? Which are the sites where lie the seeds of the future? Would not these locations have to be unique zones that contain memory and history, the reality of contemporary politics and despair, the hidden ordinary and the fierce struggle for justice, love and unconditional compassion? Can there exist such a special location?

How do you find the vocabulary for a new politics? The pursuit of an answer became a search that led to the film *A Night of Prophecy* but more critical was the realisation that poetry could be 'that unique location'.

*…when the dreams of*
*people are unfulfilled*

*the fiery spirits*
*like dreams wander*

*on the outskirts*
*of the village*

*the pungent smell*
*from the body on the pyre*

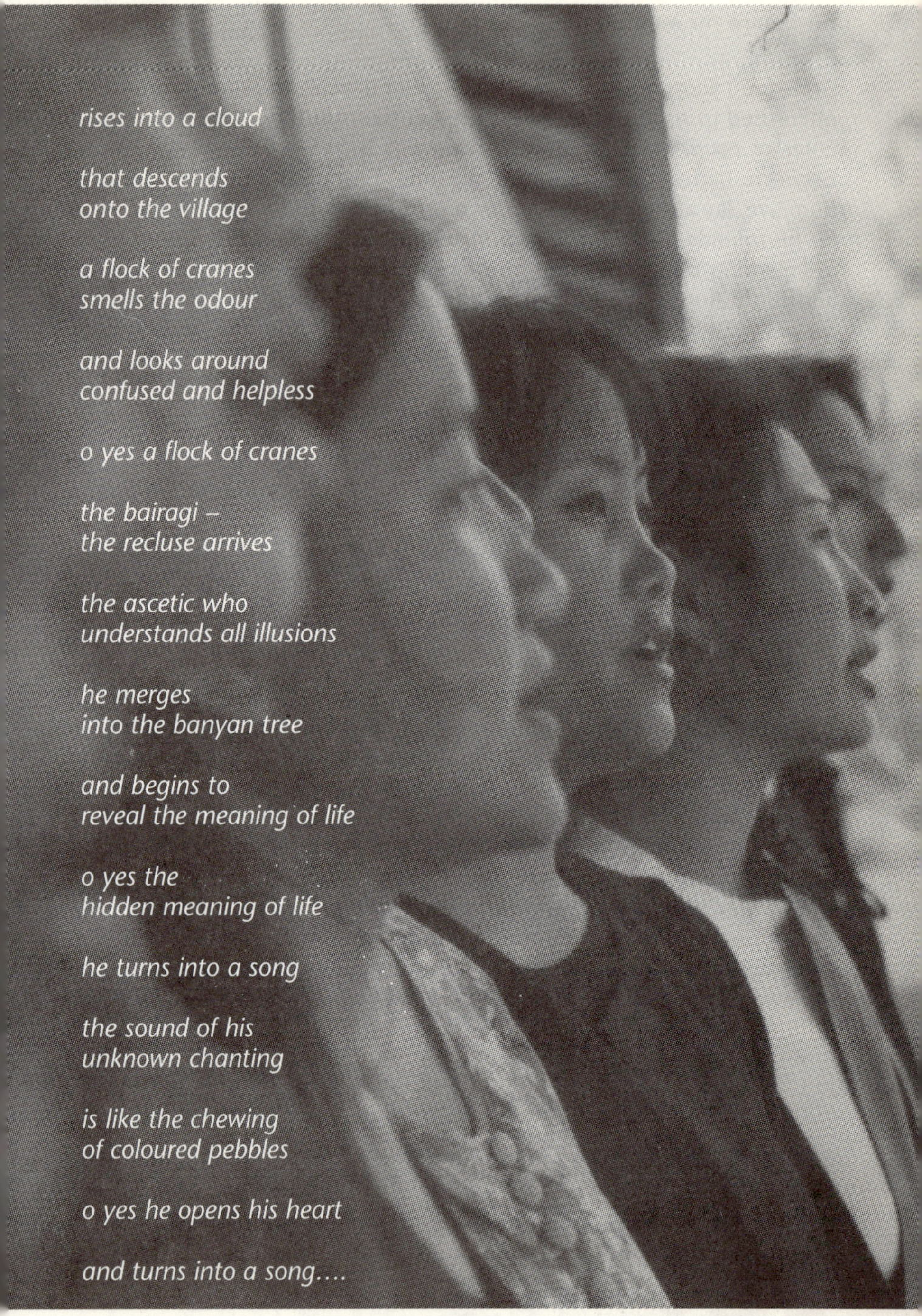

*rises into a cloud*

*that descends*
*onto the village*

*a flock of cranes*
*smells the odour*

*and looks around*
*confused and helpless*

*o yes a flock of cranes*

*the bairagi –*
*the recluse arrives*

*the ascetic who*
*understands all illusions*

*he merges*
*into the banyan tree*

*and begins to*
*reveal the meaning of life*

*o yes the*
*hidden meaning of life*

*he turns into a song*

*the sound of his*
*unknown chanting*

*is like the chewing*
*of coloured pebbles*

*o yes he opens his heart*

*and turns into a song....*

He is an accountant by profession, is that difficult to believe? As a child he often used to go to the temple on the outskirts of the village. He could not enter of course, but he liked to hang out there and watch. On the way, between barren fields and the gigantic Telengana boulders, silent and primitive, lay a small isolated rocky patch. This was the place he had chosen for his solitude, where he would dream and write his poems.

Emerging from the depths of their own worlds, where time is flung back and forth around the torment of the present. Search for new politics and travel through the faultlines of the 'great nations ' but only through poetry. Stop and look at the faint graffiti on the wall.

*...I piss in the*
*bastard gutter which*

*has links with*
*high-class sewage water*

*'who was he?*
*who's my father...'*

Silent but ever-present, adjacent to the busy main road. Open and yet hidden, exposed interior of the great city of Bombay, now Mumbai. A shanty town, a labour camp. A rising slope with bizarre lanes, rows of homes have submerged a low hill. He used to be a cargo worker in the airline, he is seriously ill now. Under his bed you can still find half-torn diaries filled with poetry. He has such a beautiful hand, the inked words are cold printed calligraphy but they will burn in the labyrinth under Dadar bridge forever.

Complex territories of severe conflict, where many lives have been slowly destroyed and minds are coerced to absorb slavery, decades of fresh blood, pain beyond generations, where no reconciliation seems possible. What would the meaning of justice be? How deep would be the wisdom of a new politics?

Like the omnipresent dust his words continue to be reborn.They said he could be anywhere between Mumbai and Aurangabad, you would be lucky to find the old man, he has almost 7000 poems to his credit but he does not write. Only recites them. For years he has travelled the villages and towns, reciting as he moved. His poetry lives with the faithful, with the angry, as an anthem, as a school choir song.

I had with me one printed poem. I went to make a xerox at a local shop. The boy there recognized the poetry. Where can I find him I asked, he said find an admirer, go from one to another for he is hardly ever home. I found a devotee, long black car, formal white attire... finally we found the old bard. Not very far, in fact within the magnetic field of the old Kala Ram temple, famous for the historic temple-entry struggle of the 'low' castes in Nasik.

A history of struggle... the accumulation of anger, the sorrow of slavery, the failure of democracy and the politics of identity. The priest and his pen.The artisan and the skin. Only the 'lowest' caste is to work with leather. The same skin makes the drum and when the doors of schools are closed and access to the world of knowledge is denied, percussion becomes the poetry of resistance.

Poetry! It opened doors to the warm comfort of many a home. The economist works with statistical data, the astrologer studies the constellations. In *A Night of Prophecy*, it is only through poetry that you understand history and the future.

The black and white photograph of his mother on the wall, adjacent to his father who was a mason. In 30 years the son became a legend. The revolutionary bard who sang for millions of poor labourers in Andhra Pradesh, the singer-performer who survived many attempts on his life.

As the auto-rickshaw driver drove me away, he asked if I was afraid. I said no, he said that's good because we are being followed. He said that if one is not afraid than one can find a meaningful death. He began to sway over the handles of the auto and then, at the top of his voice, louder than the engine that he sat on, he sang one of his favourite compositions by the bard whom we had just left behind. Weaving through traffic and red lights we disappeared into Hyderabad.

*The army of ants*
*has started marching!*

*the snakes are*
*terrified*
*the sheep and*
*cows move ahead*

*the wolves and tigers*
*are running away*

*o fire blazing from*
*hungry stomachs ...*

Poems and images stand witness to the passage of time. Here, in this passage lie hidden answers, the seeds of what shall come to pass and what must be done.

*... from beyond*
*an envious gaze*

*o Motherland!*
*I want to embrace you*

He remade the old instrument himself, adjusted it just a bit so as to play what some call the Naga folk blues. Red chillies and a piece of meat. Remember the old men and women... O lovely lady with the shawl, O silver fish in the water, O little flowers on the slope. Songs, with a weapon beside me, sorrow in my heart, anger in my mind and blood in the breeze. An axe and a Bible. A piano and a typewriter. Freedom! Simple words strung together make lines that are sung with difficulty. Carvings embedded deep in stone, warm smoke from the fire, the quiet scrape of the blade.

*...How shall we pray*

*the prayer of peace*

*when peace is a far cry ...*

Poetry from each territory becomes a reflective space for a traveller. Look at it up close or from within any bird's eye. Each territory has its own trajectory. We may remain within it and apply closure, or we may cross-connect and see the future. Separate worlds have inner narratives. They can also flow into a larger narrative, with possibilities of resonance with many nations and peoples.

*They drowned though*
*the river was dry*

*what can one say?*

*and we, hungry*
*chewed up poisoned grass!*

Poetry in paradise! Kashmir. A teacher, a student, a bullet in the window. An old man, a furious woman, a ball in a graveyard. Eyes that look at nemesis. A cracked mirror. Exodus, its significance not yet recognised. I searched the internet and found a virtual strand, made a call and found a body that offered me affection, biscuits and a refreshing cool drink.

*...our tongue our identity*
*our time our being*

*sweet myna, long necked Pine*

*ripples ... yearning*

*fell asleep disturbed*
*river Vitasta lay naked*

The different poetic narratives begin to merge together, allowing us to discern a more universal language of symbols and meanings, which may be valid for all beings.

The moment when this merger takes place in the mind is the moment of prophecy.

It is also the moment that could inspire us towards a new politics.

# The Open Space Seminar Series

University of Delhi, August 2003 – February 2004

## SESSION 1 AUGUST 19, 2003

**CULTURES OF POLITICS**: The Idea of the World Social Forum
**VENUE**: Seminar Room, Ramjas College, North Campus, University of Delhi
Panellists:
**VEENA DAS**, Professor, University of Delhi and The Johns Hopkins University, Baltimore, USA
**NIVEDITA MENON**, Department of Political Science, University of Delhi
**JAI SEN**, independent researcher and civil actor, New Delhi
A screening of **AMAR KANWAR'S** film *A Night of Prophecy* followed the seminar and a long discussion.

## SESSION 2 AUGUST 29, 2003

**EMPIRE 1**: Globalisation - Questions of Capital, Labour, and Sustainability
**VENUE**: Seminar Room, Ramjas College, North Campus, University of Delhi
Panellists:
**PRAFUL BIDWAI**, journalist and commentator, New Delhi
**JEAN DRÈZE**, Delhi School of Economics
**JAYATI GHOSH**, Centre for Economic Studies and Planning, Jawaharlal Nehru University
**MAHESH RANGARAJAN**, Fellow, Jawaharlal Nehru Museum and Library
The film *Jari Mari* was screened after the discussion.

## SESSION 3 SEPTEMBER 9, 2003

**THE WSF AND OLD VS NEW POLITICS**: Parties, Social Movements, and Civil Groups
**VENUE:** Arts Faculty, North Campus, University of Delhi
Panellists:
**MARY JOHN**, Jawaharlal Nehru University
**KAVITA SRIVASTAVA**, PUCL (People's Union for Civil Liberties), Rajasthan
**VINOD RAINA**, Eklavya, Jubilee South, and All India People's Science Network
with **ADITYA NIGAM**, Centre for the Study of Developing Societies, as Moderator
**AMAR KANWAR'S** film *Freedom* was screened after the seminar, followed by a long discussion.

## SESSION 4 SEPTEMBER 19, 2003

**EMPIRE 2:** Authoritarianism, Militarisation, & Nuclearisation : Questions of War, Peace, and Terror
**VENUE:** Indraprastha College, North Campus, University of Delhi
Panellists:
**ROHINI HENSMAN**, journalist, activist, Mumbai
**ASHIS NANDY**, author, commentator, Centre for the Study of Developing Societies, Delhi
**ACHIN VANAIK**, journalist, commentator, and anti-nuclear activist, New Delhi

## SESSION 5 OCTOBER 21, 2003

**EMPIRE 3:** Caste and Race: Questions of Identity and Exclusion
**VENUE:** Room No 1, Department of Sociology, Delhi School of Economics, University of Delhi
Panellists:
**PAUL DIVAKAR**, National Campaign for Dalit Human Rights
**V GEETHA**, Independent researcher writing on Gender, History and Culture
**KALPANA KANNABIRAN**, Feminist, Sociologist, teaching Law at the University of Hyderabad
**GAIL OMVEDT**, Sociologist and Activist working on Caste, Class and Gender

## SESSION 6 OCTOBER 31, 2003

**THE POLITICS OF BOUNDARY:** The Question of the WSF and (Non)Violence
**VENUE :** Seminar Room, Ramjas College, North Campus, University of Delhi
Panellists:
**URVASHI BUTALIA**, Author, Feminist, co-founder of Kali for Women and Director, Zubaan Publishers,
**DEEPAK MEHTA**, Department of Sociology, Delhi School of Economics, Delhi University
**SWAPAN MUKHERJEE**, General Secretary, AICCTU, CPI(ML) Liberation
**P V RAJAGOPAL**, Ekta Parishad, Chhattisgarh
**DILIP SIMEON**, Historian, Director, Aman Trust

## SESSION 7 NOVEMBER 11, 2003

**EMPIRE 4:** Fundamentalism, Communalism, and Nationalism
**VENUE:** Seminar Room, Ramjas College, North Campus, University of Delhi
Panellists:
**PURUSHOTTAM AGARWAL**, Social and cultural critic, political analyst, Professor JNU
**SWAMI AGNIVESH**, Bandhua Mukti Morcha
**ASHOK VAJPEYI**, Poet and critic, New Delhi

## SESSION 8 NOVEMBER 25, 2003, TUESDAY

**THE WSF AND NEW INTERNATIONALISMS**: The Culture and Politics of Cyberspace
**VENUE:** Sarai, Centre for the Study of Developing Societies, Rajpur Road, New Delhi
**C K RAJU**, Physicist, Author of the book 'Eleven Pictures of Time'
**SUDDHABRATA SENGUPTA**, Sarai, Centre for the Studies of Developing Societies, Delhi
with **JAI SEN**, independent researcher and civil actor, New Delhi as moderator

## SESSION 9 DECEMBER 2, 2003

**EMPIRE 5:** Patriarchy, Sexuality, and Questions of Openness
**VENUE:** Kirorimal College, North Campus, Delhi University
Panellists:
**UMA CHAKRAVARTHY**, author, feminist, and activist
**PRAMADA MENON**, Director CREA, feminist, author
**SHALIN RAKESH**, Naz Foundation

## SESSION 10 DECEMBER 12 2003

**HOW OPEN? IS SOCIALISM THE ONLY POSSIBLE OTHER WORLD?**
**VENUE:** Seminar Room, Ramjas College, North Campus, University of Delhi
Panellists:
**DIPANKAR BHATTACHARYA**, General Secretary, CPI (ML)
**KUMKUM SANGARI**, Professorial Fellow, Centre for Contemporary Studies, Teen Murti Museum & Library, New Delhi
**DUNU ROY**, Sajha Manch
Followed by the 'Open Spaces Concert' by **INDIAN OCEAN** and **PHASE DAMAGE**, a students band

## SESSION 11 DECEMBER 19, 2003

**CULTURES OF POLITICS:** The University as Open Space?
**VENUE:** Vivekanand Statue, Arts Faculty, North Campus, Delhi University
Panellists:
**ANITA GHAI**, Lecturer, Jesus and Mary College, University of Delhi, as a disability rights activist
**NANDITA NARAIN**, Reader, St. Stephen's College, University of Delhi
Testimony by several speakers from the audience, coming from different points of view and different sections within the university community (the blind and visually impaired, students from outside Delhi, Muslims, Dalits, women, students of colour from other parts of the world)
and with **MUKUL MANGALIK**, Sr. Lecturer, Ramjas College, as moderator

INFORMAL POST WORLD SOCIAL FORUM RESUMPTION OF THE SERIES:

## SESSION 12 FEBRUARY 11, 2004:

**IS THE WORLD SOCIAL FORUM HELPING TO MAKE OTHER WORLDS POSSIBLE ?**
**VENUE:** Jesus and Mary College, South Campus, Delhi University
Panellists:
**CHLOÉ KERAGHEL**, researcher, France
**EZEQUIEL ADAMOVSKY**, teacher, writer, and activist, Argentina
**LACHLAN TAN**, student, Australia

A session entitled *Contested Space? The Forum as Space, the Forum as Movement* featuring speakers from the WSF Organising Committee and other, scheduled to be held in a South Delhi college had to be cancelled.

# Frequently Asked Questions About the WSF

QUESTIONS YOU ALWAYS HAD IN YOUR MIND BUT NEVER DARED TO ASK....

### *What is the World Social Forum?*

The World Social Forum is an open meeting place where social movements, networks, NGOs and other civil organisations opposed to neo-liberalism and a world dominated by capital or by any form of imperialism come together to pursue their thinking, to debate ideas democratically, to formulate proposals, share their experiences freely, and network for effective action. For details, see the WSF website http://www.forumsocialmundial.org.br/home.asp.

The first 'World Social Forum' – the first meeting of what then became the World Social Forum process – took place in January 2001, in the city of Porto Alegre, in southern Brazil. Set up to challenge the World Economic Forum and the singular idea and future that it stands for, the WSF emphasised the social dimensions of life, and coined for itself and the world the slogan that:

'Another World Is Possible!'

Since the first world encounter in 2001, the World Social Forum has taken the form of a permanent world process seeking and building alternatives to neo-liberal policies. This definition is in its Charter of Principles, the WSF's guiding document (see page 205-208). The World Social Forum is characterised by plurality and diversity, is non-confessional and secular, non-governmental, and non-party. It proposes to facilitate decentralised coordination and networking among organisations engaged in concrete action towards building another world, at any level from the local to the international, but it does not intend to be a body representing world civil society. The World Social Forum is neither a group nor an organisation.

### *Who organises the WSF?*

In formal terms, the WSF is organised by the WSF International Council (IC), which is serviced and coordinated by the WSF Secretariat (formerly the (Brazil) Organising Committee), the body that coordinates the larger process of building and internationalising the Forum. The IC debates and resolves issues of overall policy and the directions the WSF should take, as well as the methodologies of the annual events. As of September 2004, the IC was made up of 132 'delegate' organisations and seven 'observer' organisations, mostly national and international civil organisations, federations, and movements, from many parts of the world. For the composition of the IC, see http://-www.forumsocialmundial.org.br/main.asp?id_menu=3_2_1&cd_language=2

The WSF International Secretariat (or office), which is based in São Paulo, Brazil, is responsible for supporting the operationalisation of WSF activities. For the first four years, the WSF Secretariat was made up of the eight civil organisations that started the WSF and organised the first world meeting. The eight organisations, first known as the Brazil Organising Committee are: ABONG (Brazilian Association of Non-Government Organisations), ATTAC-Brazil (Association for the Taxation of Financial Transactions for the Aid of Citizens), CBJP (Brazilian Justice and Peace Commission), CIVES (Brazilian Business Association for Citizenship), CUT (Central Workers Federation), IBASE (Brazilian Institute for Social and Economic Studies), MST (Landless Rural Workers Movement), and the Social Network for Justice and Human Rights. In 2004, this body was expanded, and now has 22 organisations. For details, see http://www.forumsocialmundial.org.br/main.asp?id_menu=3_1&cd_-language=2.

However, and as the organisers of the WSF have themselves said on many occasions, the strength of the Forum lies in the self-organised events that take place within or during the Forum. In an important sense therefore, the WSF is put together by those who take part in it: by thousands of civil groups (and also individuals), who are responsible for many of the smaller events though under the name of one or another organisation, real or virtual.

In 2004, and as a consequence of rising debate within the Forum as to just how open the Forum is, the WSF took an important step towards opening up the process of planning and organisation of certain aspects. For the first time in its history, it opened up its website to participants to take part in exchange and consultation about what the themes should be for WSF 2005, and came up with eleven thematic terrains and three transverse themes. It has subsequently created a process whereby those who wish to organise events during WSF 2005 can consult a data bank about what events have already been proposed in areas they are interested in, thus allowing them to coordinate with the authors of events similar to their own. In principle, this process has the potential of facilitating greater convergence and reduced repetition, and in this limited sense therefore allows participants to 'organise' the Forum.

### *What are the activities of the WSF?*

Since January 2001, the most visible activity of the WSF has been the annual world meetings of the World Social Forum in Porto Alegre. The meetings have grown in size and strength: From 20,000 participants in the first year to 100,000 at the third world meeting, held this year in January 2003. In January 2004, the world meeting of the WSF was, for the first time, held outside Brazil, in Mumbai, India, from January 16-21, 2004, where an estimated 130,000 people took part. In January 2003, the IC decided that from 2004

onwards, the WSF will organise the world meeting alternately in Brazil and in other countries where the necessary structural and political conditions obtain.

Since the first meeting, each one has been timed to coincide with the World Economic Forum that is held in Davos, Switzerland. The WSF has now freed itself of this link. The World Social Forum also promotes international Regional and Thematic Social Forums to pursue debates in specific regions and/or to discuss specific issues considered priorities by the International Council.

In early 2003, before the third World Social Forum in Porto Alegre in late January, as many as four regional Fora were held in various parts of the world: The Asian Social Forum in Hyderabad, India; the Palestine Social Forum; an African Social Forum in Addis Ababa, Ethiopia; and a Pan-Amazonian Social Forum in Belém, Brazil. This was aside from several thematic, national, and city fora, of which one of the most important was the World Social Thematic Forum on 'Democracy, Human Rights, War, and Drug Trafficking' that was organised in Cartagena de Indias, in Colombia, in June 2003. This practice continues to take place and to grow in strength each year, in all parts of the world.

For details of recent and upcoming thematic, regional, and national events, see http://www.forumsocialmundial.org.br/main.asp?id_menu=11_1&cd_la

### *Who takes part in the WSF events?*

Technically, WSF meetings have been open only to all civil organisations, movements and groups that declare their agreement with the WSF Charter of Principles (for example, in terms of its opposition to neo-liberal globalisation). Other activists, or interested parties not belonging to any organisation, have technically been able to participate only as spectators in the open activities.

As of the time of writing however (September 2004), and according to the WSF Newsletter of September 24, 2004, the 2005 edition of the WSF will be open also "for individuals who are not attached necessarily to an organisation. People who don't represent any organisation can be registered and can participate in all programme events, but they can't propose activities." In principle, this therefore reflects an opening up of the Forum – and this step would again appear to follow the rising debate within and around the Forum about how open it really is.

### *Who is not welcome to participate in the WSF?*

The WSF is a meeting place for civil organisations, networks and movements. For that reason, groups or individuals connected with governments or political parties are not permitted to participate as delegates in the WSF. However, the governments that host the WSF events can be partners in organising them. Members of governments and parliaments may be invited to take part in a personal capacity, providing they agree to abide by the Charter of Principles.

It is the WSF's intention to build another world without using violence and it therefore also does not allow armed or military organisations to take part.

### *Does the WSF organise campaigns or actions?*

The WSF does not see it as its place or role to promote campaigns or actions, or to produce declarations or final documents at its events. The WSF is a place where civil organisations, movements, and groups can meet to debate their ideas and proposals, and is not deliberative in nature. In this regard, the WSF argues that it does not constitute a locus of power to be disputed by the participants in its encounters.

Equally, no one is authorised to express positions on behalf of the Forum, claiming to be those of all its participants or of the Forum as a whole. However, the WSF does enable participants to network, coordinate, and propose concrete actions, and to produce documents on their positions, and it undertakes to publicise all such documents.

### *How is the WSF financed?*

The WSF raises its resources in the following manner:

- It sees Registration fees as "a political call for World Social Forum self-sustainability", because of the major role they play in keeping the WSF capable of financing its own activities. (From the WSF newsletter of September 24 2004).
- It accepts support from the State, in the form of infrastructure, security services, and facilitation in the entry of international delegates.
- It also accepts support from civil foundations. Some of the major sources have been Ford Foundation, Oxfam-Novib International, and Action Aid (although the WSF India Organising Committee elected to not accept any funds from the Ford Foundation for the Mumbai edition of the Forum).
- The WSF also sees self-organised resources -- the resources that participating organisations and individuals raise through various means, and then spend to take part in the Forum, including all the fares that delegates pay to reach the Forum site from all over the world — as being a major component of the WSF's resources in the broader sense.

This debate, especially about funds from 'foreign funding organisations', arose especially sharply for and during the WSF world meeting held in India in 2004. For details of the WSF India position, see the WSF India site http://www.wsfindia.org/Funding_Policy.php.

### *What is the WSF presence in India?*

During 2002-4, there was a WSF Organising Committee in India, set up in April 2002. During 2002-3, it was called the 'WSF India Working Committee'.

During 2003-4, it came to have three tiers, with new names: A WSF India General Council, made up of civil organisations from all over the country; a smaller WSF India Working Committee; and a select WSF India Organising Committee, acting as the executive arm. The main activity of the WSF India Committee/s so far has been the organisation of the 'Asian Social Forum', held in Hyderabad in January 2003, and then the organisation of the world meeting of the World Social Forum that was held in Mumbai in January 2004. See below for contact details.

## Some important links

World Social Forum
http://www.forumsocialmundial.org.br/home.asp

World Social Forum India
www.wsfindia.org

European Social Forum
www.fse-esf.org

**NOTES**

*The above text is adapted by* Jai Sen *and* Madhuresh Kumar *from* 'Information Sheet on the World Social Forum: Frequently Asked Questions', *prepared for the Open Space Seminar Series, New Delhi, August – December 2003; based on information available on the main WSF website during 2003-4.*

# WSF CHARTER OF PRINCIPLES

The committee of Brazilian organizations that conceived of, and organized, the first World Social Forum, held in Porto Alegre from January 25th to 30th, 2001, after evaluating the results of that Forum and the expectations it raised, consider it necessary and legitimate to draw up a Charter of Principles to guide the continued pursuit of that initiative. While the principles contained in this Charter — to be respected by all those who wish to take part in the process and to organize new editions of the World Social Forum — are a consolidation of the decisions that presided over the holding of the Porto Alegre Forum and ensured its success, they extend the reach of those decisions and define orientations that flow from their logic.

1. The World Social Forum is an open meeting place for reflective thinking, democratic debate of ideas, formulation of proposals, free exchange of experiences and interlinking for effective action, by groups and movements of civil society that are opposed to neoliberalism and to domination of the world by capital and any form of imperialism, and are committed to building a planetary society directed towards fruitful relationships among humankind and between it and the Earth.

2. The World Social Forum at Porto Alegre was an event localised in time and place. From now on, in the certainty proclaimed at Porto Alegre that "another world is possible", it becomes a permanent process of seeking and building alternatives, which cannot be reduced to the events supporting it.

3. The World Social Forum is a world process. All the meetings that are held as part of this process have an international dimension.

4. The alternatives proposed at the World Social Forum stand in opposition to a process of globalisation commanded by the large multinational corporations and by the governments and international institutions at the service of those corporations' interests, with the complicity of national governments. They are designed to ensure that globalisation in solidarity will prevail as a new stage in world history. This will respect universal human

rights, and those of all citizens — men and women — of all nations and the environment and will rest on democratic international systems and institutions at the service of social justice, equality and the sovereignty of peoples.

**5.** The World Social Forum brings together and interlinks only organisations and movements of civil society from all the countries in the world, but intends neither to be a body representing world civil society.

**6.** The meetings of the World Social Forum do not deliberate on behalf of the World Social Forum as a body. No one, therefore, will be authorised, on behalf of any of the editions of the Forum, to express positions claiming to be those of all its participants. The participants in the Forum shall not be called on to take decisions as a body, whether by vote or acclamation, on declarations or proposals for action that would commit all, or the majority, of them and that propose to be taken as establishing positions of the Forum as a body. It thus does not constitute a locus of power to be disputed by the participants in its meetings, nor does it intend to constitute the only option for interrelation and action by the organisations and movements that participate in it.

**7.** Nonetheless, organisations or groups of organisations that participate in the Forum's meetings must be assured the right, during such meetings, to deliberate on declarations or actions they may decide on, whether singly or in coordination with other participants. The World Social Forum undertakes to circulate such decisions widely by the means at its disposal, without directing, hierarchising, censuring or restricting them, but as deliberations of the organisations or groups of organisations that made the decisions.

**8.** The World Social Forum is a plural, diversified, non-confessional, non-governmental and non-party context that, in a decentralised fashion, interrelates organisations and movements engaged in concrete action at levels from the local to the international to build another world.

**9.** The World Social Forum will always be a forum open to pluralism and to the diversity of activities and ways of engaging of the organisations and movements that decide to participate in it, as well as the diversity of genders, ethnicities, cultures, generations and physical capacities, providing they abide by this Charter of Principles. Neither party representations nor military organisations shall participate in the Forum. Government leaders and members of legislatures who accept the commitments of this Charter may be invited to participate in a personal capacity.

**10.** The World Social Forum is opposed to all totalitarian and reductionist views of economy, development and history and to the use of violence as a means of social control by the State. It upholds respect for Human Rights, the practices of real democracy, participatory democracy, peaceful relations, in equality and solidarity, among people, ethnicities, genders and peoples, and condemns all forms of domination and all subjection of one person by another.

**11.** As a forum for debate, the World Social Forum is a movement of ideas that prompts reflection, and the transparent circulation of the results of that reflection, on the mechanisms and instruments of domination by capital, on means and actions to resist and overcome that domination, and on the alternatives proposed to solve the problems of exclusion and social inequality that the process of capitalist globalisation with its racist, sexist and environmentally destructive dimensions is creating internationally and within countries.

**12.** As a framework for the exchange of experiences, the World Social Forum encourages understanding and mutual recognition among its participant organisations and movements, and places special value on the exchange among them, particularly on all that society is building to centre economic activity and political action on meeting the needs of people and respecting nature, in the present and for future generations.

**13.** As a context for interrelations, the World Social Forum seeks to strengthen and create new national and international links among organisations and movements of society, that — in both public and private life — will increase the capacity for non-violent social

resistance to the process of dehumanisation the world is undergoing and to the violence used by the State, and reinforce the humanizing measures being taken by the action of these movements and organisations.

**14.** The World Social Forum is a process that encourages its participant organisations and movements to situate their actions, from the local level to the national level and seeking active participation in international contexts, as issues of planetary citizenship, and to introduce onto the global agenda the change-inducing practices that they are experimenting in building a new world in solidarity.

***Approved and adopted*** *in São Paulo, on April 9, 2001, by the organisations that make up the World Social Forum Organising Committee, approved with modifications by the World Social Forum International Council on June 10, 2001.*

ORIGINAL SIGNATORIES, SÃO PAULO, APRIL 9 2001:

| | |
|---|---|
| **ABONG** | Brazilian Association of Non-Governmental Organisations |
| **ATTAC** | Association for the Taxation of Financial Transactions for the Aid of Citizens |
| **CBJP** | Brazilian Justice and Peace Commission, National Council of Bishops (CNBB) |
| **CIVES** | Brazilian Business Association for Citizenship |
| **CUT** | Central Trade Union Confederation |
| **IBASE** | Brazilian Institute for Social and Economic Studies |
| **CJG** | Centre for Global Justice |
| **MST** | Movement of Landless Rural Workers |

# GLOSSARY

*This glossary attempts to provide basic working definitions or explanations for the key concepts and ideas that are mentioned in this book, it also offers brief biographies of the more prominent individuals, as well as profiles of organisations mentioned in the text. The words and ideas glossed here are, however, not comprehensive and for further elaboration of these the reader is referred to a number of useful websites. We would be very glad to receive comments and feedback on the definitions given here, including suggestions for improvements and additions. Please send these to: jai.sen@vsnl.com and kmadhuresh@hotmail.com*

**9/11:** September 11, 2001 ("9/11") is the date on which Islamic militants attacked and destroyed the twin towers of the World Trade Center in New York and also seriously damaged the Pentagon in Washington DC. It was the first time in history that the USA mainland had been successfully attacked. Historic policy decisions were then precipitated by this attack. In particular, the so-called 'war on terror' on Afghanistan, Iraq, and worldwide by the US and its allies, both militarily and through the introduction of new 'security' laws and policies; and more generally, the aggressive resurgence of a fundamentalist Right in the North that is in favour of militarily-backed dominance and empire that has so far been especially directed towards Muslim countries and peoples. The term '9/11' therefore now has multiple meanings, at a global level, and its meaning depends very much on who uses it and how.

**ABONG:** Associação Brasileira de Organizações Não Governamentais, the 'Brazilian Association of Non-Government Organisations', a platform for a wide range of civil/non-governmental organisations in Brazil, and one of the founding organisations of the World Social Forum.

**ABVP:** Akhil Bhartiya Vidyarthi Parishad (All India Students' Council). Inspired by the Rashtriya Swayamsevak Sangh (RSS), the key right wing organisation in India, the ABVP was founded by a group of students and teachers in the aftermath of Indian independence in 1947. Its aim is to channel the energies of students in the task of 'national reconstruction'.

**AIDWA:** All India Democratic Women's Association. Founded in 1981, a left-oriented women's organisation affiliated to the Communist Party of India (Marxist). The main focus of its work is among the poorer sections of women.

**AISF:** All-India Students' Federation. The student wing of the Communist Party of India (CPI) founded in Lucknow, India in 1936. It believes that only socialism can bring about fundamental changes in society.

**Akal Sangharsh Samiti:** Committee for Resistance Against Drought - A coalition of 80 organisations in Rajasthan, India, who are campaigning for the Right to Food and the Right to Work both within the state and nationally.

**alap:** The introductory section of any Indian classical music performance. Its length may vary from a few seconds to many hours depending upon the ability of the artist. It may be based on the raga of the song that is going to be sung. The various kinds of alap are: Anakshar alap, Sakshar alap, etc.

**Alter-globalisation (or 'alter-mondialisation' from the French word):** The name given to a widespread way of thinking that supports international / global integration but demands that values of direct democracy, economic justice, environmental protection, and human rights be put ahead of purely economic concerns. The term, implying 'another globalisation' or an alternative globalisation, is a positive spin on the more widely used and somewhat pejorative word 'anti-globalisation'. Alter-globalisation believers oppose the way international institutions (such as the WTO, the IMF, and the World Bank) promote First World economic interests. Alter-globalisation approaches and is sometimes confused with 'internationalism', as put forth by communists, since both oppose any globalisation that prioritises capitalists over ordinary people.

# GLOSSARY

**Amin, Samir:** Born 1931. Egyptian-born and Paris-trained, Amin is a Marxist economist and political scientist, an intellectual who is widely regarded as one of the foremost thinkers on the changing dynamics of capitalism. Presently the Director of the Third World Forum, based in Dakar (Senegal), Cairo (Egypt), and in Belgium, formed by a network of social scientists and intellectuals from the South. Amin has also played a key role in the formation of the World Forum for Alternatives, launched in 1997, which aims to service the needs of social movements that challenge the dominant discourse on globalisation. He is a member of the International Council of the World Social Forum. Amin's seminal work, *Accumulation on a World Scale*, was first brought to the attention of the English-speaking world in 1970.

**Anarchism:** A political theory that aims to create anarchy, a condition in which individuals freely co-operate together as equals and which does not mean 'chaos' (as is commonly held by its critics) but 'the absence of a master, of a sovereign' (P-J Proudhon, *What is Property*, p 264). As such, anarchism opposes all forms of hierarchical control — be it control by the state or by capitalism — as harmful to individuals and their individuality.

**Anti-arrack movement:** Arrack is the term for locally brewed liquor in several parts of India. Beginning in early August 1992, in the remote village of Dubagunta of Nellore district in Andhra Pradesh, India, a massive and widespread agitation by women took place, protesting against arrack auctions and demanding a ban on its production and sale. The movement ultimately spread to almost all the districts of the state, and later contributed to the toppling of the state government.

**Anti-globalisation:** A political stance of opposition to the negative aspects of (neo-liberal, economic) globalisation. The corresponding movement is known widely as the anti-globalisation movement, and is a largely grassroots effort, with some support from the intellectual elite. Many participants, however, regard the term 'anti-globalisation' as a misnomer, and prefer and advocate more precise terms such as 'anti-capitalist', 'anti-corporate', or 'alternative globalisation/alter-globalisation'.

**Anti-globalisation movement:** Also referred to as the Global Justice or Fair Trade movement, the Global Justice and Solidarity Movement (GJ&SM), the 'Movement of Movements' or simply 'The Movement'. It uses, and is known for, slogans such as 'Globalise justice!'. The movement is heterogeneous and includes diverse, sometimes opposing, understandings of this process, alternative visions, strategies and tactics. Some parts of the movement reject globalisation as such, but the overwhelming majority of its participants are aligned with movements of indigenous people, human rights NGOs, anarchism, green movements, and to a minor extent communism. Some sections of the movement object not to capitalism or international markets as such but rather to what they claim are non-transparent and undemocratic mechanisms of the market and of capitalism, and the negative consequences of unregulated globalisation.

**Ariel Sharon:** Born February 27, 1928. A long-serving Israeli political and military leader known for his ruthlessness. Has been the Prime Minister of Israel since March 2001, the 11th holder of that office. Also leader of Likud, the largest party in the governing coalition of political parties in the Israeli Knesset (parliament), in 2004.

**ATTAC:** Association for the Taxation of Financial Transactions for the Aid of Citizens. An activist organisation for the establishment of a tax on international exchange transactions. Originally a single-issue movement demanding the introduction of the Tobin Tax on currency-speculation, ATTAC now devotes itself to a wide range of issues related to neo-liberal globalisation, monitoring the decisions of the World Trade Organization (WTO), the Organisation for Economic Cooperation and Development (OECD) and the International Monetary Fund (IMF). Though ATTAC criticises the neo-liberal ideology dominating economic globalisation, it is not 'anti-globalisation'. It supports globalisation

policies that it understands as being socially just and sustainable. One of ATTAC's slogans is 'The world is not merchandise', denouncing the 'merchandisation' of society.

**Babri Masjid:** A mosque constructed in the 16th century by the Mughal emperor of India, Babur, in the town of Ayodhya in north-central India which is now in the state of Uttar Pradesh. Hindus believe that Babur destroyed an existing temple at the site, which was built to commemorate the birthplace of Rama, an incarnation of Vishnu and ruler of the then-kingdom of Ayodhya. In 1990, Lal Krishna Advani, a senior leader of the Bharatiya Janata Party (BJP) began a campaign tour (a *rathayatra*, or 'chariot-journey') to build support for a Rama temple at the mosque site. The mosque was destroyed on December 6, 1992 by large numbers of Hindu nationalists. Following the destruction, communal riots broke out between Hindus and Muslims across India. The dispute is currently before the Supreme Court of India. 'Babri Masjid', till recently a relatively less-known mosque, has therefore now become a major symbol for both fundamentalist and secular politics in India.

**Bairagi:** A raga in Indian classical music, originating from Rewati, a South Indian raga. Its use in Hindustani music has been credited to both Allauddin Khan and Ravi Shankar, two great sitarists. It is a pentatonic (a gapped scale with five notes) morning raga. The main mood of the raga is that of devotion and renunciation.

**Bhagat Singh:** Born September 27, 1907 into a Sikh family in Layallpur district, Punjab (now in Pakistan). Known for his militant revolutionary activities in the Indian Independence movement. On April 8, 1929 Bhagat Singh and Batukeshwar Dutt threw paper handouts and a bomb into the Delhi Central Assembly, and then courted arrest, shouting slogans such as *Inquilab Zindabad!* (Long Live the Revolution!). He used the trial court as a platform to launch a vigorous attack on the British government. He was executed by hanging on March 23, 1931, at the age of 24.

**Biodiversity:** Also 'Biological diversity'. A measure of the relative diversity among organisms present in different ecosystems. 'Diversity' here includes diversity within species, among species, and comparative diversity among ecosystems. It also stands for the totality of genes, species, and ecosystems of a region.

**Bretton Woods:** A small town in the state of New Hampshire, US, where World War II allies agreed, in 1944, on the shape of the post-war world economic order. The term 'Bretton Woods' now refers particularly to two multilateral organisations founded there, the International Monetary Fund (IMF) and the World Bank, which together were designed to promote exchange rate stability and economic development within a free market system. There is also a third, till recently less-prominent, arm of the BW institutions, the IFC (International Finance Corporation).

**Burqa:** The niqab and burqa are two kinds of veils that cover most of the face, except for a slit or hole for the eyes, usually won by Muslim women. The Afghan burqa covers the entire body, obscuring the face completely, except for a grille or netting over the eyes.

**Cancun talks:** Popular term for the Fifth WTO Ministerial Conference, held in Cancun, Mexico, in September 2003. Also, within the global movement, 'Cancun' refers to the largely successful protest demonstrations/actions in the streets of Cancun which were aimed at derailing the WTO talks.

**Caste/Casteism:** In ancient India, the ruling sections developed a social system in which people were divided into separate closed communities where the position of individuals in society was decided by descent. These communities are known in English as castes. The caste system in the religious form is a simple division of society made up of four castes arranged in a rigid hierarchy (Brahmins, Kshatriya, Vaishya and Shudra); and below them the outcastes or the Dalits, earlier referred to (by the upper castes) as 'untouchables', who have historically suffered and continue today to often

suffer extreme discrimination and violence. But socially the caste system is far more complicated than this, with many castes, sub-castes, and other divisions. The origin of the caste system is in Hinduism, but has affected the whole of Indian society. Because they include and suggest definite economic stratification, both the term 'caste' and the system of casteism lend themselves to a functional explanation in terms of economic roles, but they are also deeply social and defy definition only in economic terms.

**Chambal Valley:** Ravines in the border areas of Uttar Pradesh, Rajasthan and Madhya Pradesh famous for being the home and the base from where dreaded dacoits (robber gangs) make their attacks.

**Charlie Chaplin:** April 16, 1889 - December 25, 1977. The most famous actor in the silent era of early Hollywood cinema; he acted, directed, scripted, produced, and eventually scored his own films. Chaplin's political sympathies always lay with the Left. Several of his movies, notably *Modern Times* (1936), depict the dismal situation of workers and the poor. During the era of McCarthyism, Chaplin was a suspected communist and accused of 'un-American activities'.

**Chattra Yuva Sangharsh Samiti (CYSV):** A student and youth movement (literally, 'Student and Youth Struggle Brigade') that emerged as an anti-corruption movement in Bihar, and then other states in India in the early to mid-1970s, under the leadership of Socialist leader and thinker Jaya Prakash Narayan. Among other things, the movement led to the toppling of state governments in Bihar and Gujarat (called the Nav Nirman, which means 'new construction', movement in the state of Gujarat), and also to the establishment of several action groups, especially in northern India.

**Chauri Chaura (incident):** A village near Gorakhpur in Uttar Pradesh in northern India, where a procession directed against liquor sales and high food prices as a part of the Non-Cooperation Movement that had been launched by Mahatma Gandhi, attacked the police station on provocation by the police and set it on fire in 1922, burning all the policemen in it. The incident deeply hurt Gandhi's ideals, and on hearing the news, he decided to withdraw the entire movement.

**Che Guevara:** May 14, 1928 - October 9, 1967. Ernesto Rafael Guevara de la Serna (commonly known as Che Guevara) was an Argentine-born Marxist revolutionary and Cuban guerrilla leader, and a member of Fidel Castro's '26th of July Movement' which seized power in Cuba in 1959. After serving various important posts in the new government, Guevara left Cuba in 1966 with the hope of fomenting revolutions in other countries, first in the Democratic Republic of the Congo and later in Bolivia, where he was captured in a CIA-organised military operation. The CIA wanted to keep him alive for interrogation, but the Bolivian army executed him. After his death, Guevara became a hero of Third World socialist revolutionary movements, as a theorist and tactician of asymmetric warfare.

**Cold War:** Term invented by the US financier and presidential adviser Bernard Brauch in 1947, and given currency by the journalist Walter Lippmann. Denotes the state of hostility between the rival Soviet and Western blocs starting from after World War II, involving economic, political, and subversive action but without overt war (though it came close to this, several times).

**Chomsky, Noam:** Born 'Avram Noam Chomsky' on December 7, 1928. Known both for his seminal work in linguistics and his radical political criticism. He is Institute Professor of Linguistics at the Massachusetts Institute of Technology, Cambridge, Mass, USA, and creator of the 'Chomsky hierarchy', a classification of formal languages. Aside from this work, Chomsky is now especially widely known for his radical Left wing, anarchist political views, and his criticism of the foreign policy of US governments. He describes himself as a 'libertarian socialist' and a 'supporter of anarcho-syndicalism'.

**Communist (Communism):** Generally defined as a believer in communism,

which in its original meaning is a social theory and political movement for the direct and communal control of society towards the common benefits of all members. The theory of communism, one of the first comprehensive revolutionary philosophies, was first formulated and espoused in the 19th century by Karl Marx, along with his collaborator Friedrich Engels.

**Complexity Theory:** Can refer to more than one thing:

- Computational complexity theory: a field in theoretical computer science and mathematics dealing with the resources required during computation to solve a given problem
- Systems theory (or systemics or general systems theory): an interdisciplinary field including engineering, biology and philosophy that incorporates science to study large systems.

Complexity theory is sometimes also used as a broad term for the study of complex systems, including subjects such as chaos theory, artificial life, genetic algorithms, and the topics studied by the Santa Fe Institute in the US, which was originally established specifically for the study of this theory.

**CPI:** Communist Party of India. Born and took shape from 1920-22, the period when the anti-imperialist struggle in India had acquired new mass militant dimensions taking the shape of the historic first Non-Cooperation Movement of 1920-22, led by the Congress and headed by Mahatma Gandhi with workers, peasants, middle classes and students being roused to new levels of consciousness and action. Thousands of patriotic cadres had been thrown up by the national upheaval. But the disappointment and disenchantment caused by the sudden withdrawal by Gandhi of the Non-Cooperation Movement in 1922 led them to search for new, more revolutionary and consistent platforms and forms of anti-imperialist struggle that could lead the people of India towards national and social liberation. Established as a party in 1939. Forced underground in the immediate post-independence period, largely because of its role in the Telengana movement. Split into the CPI and CPI(M) in 1964. Is now the second-largest CP in India.

**CPI(M):** Communist Party of India (Marxist). Formed in 1964, after split within the former united CPI, on ideological and tactical issues. Subsequently, the CPI(M) has grown into being the largest CP in India. Strongest in the states of West Bengal, Kerala, and Tripura. Leads the ruling Left Front coalition in the state of West Bengal, and the Left Democratic Alliance in Kerala (presently in opposition, in 2004). Suffered split in the late 60s, when a section of the CPI(M) cadres led by Kanu Sanyal and Charu Majumdar broke away to form the CPI(ML).

**CPI(ML):** Communist Party of India (Marxist-Leninist). Formed by the All-India Coordination Committee of Communist Revolutionaries at a congress in Calcutta in 1969, after a break from Communist Party of India (Marxist) led by Kanu Sanyal and Charu Majumdar who had mobilised a revolutionary peasant movement in Naxalbari, in north West Bengal, which evolved into an armed uprising. The new party at first advocated armed revolution and denounced participation in the electoral process. Came to be referred in mainstream discourse in India as the 'Naxalites'. Several factions of the CPI (ML), along with the CPI (ML) Liberation, later formed the People's War Group (PWG), the Maoist Communist Centre, and others, all of which started out as underground movements. The CPI (ML) Liberation faction, with bases especially in Bihar and northern India, subsequently entered electoral politics, and is now perhaps the third-largest CP in the country; and the PWG and the Maoist Communist Centre are presently gradually coming above ground in the state of Andhra Pradesh.

**CUT:** Consumers Unity Trust. A civil organisation based in Jaipur and New Delhi, committed to consumers' rights, which has become increasingly active in relation to global trade issues in the past some years.

**Dadar:** A bustling working and middle-class locality in the north-centre of the metropolis of Mumbai, on the western coast of India. Home to several trade unions and also to Bal Thackeray, the founder of the Shiv Sena.

# GLOSSARY

**Dalits:** The so-called *achuta*, or 'untouchables', are a group of castes outside the four main categories in India's caste system. They include people such as leather-workers, sweepers (*bhangis*), etc. Mahatma Gandhi called them Harijan, a term meaning 'Children of God' (Hari is another name for Vishnu, a Hindu God). Untouchables generally consider this term to be condescending and prefer the name Dalit, variously translated as 'crushed', 'stepped on' or 'oppressed'. More recently, some Dalit groups have also raised objections to the use of Dalit, preferring the non-perjorative, and merely descriptive category of Scheduled Castes. Based on a British colonial system of categorisation, the term 'Scheduled Caste' is still used in the Indian legal system to refer to this group, along with other non-caste 'tribes' ('SC&ST' – Scheduled Castes and Scheduled Tribes).

**Davos:** A town in eastern Switzerland, in the canton Graubünden, on the Landwasse River. Earlier known mostly as a winter sports town, it has come to be host to the World Economic Forum (WEF) for its annual meetings of leaders of big business and, more recently, of select countries, in January each year. Has become a symbol of world capitalism, not unlike the former World Trade Center in New York, and WEF meetings are confronted by strong demonstrations each year from constituents of the Anti-globalisation movement.

**Dawood Ibrahim:** A powerful and notorious kingpin of the Indian underworld, based in Dubai. Said to be responsible for the Mumbai bomb blasts in March 1993.

**Developing countries:** Term coined and used from the 1950s onwards especially by economists and politicians in what was then called the West (now the North) and by their collaborators in the South, to refer to countries that had recently become independent in the wave of decolonisation that took place after the Second World War (1939-45), and which they suggested were 'under-developed' but now capable of 'developing' into greater prosperity. Part of mainstream development theory and ideology. See also NAM, South, and Third World.

**Dharavi:** An area in Mumbai, India, said to be Asia's largest slum. Major centre of the 'informal economy' in the city. Also the scene of communal riots during 1993, in the aftermath of the series of bomb blasts allegedly initiated by the Dawood Ibrahim gang.

**dharna:** A sit-down strike, a popular mode in India of protest and of demanding justice.

**'Do or Die':** Slogan ('Karenge ya marenge') given by Mahatma Gandhi during the Quit India Movement in 1942. Launching the struggle he said, "I am not going to be satisfied with anything short of complete freedom.... Here is a mantra, a short one that I give you. You may imprint it in your hearts. The mantra is 'Do or Die': '*Karenge ya marenge*'! Take a pledge with God and your own conscience as witness that you will no longer rest till freedom is achieved...".

**Engels, Friedrich:** November 28, 1820 – August 5, 1895. German. Collaborator of Karl Marx, author and co-author of several works on communism, including *The Conditions of the Working Class*. Responsible for the diffusion of Marxism as a worldview within the Socialist movement.

**Enlightenment:** Name given to the period in European history that succeeded the rise of modern science in the 17th century, culminating in the French Revolution. Essentially refers only to the 'educated' part of society. Characterised by scepticism towards traditional authority in matters of religion and politics, an openness of outlook, a respect for reason as the guiding principle and also as the most basic property of the human condition.

**Fascists:** Followers of fascism, (in Italian, fascismo). Originally referred to the Right-wing authoritarian political movement that ruled Italy from 1922-43 under the leadership of Benito Mussolini. The Italian 'Fascisti' were also known as the 'Black Shirts' for their style of uniform incorporating a black shirt. Subsequently, came to also refer to German Nazism and Spanish falangism, given their common ethos: nationalism; hostility to democracy, egalitarianism, and the values of the liberal

# GLOSSARY

enlightenment; cult of a single leader and admiration for his special qualities; and a fascination with collective organisation and symbols. Usually accompanied by violence, and in the case of Nazism, extreme anti-Semitism and anti-communism.

**Fifth International:** Term referring to the possibility of the formation of another 'International'. This term generally applies to the succession of international federations formed by parties dedicated to international socialism. The first International (the 'International Working Men's Association') was formed in London in 1864, with the support of Marx and where he wrote almost all their documents, and the second in Paris in 1899. Both were split by factionalism, decay, and hostility between participants over doctrine and policy. The Third International (the 'Comintern') was formed in Moscow in 1919, led by Lenin and Stalin, for the first time by a party that was ruling in a State-nation. The Fourth International was formed in 1938 by followers of Trotsky, who had been hounded out of the Communist Party of the Soviet Union (and finally assassinated) by Stalin. There also exists a Socialist International, formed in 1923, but which is not considered in the same tradition or line.

**Foucault, Michel:** 1926-1984. A French philosopher and historian of 'systems of thought', who attempted to show that the basic ideas which people normally take to be permanent truths about human nature and society change in the course of history. His writings, which challenged the influence of German political philosopher Karl Marx and Austrian psychoanalyst Sigmund Freud, have had an enormous impact on many fields including literary criticism and theory, philosophy (especially philosophy of science in the French-speaking world), critical theory, history, history of science (especially scientific medicine), critical pedagogy, and the sociology of knowledge, which he transformed altogether.

**Fukuyama, Francis:** Born October 27, 1952, in Chicago, USA. Professor of Political Economy at The Johns Hopkins University, USA; best known as the author of the controversial book *The End of History* and *The Last Man*, in which he argues that the progression of human history as a struggle between ideologies is largely at an end, with the world settling on liberal democracy after the end of the Cold War. He has also subsequently written Our Posthuman Future: Consequences of the Biotechnology Revolution, in which he retracts his original 'end of history' thesis, arguing that since biotechnology increasingly allows humans to control their own evolution, it may allow humans to become fundamentally unequal, and thus spell the end of liberal democracy as a workable system. Active in the Project for the New American Century think-tank starting in 1997, that also informs the policies of the present Bush presidency.

**Fundamentalism:** A tendency in social institutions and processes to 'return' to a more rigid adherence, to what they consider to be founding principles; usually in religion but also applicable to politics.

**G-77:** 'Group of 77' – a bloc of what were originally 77 'developing countries'/nation-states of the South, that emerged in the 90s during world trade negotiations and that in many ways have taken the place of the earlier NAM – Non-Aligned Movement. Holds periodic conferences, is officially recognised in the UN system and has an office in the UN building in New York. g77off@undp.org See also NAM, South, and Third World.

**Gaia Theory:** A thesis and theory that Planet Earth is, and should be regarded, as one living organism, as developed and propounded by James Lovelock and then others.

**Gandhi, Mohandas Karamchand** (known as Mahatma Gandhi or Gandhi): 1869-1948. Indian statesman and political leader during India's struggle for independence from British colonial rule, where the term Mahatma refers to the 'Great Soul' (title given to him by the great Indian poet Rabindranath Tagore). Portrayed in India as the 'Father of the Indian nation'. Responsible for the formulation under Indian conditions of the doctrines of civil

disobedience, direct action, non-violence, and passive resistance, including perhaps especially the Non-Cooperation Movement, the Quit India Movement, and the tactic of satyagraha. Assassinated on January 30, 1948 by right Hindu fundamentalists, for his alleged policy of appeasement of Muslims.

**Globalisation:** In its literal sense, a social change, an increased connectivity among societies and their elements due to transculturation; and the explosive evolution of transport and communication technologies to facilitate international cultural and economic exchange. The term is applied in various social, cultural, commercial and economic contexts. Historically, has taken place across the centuries, in the course of human migration, the building of empires, and the expansion and spread of technologies, Ideologically and conceptually, it shares a number of characteristics with internationalisation and the terms are widely used interchangeably. Since the early 1990s, the term has been increasingly used to refer to neo-liberal economic globalisation, leading to the erosion of the nation-state and of national boundaries and the overwhelming destruction of local economies by the global economy dominated by huge multinational corporations, something that has spawned protest and resistance all over the world. See also Alter-globalisation, Anti-globalisation, and Anti-globalisation movement.

**Green Revolution:** The 'Green Revolution' is a process of accelerated technological development of agriculture that was started in the 1960s, including in India, and has now spread throughout the world. The goal of the Green Revolution was to increase the efficiency of agricultural processes so that the productivity of crops was increased and this could help developing countries face the needs of their growing populations. The reality of this accelerated change however, has been complex and controversial, since it also led to massive labour displacement and unemployment, ecological degradation and instability (because of the heavy use of chemical fertilisers and pesticides), and the concentration of wealth and landholdings – it has now also been widely shown that the productivity of areas covered by these technologies was, at its best, no better than that achieved by intensive organic and traditional agricultural techniques, and that it is now dropping.

**Greens:** Earlier referring (in the 1960s and 70s) to all ecologically minded people, later came to refer more to members of the Green Party, initially formed in Germany, and subsequently in several European countries and also the US. The Greens generally view grassroots democracy, pacifism, and social justice causes — especially those related to the plight of indigenous peoples — as inherently related to ecology and human bodily health. They see thriving natural eco-regions as the way to prevent global climate change and to preserve other aspects of the natural environment, and as essential to maintain human life and life on Planet Earth.

**Gujarat:** Located in western India near the border with Pakistan, Gujarat is now the most industrialised state in the country after Maharashtra. Also the home of a rich culture of craft. The state was witness to extreme communal violence between Hindus and Muslims in March 2002.

**Hannah Arendt:** October 14, 1906 - December 4, 1975. German political theorist, philosopher, and social critic. Her work deals with the nature of power, and the subjects of politics, authority, and totalitarianism. In her book *Eichmann in Jerusalem*, she raised the question whether evil is radical or simply a function of banality; of the failure of good people to take risks. In *The Origins of Totalitarianism*, she attempted to trace the roots of communism and fascism and their link to anti-Semitism.

**Imperialism:** The extension of power through conquest, or the pursuit of 'empire'; the policy of extending the control or authority over foreign entities as a means of acquisition and/or maintenance of empire, either through direct territorial control or through indirect methods of exerting control on the politics and/or economy of other countries. The term is sometimes used to describe the policy of a country in maintaining colonies and dominance over distant lands.

regardless of whether the country calls itself an empire. Was used as a positive term in the 19th century, by politicians of colonial countries such as Britain. The popular meaning of the term has now changed, however. According to Lenin, imperialism is an economic necessity of capitalism, in order to overcome the otherwise inevitable falling rate of profit that would spell its doom, and is accordingly the highest stage of capitalism (1917), leading to 'imperialist war', and the term is now associated with oppression. Largely as a consequence of Lenin's theory and the communist usage of the term however, it has also come to be given a particular ideological slant: armed invasion by communist powers, for example, is generally not called by this name even though it meets all the basic criteria.

`Imperialist globalisation:` Marxist term for economic globalisation.

`(WSF) India General Council (IGC):` The decision-making body of the WSF India process. The membership to the IGC is open to all social movements and organisations that are committed to the WSF Charter of principles. In 2003, there were 135 members in the IGC.

`(WSF) India Organising Committee (IOC):` The executive body for the organisation of WSF 2004. In 2003-04, the IOC consisted of 45 individuals, chosen from among those on the WSF India Working Committee, each being a member of one of the eight working groups

`(WSF) India Working Committee (IWC):` Responsible for formulating policy guidelines that form the basis for the functioning of the WSF India process. In 2003-04, the IWC consisted of 67 organisations nominated from and by the IGC, and aimed to be representative of the diverse social, political and economic reality of the country. In 2003-04, the IWC comprised 14 national trade unions and workers' organisations, eight national women's organisations, six national farmers' networks, and four national platforms each of Dalits and Adivasis, four student and youth bodies, as well as 27 social movements, other organisations and NGOs.

`Internationalism:` A political movement that grew out of a revulsion for the intense and brutal nationalism that led to World War II; which advocates a greater economic and political cooperation between nation-states for the benefit of all. Partisans of this movement, such as supporters of the World Federalist Movement, claim that nations should cooperate because their long-term mutual interests are of greater value than their own individual short-term needs. Internationalism is by nature opposed to ultra nationalism, jingoism, and national chauvinism as well as to strict economic globalisation, which deny the value of individual cultures and the differences that exist between societies. Internationalism presupposes the recognition of other nations as equal, in spite of all their differences, as well as a total respect of each other's nationalism.

`Internationals:` See 'Fifth International'.

`Israel-Palestine conflict:` The long-running conflict in the Middle East in regard to the existence of the states of Israel and Palestine. The roots of the conflict are in the creation of the Israeli state by Britain and other colonial powers after World War II and the subsequent unjust and illegal occupation of the Palestinian territory by Israel and denial of sovereignty of the Palestine state.

`Ivan Illich:` Born in Vienna, 1906. Theologist, philosopher. Considered one of the most radical political and social thinkers in the second half of the 20th century. Co-founder of the widely known and controversial Center for Intercultural Documentation (CIDOC) in Cuernavaca, Mexico. His aim was to analyse the institutional structures of industrialised society and to provide both rigorous criticism and a set of alternative concepts. Became well known in 1970 when he published *Deschooling Society*, in which he argued that the top-down management of schools makes students powerless — and that the same

top-down management is typical of the modern, technological economy that prevents people from learning. *Tools for Conviviality* made the same criticism of technology in general. Along with *Energy and Equity*, this book made Ivan Illich one of the most important theorists of the radical ecology movement of the 1970s.

**Jubilee South:** Formally constituted in November 1999 in a South-South Summit held in Johannesburg, at Gauteng, South Africa. A network of jubilee and debt campaigns, social movements, people's organisations, communities, NGOs and political formations, Jubilee South is in the process of emerging and developing as an international movement of the South on debt. It has members from over 40 countries from the regions of Latin America and the Caribbean, Africa and Asia/Pacific, and is composed of 85 groups. The network's concept of 'Jubilee' is the Biblical concept — of justice, in particular of economic (*Oikonomia*, in Greek) justice. Apart from debt cancellation, it embraces restoration and reparation, arguing that there is nothing like 'unpayable' debt; that all debt must be cancelled, and the poor must take precedence. "There is a command from God to ensure that the poor are not kept deliberately poor. This Jubilee is a Jubilee that tries to deal with the oikos, with the economic structure of the world."

**Kashmir:** A region in the northern part of the Indian subcontinent, currently divided amongst three countries: Pakistan controls the northwest portion (Northern Areas, Pakistan, and Azad Kashmir), India controls the central and southern portion (Jammu and Kashmir), and the People's Republic of China controls the north-eastern portion (Aksai Chin). Though these regions are in practice administered by their respective claimants, India has never formally recognised the accession of the areas claimed by Pakistan and China. Pakistan views the entire Kashmir region as disputed territory, and does not consider India's claim to it to be valid.

**Korean War:** A military conflict between communist North Korea and anti-communist South Korea, which was a proxy war between the United States and the Soviet Union. Took place from June 25, 1950 to July 27, 1953.

**Kosovo:** An autonomous province in the south of Serbia (which together with Montenegro constitutes 'Serbia and Montenegro'); part of the former Federal Republic of Yugoslavia. Also a synonym for the Kosovo War: essentially two armed conflicts — a civil war between Albanian separatists and the Serbian and Yugoslav security forces from 1996-99, which Albanians characterised as a national liberation struggle and Serbs saw as terrorism; followed by an international war in 1999 between Yugoslavia and NATO; the latter invaded the region on the argument of a gross violation of human rights, under the rule of Slobodan Milosevic. The majority of the mostly Albanian population had earlier declared the independence of the Republic of Kosovo in 1990, but this parallel government is not recognised internationally except by Albania. It is currently administered by the United Nations following the war. The final status of the region is as yet undetermined.

**Kurds:** An ethnic group of Medes origin, comprised of approximately 35 million people, primarily in Iraq, Iran, Turkey, and Syria. There are also Kurdish communities in Armenia and Georgia. Traditionally nomadic herdsmen, but are now semi-nomadic or sedentary. The majority of Kurds are Sunni Muslims. For over a century, one section of Kurds has been campaigning for the right to their own state, which they would call Kurdistan. By some accounts, the Kurds are the world's largest ethnic group without their own state. However, despite promises of the creation of such a state made in the early 20th century, all the region's governments are opposed to it.

**Land Ceiling Act:** Central legislation introduced in India in 1976 to set a ceiling on urban land holdings during the Emergency (involving the promulgation of central rule throughout the country and suspension of all democratic process). Never put into effect. Part of a family of populist legislation introduced by then Prime Minister Indira Gandhi from 1970 onwards. The law has been repealed at the central level since 1991, while attempts to have state governments repeal the law still continue.

# GLOSSARY

**Le Monde Diplomatique (The Diplomatic World):** Influential monthly journal in France (nicknamed 'Le Diplo' by its readers), offering well-documented analysis and opinion on politics, culture, and current affairs. The journal takes a critical offers a decidedly Left-wing viewpoint, particularly of the effects of neo-liberalism on the world and its population.

**Leninism:** A political and economic theory, a further development of Marxism, formulated and put into practice by the Bolshevik leader Vladimir Lenin after the Russian Revolution in 1917. Hotly contested since its inception, both by critics on the Left, particularly Social Democrats, and also by liberals and conservatives. Lenin argued that the proletariat could only achieve revolutionary consciousness through the efforts of a communist party that assumes the role of 'revolutionary vanguard', formed by disciplined organisation and practice known as 'democratic centralism'. Lenin's other arguments included the necessity to spread the communist revolution to other countries in order for it to survive, and an analysis of, and opposition to, imperialism. He argued that imperialism is the highest stage of capitalism.

**Lesbian:** A homosexual woman, one who prefers to have romantic and sexual relationships with other women. In relation to feminism, and arising in relation to the Radical Feminism Movement, 'lesbian separatism' became popular, with groups of lesbian women coming together and living in communal societies.

**Lula (Luiz Inácio Lula da Silva):** Born October 27, 1945. A trade unionist and Left-wing Brazilian politician, leader of the Worker's Party (PT) who was elected the President of Brazil in 2002 and took office on January 1, 2003. In his 2002 campaign he abandoned his style of informal clothing, as well as his platform position of refusing to pay the Brazilian foreign debt. This last point had worried US economists, businessmen and banks, who feared that a Brazilian default, along with the already ongoing Argentine default, would have a massive ripple effect upon the world economy.

**Manchurian War:** The Russo-Japanese War of 1904-05, which began with the Japanese naval attack on Port Arthur (now Lu Shun, in northern China) and had its roots in the simultaneous determination of both Japan and Russia to develop 'spheres of influence' in the Far East, mainly at the expense of China. Japan became the first Asian power in modern times to defeat a European power.

**Mao Zedong (Mao Tse-tung):** 1893-1976. Communist revolutionary, leader of the popular revolution in China in the late 1940s, and the founder of the People's Republic of China. Chairman of the Communist Party of China and one of the most prominent communist theoreticians; his ideas on revolutionary struggle and guerrilla warfare were extremely influential, especially among Third World revolutionaries. He developed a brand of Marxism-Leninism known as Maoism. While in power, he collectivised agriculture under the 'Great Leap Forward' which, however, failed and 20 million people starved. After this Mao temporarily withdrew from public view. The failure of this programme also resulted in a break with the Soviet Union, which cut off aid, and Mao accused Soviet leaders of betraying Marxism. He subsequently launched the 'Cultural Revolution' to reassert his leadership and ostensibly to purge the party of Rightists.

**Marx, Karl:** 1818-94. A German philosopher turned social scientist, and founder of a school of thought based on dialectical materialism, 'Marxism'. Marx lived much of his life in exile. Together with Engels, he wrote the *Communist Manifesto*, and developed a philosophy of human beings, history, and politics that would give unprecedented authority to the communist cause.

**Milosevic genocide:** Slobodan Milosevic, former Yugoslav President and Serbian leader during the Kosovo War (1996-99) has been accused of responsibility for mass killings and expulsion of ethnic Albanians, and of the genocide of Muslims and Croats in Bosnia during 1992-95. He has been charged with crimes against humanity, and is presently being tried by

the International War Crimes Tribunal.

**MKSS:** Mazdoor Kisan Shakti Sangathan (Organisation for Workers & Peasants' Power). Mass organisation in Rajasthan, well known for raising issues for the rights of workers and peasants to information from the state regarding programmes and policies that benefit them.

**MNC, or multinational corporation, or transnational corporation (TNC):** A corporation, or company, that spans multiple nations. These corporations are often very large, and have offices and/or factories in different countries. They usually have a centralised head office where they coordinate global management. Very large multinationals have budgets that exceed those of many countries. They are today seen as a major power in global politics. The first multinational appeared in 1602 and was the Dutch East India Company.

**NAM/Non-Aligned Movement:** Formed in 1961 on the initiative of Josip Broz Tito, then president of Yugoslavia, who brought together the states of the world which did not wish to align themselves with either of the Cold War superpowers. Important members included India (led by Prime Minister Jawaharlal Nehru), Egypt (President Abdul Nasser), Indonesia (President Suharto), and, for a time, the People's Republic of China. (Brazil has never been a formal member of the movement.) On the one hand, NAM constituted a major and bold new concept in world politics, historically unprecedented, when seen in the context of colonialism that had dominated and oppressed most of the world till just the decade before, and in this sense, was a direct outcome of anti-colonial freedom struggles and their aspirations. On the other, while the organisation was intended to be as close an alliance as NATO or the Warsaw Pact, it never had much cohesion and many of its members were induced into aligning with one or another of the great powers, or were unable to resist doing so.

**Narendra Modi:** Born September 17, 1950. Member BJP (Bharatiya Janata Party — 'Indian People's Party'), former ABVP activist. Chief Minister of the state of Gujarat in India since October 7, 2001. His tenure has been marked by the communal riots in Gujarat in March 2002 in which over 3,000 people, mostly Muslims, lost their lives. There is evidence showing complicity of the police and state administration in a massacre that saw some of the worst human rights violations ever witnessed in India.

**Narmada Bachao Andolan / NBA:** Literally, 'Save the Narmada Movement'. A national coalition of environmental and human rights activists, scientists, academics, students, and project-affected people, that has been working since the mid 80s to stop several dam projects in the Narmada River Valley in western India. Since the late 80s, has been supported by an international campaign based in most countries of the North, as a consequence of the fact that the project was receiving finance from the World Bank and the primary shareholding countries in the Bank – therefore having the greatest clout – are in the North. Collectively, one of the most creative and influential environmental and social campaigns, in India and worldwide, and led to both the World Bank and Japan, which was semi-independently providing some finance, withdrawing from supporting what was then the biggest dam in the project, the Sardar Sarovar Dam. But the government of India elected to continue the project even without this aid, and the project has now considerably progressed. The campaign also included a major case in the Supreme Court of India, The NBA is also opposing several of the other dams in the valley project, including the Bargi dam and the Maan dam, and has put forward alternatives both for irrigation and power, the main declared objectives of the project. For details: www.narmada.org.

**NATO:** The North Atlantic Treaty Organisation (NATO), sometimes called North Atlantic Alliance or Atlantic Alliance, is an international organisation for defence collaboration between European and North American states. Established in April 1949.

**Nazism, or National Socialism (German Nationalsozialismus), or Hitlerism:** The totalitarian ideology of

the dictatorship which ruled Germany from 1933 to 1945, led by Adolph Hitler. In this ideology, the German nation and the purported 'Aryan' race were considered superior to all other races. Nazism is usually associated with Fascism. Key elements of the Nazi ideology are: Racism (especially anti-Semitism), including anti-Slavism and a belief in the superiority of the German and Aryan/Nordic races; Euthanasia and Eugenics with respect to 'Racial Hygiene'; Anti-Marxism, Anti-Communism, and Anti-Bolshevism; the denial of democracy, and effectively killing all opposition parties, labour unions, and the free press.

**Neo-liberalism:** A political philosophy and a political-economic movement that emerged in the 1970s, and grew more prominent since 1980, which de-emphasises, or rejects, government intervention in the economy. Instead, it focuses on achieving progress and even social justice by free-market methods, especially through an emphasis on economic growth, as measured by changes in so-called 'real gross domestic product'. This is the philosophy that underpins and drives the current phase of economic globalisation (therefore also known as 'neo-liberal globalisation'). The four pillars of this philosophy involve liberalisation (or the reduction of rules and restrictions): capital account liberalisation, trade liberalisation, domestic liberalisation, and privatisation.

**New International Economic Order (NIEO):** Two closely related terms, the 'New International Economic Order' and the 'New International Information Order', popular in the United Nations and its specialised agencies (especially UNESCO) in the 1970s and 1980s. Used mainly by developing country groups (for example NAM and the G-77) to refer to the redistribution of wealth on a global scale and to the international control of the media, the latter to stop distorted reporting of developments in Third World countries and to develop independent, South-based media. Western countries attacked these initiatives as attempts to destroy the free market and freedom of speech and threatened to withdraw from United Nations bodies, after which the programmes faded.

**New Social Movement (NSM):** The term refers to the plethora of social movements that have come up in various societies, initially (in the mid-1960s) especially in the North but more recently also in the South, and which have departed significantly from the conventional paradigm of social movements. In particular, traditional social movements, such as the labour movement, were centred on economic concerns. The new movements include the women's movement, the human rights movement, the ecology movement, various peace movements, and others. NSM theorists have argued that many of these NSMs tend to emphasise changes in lifestyle and culture rather than pushing for changes in public policy or in areas of economic or social structure. They also argue that the key actors in these movements tend to be members of the 'new middle class' or service-sector professionals (such as academics). Some have also related the emergence of these new movements with the post materialism hypothesis as put forth by Ronald Inglehart and others. Other sociologists who have contributed in this field include Alain Tourraine, Claus Offe, Jürgen Habermas, Jean Cohen, and Sidney Tarrow. But the actual reality of social movements across the world has now dramatically exploded, encompassing also the political, and requires constant further and new theorisation.

**New World Order:** The phrase first used by Woodrow Wilson in the period just after World War I (1914-1918), during the formation of the League of Nations. It has subsequently come to have different meanings. In the South the term is associated with the New International Economic Order, and in the North to refer to post-Cold War conditions and to represent a dramatic change in world political thought and balance of power. See also Wilsonian World Order.

**Non-Cooperation Movement:** A mass civil disobedience movement against colonial British rule launched throughout India by the Indian National Congress in 1920, following its Nagpur Conference where Mahatma Gandhi assumed leadership of the Congress. The launching of this movement, which sought to

paralyse the colonial government and at the same time to turn the movement towards pacifist struggle, marked a major new phase in the struggle for India's independence.

North: A geo-political concept that gained currency in the 1980s, to collectively describe advanced capitalist countries as a collective political force in world politics, overtaking the idea of a 'West' – by making room for Japan, which had by then emerged as a world economic power – and by also using its opposite, the 'South', composed of what had till then been termed 'developing countries'. This established a dynamic and dialectical opposition of richer and poorer countries as collectivities that respectively had common interests in world politics. Now also includes Russia, but the duality still fails to account for wealthy countries such as those in the Middle East, which are still 'developing' but that do not see themselves as belonging to the 'South'.

NSUI: National Students Union of India. The student wing of the Indian National Congress, one of the main political parties in India.

Osama bin Laden: Saudi Arabian, a member of the wealthy bin Laden family. He turned to fundamentalist politics in the 1990s and backed the Taliban in Afghanistan. Is now best known for masterminding the '9/11' attack on the World Trade Center in New York and the Pentagon in September 2001, which led to the 'war on terror' launched by the US, the UK, and their allies.

Panchayat: The lowest administrative unit of local self-government in modern India as mandated by Article 40 of the Indian Constitution. The panchayat is an old institution, part and parcel of Indian villages, used for solving local disputes such as around land. Traditionally, different castes in villages also had (and some still have) their own panchayats that decide the rules and regulations of their own communities and also help resolve minor disputes. Until the late 1970s, the panchayats were largely inactive in most states. The exceptions were Karnataka and West Bengal, where the respective state governments since the late 1970s – the Janata Party in the former, the Left Front in the latter – took vigorous steps to enact and enable them. The situation in the country as a whole changed when the 73rd (Constitutional) Amendment in 1992 gave panchayats constitutional status (previously panchayat matters were considered only a state subject), leading to local elections and significant devolution of power in some parts of the country. A significant further step was the reservation of one-third of these seats for women.

Patriarchy: The political structure that privileges men at the expense of women; used sometimes as a synonym for male domination. Literally means 'rule of the father' (in Latin) and was originally used by anthropologists to describe the social structure in which one man, usually an elder, the (patriarch) had absolute power over everyone else in the family.

Patta: Legal document in India, containing the details of land deeds, ownership records and rights, etc.

People's Movement against Violence against Women (Mahila Atyachar Virodhi Jan-Andolan – MAVJA): Formed in 1996, an informal network of more than 40 organisations seeking justice and working for protection of rape victims in Rajasthan.

Pokhran: Remote village in the Thar Desert, in the state of Rajasthan. Chosen by the government of India as the test site for India's nuclear programme, first in 1974 and subsequently on May 11 and 13, 1998.

PWG/People's War Group: Maoist group engaged in armed struggle over the question of land for the landless and other issues in various states of India including Andhra Pradesh (a state where they have a wide influence, especially in Telengana), Bihar, Jharkhand, etc. Following the initiation of peace talks with the Andhra Pradesh state government in 2004, it merged with another political grouping, the Maoist Communist Centre to form the Communist Party of India (Maoist).

## GLOSSARY

**Raga:** Composition based on an intricate Vedic philosophy of sound that details the melodic modes used in Indian classical music. It specifies rules for movements up (*aarohanam*) and down (*avarohanam*) the scale, notes that should be used in abundance or sparingly, phrases to be used, phrases to be avoided, and so on. The result is a framework that can be used to compose or improvise melodies, allowing for endless variation within a set of notes. There are specific ragas for each time of the day — morning, afternoon, evening and night. This distinction is strictly followed in Hindustani music (North India), but not in Carnatic music (South India).

**Ranvir Sena (also spelt Ranabir Sena):** Militia of feudal caste peasantry active in central Bihar, a state in eastern India, formed to protect their landed property from Maoist groups.

**RAND Corporation:** The RAND Corporation, based in San Diego, California, presents itself as 'a non-profit institution that helps improve policy and decision-making through research and analysis.' Set up in the 1950s as a low profile, shadowy, and high-security think-tank, decision-makers in the public and private sectors in the US have turned to the RAND Corporation for analysis and solutions to key social, economic, technological, and policy challenges.

**Rights to due process:** The rights of all persons to all provisions in law.

**Russian Revolution:** A communist uprising in 1917 led by Lenin's Bolshevik party that succeeded in overthrowing the provisional government that had replaced the Russian Tsarist regime, and that led to the establishment of the Soviet Union, the world's first communist state. This revolution, the theory that accompanied it (Marxism-Leninism), and its success, played a major role in inspiring revolutionary movements and uprisings throughout the world over the next half-century and more. However, on account of intense internal contradictions as well as the sustained pressure of the Cold War over 40 years, this first communist state collapsed in 1991.

**Rashtriya Swayamsevak Sangh (RSS):** Nationalist Volunteer Organisation, or Force. Militant Hindu-supremacist organisation in India, formed in 1925. Has consistently worked on its long-term ideal of transforming the Indian democratic State into a hegemonic nation representative of one people, one faith, one language, one culture. Mahatma Gandhi was assassinated by one of its members, Nathuram Godse.

**Sahlins, Marshall:** One of the most prominent US anthropologists of our time. Holds the title of Charles F. Grey Distinguished Service Professor of Anthropology at the University of Chicago, where he currently teaches.

**Sati:** Widow immolation; the practice of death of widows on the funeral pyres of their husbands in India. Though supposedly a voluntary act, it is often enforced on the widow by traditional social pressures. Sati is known to have been practised in many different regions of India from medieval times, but was more common in Rajasthan and in parts of the Gangetic plain till the early 19th century. It was banned in the Bengal Presidency on December 4, 1829, during British colonial times, following a campaign to outlaw it, and is today a punishable offence in Indian law; but the practise of sati continues sporadically, campaigns continue against it, and it remains an issue in modern India.

**Sati-hood:** The woman who commits sati is said to achieve sati-hood. (Word used in English. Combination of the Hindi sati and the English ending denoting status, -hood).

**Sathin:** Term in Hindi for women comrades in a struggle.

**Satyagraha:** (Sanskrit: truth + grasp/hold). The philosophy of non-violent resistance most famously employed by Mahatma Gandhi to end British rule in India. Also rendered as 'civil disobedience', 'passive resistance', 'truth-force', or 'the willingness to endure great personal suffering in order to do what's right'.

**Sexuality:** The expression of sexual

feelings due to genetic predisposition or one's own personal experimentation. Sexuality, which can be influenced by hormonal changes in the development of the foetus during pregnancy, strongly influences social behaviour. Human sexuality can also be understood as part of the social life of humans, governed by implied rules of behaviour status in quo.

**Shiv Sena:** Meaning Army of Shiva, referring to mediaeval Maratha king Shivaji, in India. A regional Hindu nationalist political party in Maharashtra, India, founded in June 1966 by Bal Thackeray. Cadres of the party are called Shiv Sainiks.

**Socialist:** The terms socialist, or socialism refer to several related things; an ideology, and economic system, a nation-state, and in Marxist theory, the society that will succeed capitalism and develop further into communism. The terms essentially refer to societies operating according to principles of solidarity and egalitarianism. The philosophy dates back to the first half of the 19th century. Originally included Marxists and non-Marxist followers of the Second International, who subsequently parted ways with the Marxists forming the Third International and the Socialists going on to form the Socialist International. Socialists have led industrial and agricultural workers' struggles and have formed governments in both the North and the South.

**South:** A geo-political concept that gained currency in the 1980s, to collectively describe what had till then been described as 'developing countries' as a collective political force in world politics. Together with its opposite, the 'North' — composed of advanced capitalist countries — this duality established a dynamic and dialectical opposition of wealthier and poorer countries as collectivities that respectively had common interests in world politics. The duality however fails to account for (wealthy) countries such as in the Middle East, which are still 'developing' but do not see themselves as belonging to the 'South'. See also 'North', 'New International Economic Order', NAM, and Third World.

**Soviet:** Workers' councils that emerged in Russia during the first revolution in 1905. The first soviets were organised by the Russian revolutionary and theorist Trotsky. The idea of 'sovietisation' was that all economic, political, and administrative powers would be transferred to such councils, in theory to facilitate grassroots democracy, but in practice permitting control by the Central Party, which acted in the name of the 'Supreme Soviet', the highest organ of state in the former USSR (Soviet Union). A century later, the term has come to be almost completely associated with the nation-state earlier known as the Soviet Union, losing its original meaning.

**Spanish Civil War:** 1936-1939, between the Republicans —supporters of the Second Spanish Republic, subscribing to electoral democracy — and the Fascists led by Francisco Franco who finally seized power and established dictatorship. The war attracted widespread support from international intellectual and political communities, resulting in the formation of an International Brigade in support of the Republicans.

**Taliban:** Literally meaning students of Islam. A fundamentalist Islamic movement in Afghanistan formed in the 1980s with the support of the US in its covert war against the Soviet Union, to oppose and bring down the Soviet-supported government in the country. The movement seized power in Afghanistan in 1995-96, following the collapse of the Soviet Union in 1991 and the withdrawal of Soviet support to the regime. It ruled most of the country with an extreme interpretation of Islamic doctrine until 2003. Following 9/11 and the 'war on terror' that the US declared against Osama bin Laden, who was then based in Afghanistan and had been given refuge by the Taliban, it was militarily hunted and defeated. The regime had diplomatic recognition only from United Arab Emirates, Pakistan and Saudi Arabia, all of which then turned against it under US pressure, post-9/11.

**Telengana:** A region in Andhra Pradesh, a state on the eastern coast of India, with a substantial Adivasi (tribal) population, where the PWG (People's War Group) is very active. A

major movement in the region in the 1940s, led by the-then undivided Communist Party of India, the 'Telengana Movement', played an important role in the establishment of the state of Andhra Pradesh in 1956. More recently, the demand has emerged for a separate Telengana state, growing out of a sense of regional identity rather than of ethnic identity, language, religion, or caste. The demands of the movement for a separate state are redress for economic discrimination, the writing of a separate history, and the recognition of cultural distinctiveness.

**Thatcher, Margaret:** Born October 13, 1925. Nicknamed the 'Iron Lady', a British politician, the first woman to become leader of the British Conservative Party and the first woman Prime Minister of the United Kingdom, a position she held from 1979 to 1990. Thatcher's domestic policy was markedly conservative — she reduced public spending and privatised many government-owned companies. In 1984, she used police to crush the miners' strike, breaking the power of trade unions in Britain. In foreign relations, Thatcher maintained the policy of a 'special relationship' with the United States, especially under the presidency of Ronald Reagan.

**Third World:** A term used to distinguish those nations that neither aligned with the West nor with the East during the Cold War – therefore constituting a 'third' sector, or world. These countries are also known in academic circles as the Global South, developing countries, or 'least developed countries'. Development workers and activists also tend to call them The South. Many dislike the term developing countries as it implies that industrialisation is the only way forward, which they believe is not necessarily the most beneficial route to equality, justice or to 'development'. The term 'third world' was coined by economist Alfred Sauvy in an article in the French magazine *Le Nouvel Observateur* of August 14, 1952. It was a deliberate reference to the 'Third Estate' of the French Revolution. The term gained widespread popularity during the Cold War when many 'poorer nations' of the South adopted the term to describe themselves as being aligned neither with NATO / the West nor the USSR, but instead composing a non-aligned 'third world'. Leading members of this original 'Third World' movement were Yugoslavia, India, and Egypt – the founders of NAM, the Non-Aligned Movement. The term 'First World' was generally understood to mean the United States and its allies in the Cold War, which would have made the Eastern or Soviet bloc the 'Second World' by default; however, the latter term was seldom actually used. Most 'Third World' countries, as the term is understood now, are located in Africa, Latin America, and Asia.

**Tobin tax:** First proposed by James Tobin, an American economist, this is a tax (between 0.05 and 1.0 per cent) on foreign exchange transactions viewed as a penalty on short-term speculation in currencies. The idea has received support from and been promoted by many anti-globalisation movements, especially ATTAC, who advocate that the proceeds of the tax be used for funding development projects in the Third World.

**Trotskyites:** Followers of Russian communist revolutionary, writer, and orator Leon Trotsky (1879-1940), who organised the first soviets in 1905, first opposed and then supported Lenin, and was then later Stalin's unsuccessful rival for leadership of the USSR Communist Party after Lenin's death. He severely criticised Stalin's Soviet regime for replacing the 'dictatorship of the proletariat' with the 'dictatorship of the party', and advocated the theories of 'permanent revolution' and world proletarian revolution and international socialism as opposed to Stalin's idea of 'socialism in one country'. He was exiled from the USSR in 1929, but continued to organise opposition to Stalin among exiles, and founded the 'Fourth International' in 1938. He was assassinated in Mexico in 1940, at the instigation of Stalin.

**Uniform Civil Code:** A common civil code proposed in India to replace different codes for different religious communities such as Hindus, Muslims and Christians to be followed in personal law matters of marriage, divorce, inheritance, etc. The debate over a UCC has been going on for decades and the issue is still unresolved.

## GLOSSARY

**Vietnam war:** The war between the USA and the Vietnamese communist guerrillas between 1957 and 1975 in South Vietnam, parts of North Vietnam and bordering areas of Cambodia and Laos. The US government faced strong opposition to the war both at home and abroad, and was finally driven out of Vietnam.

**Vitasta:** Also known as the Jhelum, an important river of Jammu and Kashmir in India; has important symbolic meaning for Kashmiris. Also the source for water supply to most parts of the Srinagar valley.

**Warsaw Pact, or Warsaw Treaty:** A former military alliance of the Eastern European Soviet Bloc countries, to organise against the perceived threat from the NATO alliance (established in 1949). The creation of the Warsaw Pact was prompted by the integration of a 're-militarised' West Germany into NATO. The Warsaw Treaty was drafted by Nikita Khrushchev, leader of Soviet Union after the death of Joseph Stalin, and signed in Warsaw on May 14, 1955. The pact came to an end on March 31, 1991 and was officially dissolved at a meeting in Prague on July 1 1991.

**Wilsonian World Order:** An ideological perspective on foreign policy expounded by US President Woodrow Wilson for world peace. Wilsonian principles include self-determination by ethnic groups, spread of democracy, anti-isolationism, and intervention to help create peace and freedom.

**Workers' Party (PT - Partido dos Trabalhadores):** Coming out of a broader struggle in Brazil against the military regime and its economic and social policies, the PT – broadly 'socialist' – was founded in 1979 by a group of trade unionists and headed by Luís Ignácio da Silva, popularly known as 'Lula'. The PT is not a traditional political party but rather a rainbow coalition of several different issue-based social and political movements. It then went on to become one of the country's largest and most popular parties, and came into power in several major municipalities and states, and Lula was finally, after three attempts through the 90s, elected as President of Brazil in 2001. As of November 2004, the PT remains in power at the federal level but has lost power in several local and state elections, in part because of reversal of electoral policies and programmes and also because of splits and rivalries within the party.

**WTO (World Trade Organisation):** An international organisation that oversees a large number of agreements covering the 'rules of trade' between its member states. Created in 1995 as a secretariat to administer the General Agreement on Tariffs and Trade, a post-war trade treaty that laid much of the groundwork for the WTO. The WTO is the long-delayed successor to the project of the International Trade Organization, which was intended to follow GATT and whose charter was agreed at the UN Conference on Trade and Employment in Havana in March 1948, but which was blocked by the US Senate. The WTO headquarters are located in Geneva, Switzerland. Its current Director-General is Supachai Panitchpakdi. As of October 13, 2004, there were 148 members in the organisation. All WTO members are required to grant one another Most Favoured Nation status. In the late 1990s, the WTO became a major target for protests by the anti-globalisation movement.

**Zapatista:** The Zapatista Army of National Liberation (Ejército Zapatista de Liberación Nacional, EZLN) is an armed revolutionary group based in Chiapas, one of the poorest states of Mexico. The EZLN claims to represent the rights of the indigenous population, but also sees itself (and is widely seen) as part of a wider anti-capitalist movement, fighting for democracy, peace and justice for all Mexicans and for people all over the world. The Zapatistas are consciously opposed to neo-liberalism, the economic system advocated by the Mexican presidents from 1982 to 2000. The group takes its name from the Mexican revolutionary Emiliano Zapata; they see themselves as his ideological heirs and the inheritors of 500 years of indigenous resistance against imperialism. The EZLN breaks from the ordinary mould of revolutionary groups. Except for the initial uprising in the first two weeks

of 1994, they have not been known to use any weapons or bombs and have remained primarily in Chiapas. They refuse to use the normal political channels and institutions available in Mexico, including running for public office or endorsing political parties which they believe have been ineffective for too long, particularly, in their understanding of the 500 years since the invasion of the Americas. Thus the EZLN motto: ¡Ya Basta! ('Enough!').

USEFUL WEBSITES:

http://www.dingwall.bc.ca/history/about.php3
http://www.emory.edu/SOC/globalization/glossary.html#top
http://en.wikipedia.org/wiki
http://www.google.com
http://itlocus.com/glossary/globalization.html
http://www.sociology.emory.edu/globalization/glossary.html
http://www.who.int/trade/glossary/en/
http://www.worldbank.org/globalization
http://www.wordiq.com/definition/Main_Page

*Prepared by Madhuresh Kumar and Jyoti Sinha, October-November 2004, with inputs from Mayuri Saini and Jai Sen.*

**Cover:** Action and inauguration at the WSF, Porto Alegre, Brazil, January 2002, overlaid on extract from 16th century map of South America.
Photograph: Jai Sen
Map: Mappa Atlantica di Luis Texeira, 1600 circa

Page 2: Planet earth, NOAA.
Photograph: Greg Hernandez
Page 3: The Moon.
Photograph: John French
Pages 4-5: Pictures of children.
Photographs: Madan Mohan Jain
Page 25: Plenary session, Mumbai, India, January 2004.
Photograph: Jogi Panghaal
Pages 26-27: Dispute between Serra Pelada Goldmine Workers and Military Police, Brazil, 1986.
Photograph: Sebastião Salgado/Amazonas Images
Page 30: Action at the WSF, Porto Alegre, Brazil, January 2002.
Photograph: Jai Sen
Page 34: Action at the WSF, Mumbai, India, January 2004.
Photograph: Jai Sen
Page 39: Inauguration of the second WSF at Porto Alegre, Brazil, January 2002.
Photograph: Jogi Panghaal
Pages 42-43: Insider-Outsider.
Photograph: Achinto
Page 45: Popular notice-board at the WSF, Mumbai, India, January 2004.
Photograph: Jogi Panghaal
Page 48: Pakistani delegation celebrating, WSF, Mumbai, India, January 2004.
Photograph: Jogi Panghaal
Page 52-53: Dancing in the round, WSF, Mumbai, India, January 2004.
Photograph: Jogi Panghaal
Pages 54-55: The world is not for sale: Rally in Mumbai, India, following the closure of WSF 2004.
Photograph: Jogi Panghaal
Page 56: Demonstrators at the end of the WSF, Mumbai, India, January 2004.
Photograph: Jogi Panghaal
Page 60: Death man, demonstrator at the WSF, Mumbai, India, January 2004.
Photograph: Jogi Panghaal
Page 64: Open Forum Meeting of the WSF International Council, Porto Alegre, Brazil, January 2003.
Photograph: Jai Sen
Page 71: Mass rally in Pathrad, Madhya Pradesh, India against the Maheshwar dam on the Narmada river, July 25, 2000.
Photograph: Narmada Bachao Andolan
Pages 72-73: Poster from 'Carnival Against Capitalism'.
Page 74: Rally before the opening of the WSF, Porto Alegre, Brazil, January 2002.
Photograph: Jai Sen
Page 78: Anti-war demonstration, Edinburgh, Scotland.
Photograph: Paul Stevens
Pages 78-79: *Satyagrahi* (demonstrator) belonging to the Narmada Bachao Andolan, faces the rising waters of the Sardar Sarovar dam at Domkhedi village on the bank of the Narmada river, India, 2001.
Photograph: Hari Krishna
Page 80: Intervention at the WSF International Council meeting in Porto Alegre, Brazil, January 2003.
Photograph: Jai Sen
Pages 84-85: Shifting sands.
Photograph: Madan Mohan Jain
Page 86: Demonstrators WSF Mumbai, India, January 2004.
Photograph: Jogi Panghaal
Page 90: Demonstration by people displaced by a project in Orissa, India, at the WSF Mumbai, India, January 2004.
Photograph: Jogi Panghaal
Page 94: Panellists at the Open Space Seminar Series session on 'Old vs New Politics', Delhi University, India, September 2003.
Photograph: Jai Sen

## CAPTIONS AND PICTURE CREDITS

Pages 96-97: Women handpump mechanics in Gujarat, India.
Photograph: Joep Verhagen
Page 98: Demonstrators at the WSF, Mumbai, India, January 2004.
Photograph: Jogi Panghaal
Page 102: Demonstrator at the WSF, Mumbai, India, January 2004.
Photograph: Jogi Panghaal
Page 104-105: Open Forum Drummers, WSF, Mumbai, India, January 2004.
Photograph: Jogi Panghaal
Page 113: Street theatre in Delhi, India.
Photograph: Madan Mohan Jain
Pages 114-115: Woman speaking at protest action.
Photograph: Maria Sorderberg
Page 116: Silenced: Faces on a display, WSF, Mumbai, India, January 2004.
Photograph: Jogi Panghaal
Page 120: Demonstration at the close of the WSF, Mumbai, India, January 2004.
Photograph: Jogi Panghaal
Pages 124-125: Police action at a demonstration in India.
Photograph: Madan Mohan Jain
Page 126: Panellist at the Open Space Seminar Series session on 'The Politics of Boundaries', Delhi University, India, September 2003. Photograph: Jai Sen
Pages 130-131: The Open Space Seminar Series session on 'The Politics of Boundaries', Delhi University, India, September 2003.
Photograph: Jai Sen
Pages 134-135: 200,000 people say No! to the war against Iraq. The largest anti-war protest in the US since the Vietnam War, San Francisco, California, USA, on January 18, 2003.
Photograph: Bill Hackwell
Page 136: Street scene, WSF, Mumbai, India, January 2004.
Photograph: Jogi Panghaal
Pages 140-141: The Pink and Silver Protest March against Europe's biggest Arms Fair.
Photograph: Indy Media
Page 142: Nepali Dalit rally, Asian Social Forum, Hyderabad, India, January 2003.
Photograph: Jai Sen
Page 146: Preparing for a demonstration, WSF Mumbai, India, January 2004.
Photograph: Jogi Panghaal
Pages 148-149: Dinosaurs.
www.10thhussar.co.uk/KylesWallpaper.htm
Pages 150-151: Violence at a planetary level, display at the WSF, Mumbai, India, January 2004.
Photograph: Jogi Panghaal
Pages 158-159: Open Forum Conference Hall at the WSF, Mumbai, India, January 2004. Photograph: Jogi Panghaal
Page 167: Tribal Woman, India.
Photograph: Madan Mohan Jain
Pages 168-169: Tablas
Photograph: Christine Anderson
Page 170: Diversity and variation: A range of banners at the WSF in Mumbai, India, January 2004.
Photograph: Jogi Panghaal
Pages 174-175: Children
Photograph: Madan Mohan Jain
Pages 176-177: Alternatives to globalisation at the WSF in Mumbai, India, January 2004.
Photograph: Jogi Panghaal
Pages 178-179: Evicted Palestinian woman and her children, sitting amidst the rubble of her demolished home.
Photograph: Simon Hendrix
Page 180: Rally at the WSF, Mumbai, India, January 2004.
Photograph: Jogi Panghaal
Page 184: Delegate at the WSF in Mumbai, India, January 2004.
Photograph: Jogi Panghaal
Pages 186-187: Dalit gathering, WSF, Mumbai, India, January 2004.
Photograph: Jogi Panghaal
Pages 190, 192, 194:
Photographs: Amar Kanwar

■

zubaan

ZUBAAN
K-92 Hauz Khas Enclave - First Floor
New Delhi - 110 016, INDIA

# other

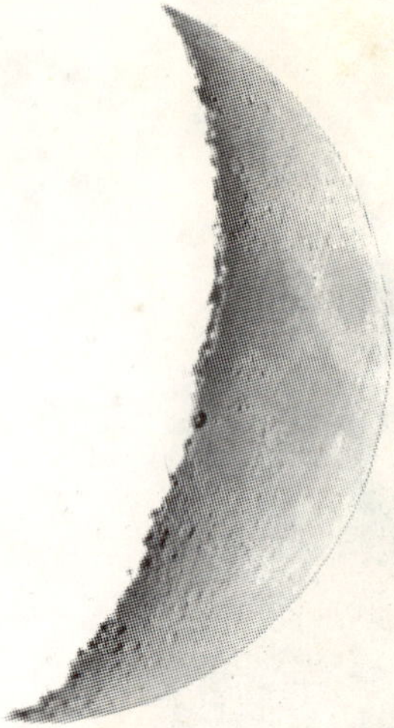

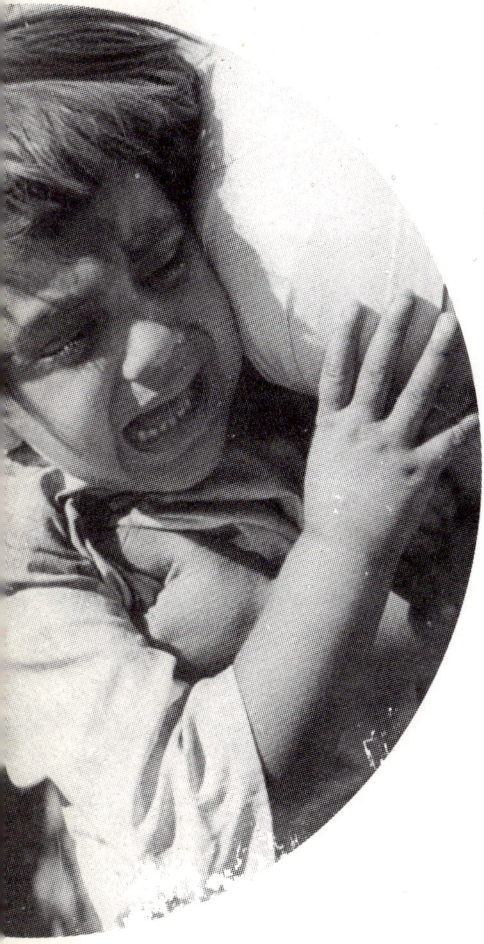

# worlds

# Are

# TALKING NEW POLITICS